P9-CFW-172

# Advance praise for *Stalking Elijah*

"*Stalking Elijah* is filled with remarkable speculations, questions, and flights of mystic fancy. . . . Every reader who cares for the vagaries of the human spirit in our confused age will find this work unsettling, important, and never less than fascinating."
—Rabbi David Wolpe, author of
*The Healer of Shattered Hearts* and *Why Be Jewish?*

"Kamenetz gracefully moves in the narrow corridor between two great spiritual traditions, guiding seekers on a great voyage of the soul."
—Rabbi Lawrence Kushner, author of
*Invisible Lines of Connection* and *Honey from the Rock*

"When a poet like Kamenetz meets an emerging mystical community like the teachers of Jewish renewal, the text that emerges is something more than lyrical sociology: it teaches without lecturing, wrestles without conquering, and dances without posturing. So to read it is to learn with a light heart."
—Rabbi Arthur Waskow, author of
*Godwrestling, Godwrestling Round 2,* and *Down-to-Earth Judaism*

"Reb Rodger invites us on a journey to sit at the feet of the great Jewish spiritual teachers and sages of our generation. What we discover is profound learning, rich inspiration, and the way to touch our souls at their deepest and most holy places."
—Rabbi Wayne Dosick, author of
*Dancing with God* and *Living Judaism*

## Praise for *The Jew in the Lotus*

"*The Jew in the Lotus* is the kind of book that seems, at first glance, to have been written for a carefully delimited audience: Jews, Buddhists, and Jewish Buddhists. But that is an illusion. It is really a book for anyone who feels the narrowness of a wholly secular life or who wonders about the fate of esoteric spiritual traditions in a world that seems bent on destroying or vulgarizing them. It is a narrative about an extraordinary moment in history, of course, but it is also the chronicle of Rodger Kamenetz's discovery of what he says is a more nourishing Judaism."
—*New York Times Book Review*

"Splendidly written from beginning to end, this is a book that might and should be read for the simple pleasure of watching an honest intellect confront its own image. . . . *The Jew in the Lotus* is a book that should be read and discussed by those interested in the marvelous complexity and resilience of the human soul."
—New Orleans *Times-Picayune*

"I found every page of *The Jew in the Lotus* enlightening and engrossing. It should be required reading for those of us who, like the author, have a stake in understanding who we are, whose history resonates with ours, and who we could become if we chose to."
—Rosellen Brown, novelist and author of
   *Before and After*, *Civil Wars*, and *Tender Mercies*

"This fascinating tale of two worlds, the Jewish and the Tibetan, is also a profound discussion of religion, exile, and survival in our time. Rodger Kamenetz has written a spiritual adventure story that brings to life the mystery of connections between seemingly different gods. But this is also a poetic manifesto calling for the creative re-thinking of religion and ritual."
—Andrei Codrescu, poet and National Public Radio commentator

# Stalking Elijah

ALSO BY RODGER KAMENETZ:

*The Jew in the Lotus*
*Terra Infirma*
*Nympholepsy*
*The Missing Jew*

# Stalking Elijah

## Adventures with Today's Jewish Mystical Masters

**RODGER KAMENETZ**

HarperSanFrancisco
*A Division of* HarperCollins*Publishers*

STALKING ELIJAH: *Adventures with Today's Jewish Mystical Masters.* Copyright © 1997 by Metaphor, Inc., Anya Kamenetz, and Kezia Kamenetz. All rights reserved. Printed in the United States of America. No part of this book may be used or reproduced in any manner whatsoever without written permission except in the case of brief quotations embodied in critical articles and reviews. For information address HarperCollins Publishers, 10 East 53rd Street, New York, NY 10022.

HarperCollins books may be purchased for educational, business, or sales promotional use. For information please write: Special Markets Department, HarperCollins Publishers, 10 East 53rd Street, New York, NY 10022.

HarperCollins Web Site: http://www.harpercollins.com
HarperCollins®, ♨ ®, and HarperSanFrancisco™ are trademarks of HarperCollins Publishers Inc.

Book design by Martha Blegen

FIRST HARPERCOLLINS PAPERBACK EDITION PUBLISHED IN 1998

*Library of Congress Cataloging-in-Publication Data*
Kamenetz, Rodger
Stalking Elijah : adventures with today's Jewish mystical masters / Rodger Kamenetz. — 1st ed.
Includes bibliographical references.
ISBN 0–06–064231–9 (cloth)
ISBN 0–06–064232–7 (pbk.)
1. Judaism—United States. 2. Mysticism—Judaism. 3. Mystics—United States—Biography. I. Title.
BM205.K36 1997
296'.0973'09049—dc21          97–2573

98  99  00  01  02  ❖  RRDH  10  9  8  7  6  5  4  3  2  1

for Rabbi Zalman Meshullam Schachter-Shalomi

"The very becoming of time is through deeds of true kindness."

R. NACHMAN OF BRATZLAV

# Contents

## Acknowledgments

I want to thank my many teachers and friends who were generous with me in the course of writing this book. To His Holiness the Dalai Lama, whose time is so immeasurably valuable, and to Rabbi Zalman Schachter-Shalomi, who gave to me as he has given to so many of my generation, I am deeply grateful. Thank you too to Eve Ilsen for our time together. Rabbi Jonathan Omer-Man both taught and generously hosted me during my visits to Los Angeles—he is my teacher and friend; Rabbi Judith Halevy was gracious in giving time from her busy schedule; Paul Wolff and Mark Borovitz taught and delighted me. I am also grateful to Mark Lerner, to Miriyam Glazer, to my old friend Nancy Goldberg Weiss, to Greg Stock and Lori Fish, and to Anne Brener and to Rabbi Mordecai Finley, all of whom added to my knowledge and understanding while I was in Los Angeles. In New Mexico, I'd like to thank Rabbi Shefa Gold and Andy Gold, Greg Burton and Wendy Pedersen, and Rabbi Lynn Gottlieb.

To Dr. Marc Lieberman, who brought me to Dharamsala the first time and came with me again, thanks immeasurably, old friend. Sylvia Boorstein opened my eyes to the meaning of prayer. Joseph Mark Epstein of Toronto and now Vancouver is a kabbalist extraordinaire. Laurel Chiten, whose film inspired by *The Jew in the Lotus* is now in the making, brought me back to India with her terrific energy, and to her I'm especially indebted. In Dharamsala, I want to thank Geshe Sonam Rinchen, who is a beautiful, wise teacher, and Ruth Sonam, whose modesty and kindness inspire me; thanks as well to Alex Berzin and to the Venerable Thubten Chodron for breaking matzah with me. I'd also like to thank Arnie Kotler of Parallax Press for sharing his anecdote about the trees and much else.

In Boston, not only did Rabbi Dr. Arthur Green bless me with his teaching, but he and Kathy Green were generous and kind in hosting me. Thanks too to Rabbi Moshe Waldoks and Anne Waldoks, who not only put up with me but put me up. Rabbi Nehemia Polen was stimulating and generous in our conversations, and I am deeply grateful for his book *The Holy Fire*, which has brought to light the teachings of Rabbi Kalonymus Kalman Shapira, the martyred rebbe of the Warsaw Ghetto.

During the course of writing this book I attended the Association of Jewish Studies gathering in Boston in 1995 and learned from many speakers there, including especially Professor Elliot Ginsburg, Professor Miles Krassen, Rabbi Lawrence Kushner, Rabbi Irving "Yitz" Greenberg, Rabbi Ellen Umansky, and Rachel Adler. I've also benefited from conversations with Marcia Falk.

Part of this book included material from interviews I conducted for an article in *Moment* on the havurah and Jewish renewal movements. Among those I spoke to then were Rabbi Leonard Gordon and Judith Plaskow. I am very grateful for their teaching.

For my friends at Aleph, especially Rabbi Arthur Waskow and woman of wisdom Phyllis Berman, my thanks are boundless. Also to Rabbi Jeff Roth and Rabbi Joanna Katz, whose work in creating Elat Chayyim is so important to me and to many of us.

I want to thank my agent, Katinka Matson, for getting this project going and Kandace Hawkinson, who believed in this book when it was only a proposal and acquired it. My editor at Harper San Francisco, Caroline Pincus, has been wonderfully encouraging and sweet as Hillel; her able assistant Sally Kim has helped me mind my deadlines. Special thanks to Muriel Jorgensen for her assistance with the text, to Carl Walesa for copyediting, and to Daniel Pincus and Jonathan Schwartz for proofreading. Thanks to Terri Leonard, who supervised production.

Steve Hanselman of Harper has been in my corner for years and made my time in Los Angeles possible—thanks, Steve.

Finally I'd like to thank Howard Schwartz for his constant inspiration—his sweetness is legendary. My sister Sylvia Scherr made it possible for me to return to India—thank you, dear one. To my children, Anya and Kezia, thanks for putting up with my absence and thanks for being here when I came home—I love you. And for my wife, Moira, who traveled with me all the way to Dharamsala on a second-class train, and who is my own true and constant teacher, all my love.

New Orleans
May 1997; Iyar 5757

## Note on Transliteration

If translation is treason—transliteration is Babel: *hasid, chasid, chassid, Hasid, ḥasid* are five valid spellings of the same Hebrew word. In the text I've followed the following conventions.

Foreign language words are in italics (*ḥasidut*). Words in the English dictionary are in roman, as are foreign words with English affixes (e.g. hasidic) and a few words I've judged ripe for entry in the dictionary (e.g., havurah, Rosh Hodesh). For italicized words, I've used the following equivalencies for Hebrew consonants: k=koof [*kadosh*], k=hard kaf [*mishkan*], kh=khaf [halakhah], ḥ=ḥet [ruaḥ] The ḥ is pronounced like "ch" in the Scots word *loch;* the "*kh*" is a somewhat harsher version of the same sound. For words in roman, I do not use the ḥ. Instead, for some words with a transliteration history *(Pesach, chutzpah, Chabad, Yechiel)*, I've used the "ch" spelling, for others *(havurah)*, "h". Moreover, out of respect to those I quote, I preserve the author's orthography though it clashes with mine.

## Hidden Gold

Dharamsala, a small town in northern India, shelters a community of several thousand Tibetan refugees. It's where my life changed dramatically in 1990 when I witnessed a dialogue between religious Jews and the Dalai Lama.

Going back to a place where your life changed is risky. Especially if it changed for the better. Suppose the magic isn't there? Suppose it was invented in the first place? I knew one thing: I wanted to make up for the last time I met His Holiness.

At the end of the 1990 dialogue, the Jewish delegates lined up to give him gifts. I hadn't brought one, so I hastily pulled out a paperback copy of *Terra Infirma* from my knapsack. A photograph shows me grinning and handing him the book: it happens to be one of the stupidest moments of my life. I am saying to this wonderfully humble Buddhist master, "I read your autobiography. Here's mine."

I hoped to do better this time.

It was two weeks before Passover 1996. I'd been traveling a long way to this moment. In the last six years I had learned something of Buddhist meditation, and explored the richness of Jewish meditation and Jewish renewal. My brief encounter with the Dalai Lama had opened a door to a new inner life. I wanted to thank him.

Now I waited eagerly in his comfortable meeting room. He smiled as he entered from the back, bowed slightly as I bowed to him, and sat in a yellow armchair. My friend Dr. Marc Lieberman introduced me, explaining that I had written about the Jewish Buddhist dialogue in *The Jew in the Lotus*. Then it was up to me.

"Your Holiness," I said, "people ask me, why did I have to go all the way to Dharamsala to look more deeply into my Jewish tradition? Why did I have to meet with a Buddhist master to see Judaism more deeply? I heard a story from Nachman of Bratzlav, a great hasidic rabbi from the last century. May I tell it to you?"

He nodded slightly and I began. A poor rabbi, Reb Yechiel, wants to build a new synagogue for his town. Every night he dreams of a certain bridge in Vienna. Hidden gold lies under it. Finally—the dream is driving him crazy—he makes the difficult journey to Vienna. He finds the bridge and searches around it. A guard asks what he's doing. Reb Yechiel explains his dream and the guard laughs.

"'Oh, you Jews are such dreamers. I'll tell you what dreams are worth. Every night I dream of a Jew—Reb Yechiel. And hidden behind his stove there's gold.'"

As I gave him the story, the Dalai Lama's face captivated me. Every emotion, every nuance registers there. He samples the feeling in your words and gives it back to you: this is sadness, this is joy. He listens with his whole being. I came to the punch line. "So Reb Yechiel returned home, looked behind his stove, and under the floorboards he found gold." The Dalai Lama's rich deep laughter filled the room. Behind him I noticed the golden statue of Avalokiteshvara, the Buddha of compassion.

"Rebbe Nachman told this tale," I said, "to explain why a person might journey far away to find a teacher, who will show the student what is already close at hand. For me," I said, looking into his eyes, "and for many Jews, you have become such a teacher. By making us look more deeply into Judaism, you have become our rabbi."

Cupping his hand, the Dalai Lama reached for the dome of his shaven head, laughing, and said, "So you will give me a small hat?"

I promised him a yarmulke. Then I closed my mouth. I had learned something from transcribing the 1990 dialogue: always leave him time to respond. In the silence, he's thinking. If you fill it with your own chatter, you may never get the benefit of that thought. So I contravened forty-six years of my own noisy cultural conditioning and let the silence alone.

Soon he replied that "all major religions can help each other. Each tradition has some specialty or uniqueness which can be very useful for other traditions." He added that sometimes the communication is not necessarily through words, but also through close feelings. "So," he concluded modestly, looking at his fingernails, "if you find some little contribution from my part to our Jewish brothers and sisters, I am very happy." He laughed and said thank you softly twice.

But though the Dalai Lama seemed bemused at being called a rabbi, I knew he had taught Jews through our 1990 dialogue, especially with his questions about the Jewish inner life. From the Tibetan perspective, religions exist to benefit humanity. The Tibetan path includes particular practices—mantras, prostrations, meditations, and visualizations—meant to purify the mind of negative emotions such as hatred, anger, lust. What practices, he had wanted to know, does the Jewish tradition teach to purify afflictive states of mind?

The phrase "afflictive states of mind" was new to me in 1990. I understand it now as the anguish that keeps us awake at night, the gnawing within that makes life difficult, the fresh pain, or the old pain, each carries in the heart. Until I heard his question, it had never occurred to me to look within Judaism for an answer.

For many reasons—the prospects of peace in the Middle East, the changing of generations—Jews today are turning from issues of identity and politics and are looking more deeply inward. Through accounts of the 1990 dialogue, including my own, the Dalai Lama's curiosity about the Jewish inner life stimulated thought and debate. I told him Jews were very grateful for his questions.

The Dalai Lama generously replied that he felt all traditions, including his own, sometimes focus too much on external rituals or ceremonies. "Then they neglect the real end of spirituality—

transformation within ourselves." He added with a playful smile, "If you make a short visit to a monastery, everything is beautiful. But if you listen to the story of what is happening—just as with normal human beings, there's fighting." He laughed, adding, "That is a clear indication we are neglecting genuine transformation, or spiritual development, inside."

O

Which Jewish practices foster "genuine transformation, or spiritual development"? I remember vividly in the 1990 dialogue when the Dalai Lama asked the delegates about the inner life of Jews today. He held his right hand in the air and turned his wrist, as if opening a door.

In the six years since, I've traveled hard, seeking Jewish teachers who have passed through that door. I asked questions about their inner life—and mine. I sought secrets of Jewish meditation and deeper prayer. I studied Torah and debated its relevance. As a frankly heterodox, somewhat anarchic, and self-educated Jew, I was asking not only for myself, but for others who might feel excluded, alienated, or on the margins. I wrestled with authenticity, my own and my teachers', wondering whether there's an entry-level test for being a good Jew, or whether the rich language of kabbalah and hasidic teaching, or ḥasidut,* can properly be understood in the context of a liberal Judaism.

My questions are not academic: they rise from the confusions and struggles in my own life. Challenged by the beauty of a frankly mystical tradition like Buddhism, I could no longer maintain my Judaism as a carefully preserved nostalgic monument to my immigrant grandparents. I wanted direct experience—to know what is useful and real about Jewish practice today.

Such questions prompted my round-trip journey from Dharamsala, from 1990 to 1996, and back and forth across the

---

* For Hebrew words, ḥ=ḥet, the sound of the "ch" in Lo*ch* Lomond.

United States, from Beverly Hills and Hollywood to Philadelphia and Boston, learning from teachers of a Jewish inner life.

Like Reb Yechiel I have journeyed far, stalking a dream. In the end I also found gold hidden behind the stove—in basic Jewish texts, prayers, and practices. The trick is to bring them inward, to take them to heart.

The Tibetan Buddhist path presents itself as a *lam rim,* a guided path to enlightenment. My own path has been more like a roller coaster, with lost luggage and airports, and intense teachings crammed between the sound of video games and honking horns. My teachers are not serene monks, but vulnerable, busy, intense women and men with financial burdens and personal problems to wrestle with, and sometimes complicated households. But that's the American way, and the Jewish way, I suppose: a Jewish path cannot be apart from, but must be in, life.

In life, the Jewish path to God can seem no more certain than a flash of lightning. Yet it is my path, something I first realized early one morning, in Dharamsala, in the fall of 1990.

## God, One: Nothing, Nothing

OCTOBER 26, 1990

According to the great Jewish philosopher the Rambam,* God is reality, or, as he writes, "there is no reality like his reality"— a point driven home to me personally one morning by Rabbi Zalman Schachter-Shalomi while we prayed together on the slopes overlooking the Kangra Valley in Dharamsala. "Your God," he said, looking straight into my eyes, "is a true God."

In some ways I'm still tracing the implications of that moment when Reb Zalman, the architect of Jewish renewal in our time, had the chutzpah to accuse me of God.

Until then I did not know I was on a search for God. Or that I would return to that same spot in Dharamsala six years later to finish a mission Zalman began. I surely didn't know I would study Jewish meditation, explore Jewish renewal, or end up shouting to heaven on the San Bernardino Freeway.

Kierkegaard remarks that life is lived forward and understood backward. Certain events fall into place only in retrospect. Their meaning hides in the details of our lives, just as God hides. The great nineteenth-century hasidic master Rabbi Nachman of Bratzlav taught that in fact, God hides in two ways: God hides from us; and then, for many of us, it's hidden from us that God hides from us. Until Reb Zalman stuck his finger in my chest, I lived in second-degree hiding.

God hides pretty well in the word *God.* I see the wisdom of writing it "G-d," as my Orthodox friends do, see the further wisdom of not writing it at all, preserving as a nameless name the

---

* The acronym for Rabbi Moses ben Maimon, or Maimonides.

four-letter suite of Hebrew breath sounds that is the secret un-pronounceable proper name of God—rendered in English as YHVH.

I agree with the Rambam, who argues strenuously that God can best be described in negatives. As a philosopher anxious to reconcile Aristotle and Torah, he devotes many chapters of his masterpiece, *The Guide of the Perplexed,* to the inadequacy of biblical terminology for God. While this might seem a peculiar enterprise for a Jewish sage, his point is that expressions like "the hand of YHVH" and "the anger of YHVH" lead to serious problems if read literally. And evidently throughout our history, we Jews have pretty much been knuckleheads in regard to such corporeal metaphors. No matter how hard we try, we keep reverting to an image of God as a fierce old man in the sky with a long white beard.

One school of mystics especially enraged the Rambam by purporting to measure the length of that beard[1] and other anatomical features. Even in our own time, some Jews, consciously or not, fixate exclusively on male images of God. A pervasive literalism grips Jewish hearts and minds. Atheists can also be quite literal minded: often the God they can't believe in is this same corporeal all-powerful white-bearded old man in the sky.

Hence the Rambam opens his masterpiece by meticulously examining expressions that mean one thing in human terms, but that must be construed quite differently when referring to God. He patiently sorts through metaphors of divinity in the Torah, hoping to wean Jews from their folk literalism by illustrating the endless failure of human language to ever mirror reality.

But if God is reality, as Reb Zalman's bold challenge to me suggested, then certain phrases in the prayer book had blocked my view, and many others', especially women's. Phrases like King of the Universe, Father, Lord. The talmudic sages offer one answer. The Bible, they say, speaks a language of human beings.[2] We launch fleets of words at the ultimate and watch them sink, give many names to our experiences, and tell stories on stories. Until that morning in October with Reb Zalman, all such language flooded and diluted my personal experience of the divine—pure absence.

In fact, my susceptibility to the wily charm of Buddhist teaching arose from the turmoil of absence, my despair, my private nowhere, my nothing.

O

I first came to Dharamsala in October 1990. A month before, I heard two years of excruciating work go down the tubes in a five-minute phone-call rejection from a tough New York editor. Books get rejected all the time, but this tore open a wound that the writing had been meant to heal. My manuscript told the story of my infant son's death and of how my wife, Moira, and I struggled to have another child. Now the manuscript, too, was dead.

The rejection left me in a delicate state of mind to be flying halfway around the world, a writer certain he couldn't write.

One night, lying in my room in a Tibetan guest cottage, a familiar gnawing voice spoke, a frequenter of many nights of insomnia over the five years since my tiny son had died so unexpectedly. The voice gathered strength from all my defeats. "You're not going to make it," I heard. "You're no good. You'll never be able to write about this." What a weirdly confident demon. I felt myself lending energy to this voice, pushing it to be louder and stronger, to see where it would go. A dangerous game to play in a dark room in the foothills of the Himalayas.

The next morning I woke, dazed and ruined, washed my face, drank tea, and opened my eyes wide. They say a man lying at the bottom of a well can see the stars even in broad daylight. I saw something brilliant those days in Dharamsala.

I never considered myself a spiritual seeker. So I was stirred and confused by this unprecedented dialogue between two major world religions. I bounded between the serene and penetrating presence of His Holiness the Dalai Lama and the frenetic and exuberant debates and teachings of the rabbis. Over the net to the Buddhist side, where calm meditation brings peace and clarity; over the net to the Jewish side, where, as we prayed outdoors overlooking Dharamsala's Kangra Valley, I heard the beauty of all creation sing with one voice. Buddhism? Judaism? Buddho-Judaism? Jewish Buddhism? Is there a God or is there nothing? Or, as the Jewish mystics seem to whisper, is God nothing?

The match was called early on account of darkness. The score: God, one; Nothing, nothing.

I sought Reb Zalman out for advice. We walked along the winding cutbacks that pass for roads in Dharamsala. Zalman comes from the Lubavitch tradition of rabbinic counseling, and his advice had range, from body to mind to soul. He peered into my psyche and also asked after my sex life. In hasidic thought, joy in everyday life is meat for the spirit. Then he moved on to my Jewish soul, my *neshamah*. He said, using Native American language, that I ought to go on a spirit quest. For a moment I pictured myself in the New Mexico desert, tied to a pole in the hot sun and pierced by arrows. But he meant a retreat, to think about one question:

*What do I want, what do I really want?*

To ask this question for a day deepens the sense of an interior life and strengthens inner listening. Later I met a teacher in Jerusalem, Susie Schneider, who explained that even seemingly trivial physical needs and wants are not to be dismissed out of hand. In Jewish thought, the prompting of the heart, even for a bagel with cream cheese, is a serious message. Because only by listening carefully to what we want can we begin to hear what is wanted of us.

Reb Zalman gave me a second way of approaching the question: "Find your risk."

That is good advice. But how much risk? Buddha left his family and palace behind to become a wandering contemplative;

Abram obeyed the startling command *Lekh lekha*—go and leave your father's house, and the land of your birth. What sort of voice was he hearing? Did it come from within or without? Should I too quit my job, leave my home, start over?

Reb Zalman stopped walking, smiled, and looked serious. "No," he said quietly. "Have the *ḥokhmah* to change your life from where you are."

*Ḥokhmah* is wisdom.

## Meditations on the Breath

Where I was was Baton Rouge, Louisiana, teaching poetry at Louisiana State University. I landed there in a heap after a twenty-four-hour flight, still clinging to the radiance of that lost world of Dharamsala. I carried Tibetan prayer beads and a Jewish prayer Reb Zalman taught me in an airport lounge.

Baton Rouge is a deeply conservative town that grew from forty thousand after the war to almost half a million. It's the state capital, where Huey Long ruled and was murdered; the home of two large universities, LSU and Southern, one mainly white and one mainly black; and in the fall of 1990, a theater for the deeply sick politics of David Duke, who in two years ran for senator, governor, and president. A strange place for a Jew to sample Buddhist meditation.

But I'd been impressed by a quality Tibetans call "quiet mind." I knew I didn't have one. My mind was more Philip Roth novel than meditation manual. It had voices within that raged and insinuated, shouted and mocked in general echoes of a fierce family argument. Yet in Dharamsala I glimpsed actual people who lived from moment to moment in equanimity. They hadn't gotten there by magic, but through specific meditation practices. That was the exciting part.

I looked for a cookbook to teach me basic meditation and, being a loyal Jew, found one written by two Jewish Buddhists, Jack Kornfield and Joseph Goldstein.[1] The directions were clear and helpful. Later, I checked in with other practitioners. I learned a proper sitting posture from the local Tibetan Buddhist community—three lonely souls in Baton Rouge who meditated on Sunday mornings in a T-shirt shop on Government Street, wedged between a "nails" boutique and a yogurt store. They sat before a life-size brass Buddha and recited Tibetan prayers to put themselves in the proper mood. Extremely squeamish around idols of any kind, I held back on the chanting. Then we sat, legs crossed, eyes open and staring straight ahead, backs of our hands resting gently on our knees. We breathed and I watched my breath.

I benefited from this experience, as a Jewish human. Was I also a T-shirt-shop Buddhist? I put aside questions of identity for a time. A very new space was opening within me, a calm space I had previously visited only on brief stopovers. For months I spent thirty minutes a day meditating Buddhist-style. I learned to follow my breath. After a while the muddy water settled, silt sinking to the bottom, clarity pooling on top. That was very good. I could hold that clarity for a moment—a breath—and then another, then a minute, even minutes. In time a certain distance arose, a separation, an inch between observer and observed. I am an excitable human. That inch was very, very good.

In *vipassana*, or insight meditation, one observes whatever arises and notes it. A body sensation—a twinge in the knee, or a scratch on the nape of the neck—and one notes *sensation, sensation*. Thinking? One notes *thinking, thinking*. Feeling? One notes *feeling, feeling*. The moment of attention is like a good-bye kiss as the stimulus fades away. What a sparkling fountain of thoughts and feelings and sensations, each rising, peaking, and fading away, each illustrating the profound impermanence of the mind, the self, and the equally profound nothing hiding behind it all.

After some practice, the rushing fountain subsides. One observes the observer—a tricky process, subtle, lovely. This observer, unlike ME, has no particular opinions, attachments, emotions. Certainly the observer has no gender. Certainly the observer is not a Jew. It is just awareness, a pure spot of light on the page of mind.

So sometimes anger arises. While one sits on a pink carpet in a bedroom. With the sensation of a flame in the lower belly. While the rest of the household sleeps. Anger rises like a bad taste of acid in the stomach, peaks with a strong burning sensation, then slowly losing its intensity, fades. *Feeling, feeling.*

And anger, I learned through meditation, does not require action. It does not require the vote of my body. The anger motor can rev in neutral, but need not be put in gear. So it is with other thoughts and feelings. None absolutely require my participation, none are solidly real or necessarily me.

Such knowledge is freedom.

In spring 1991, I attended bodhisattva teachings given by the Dalai Lama at a Chinese Buddhist temple in Houston. He sat before a Buddha carved from an enormous block of white jade. The Westerners asked him theoretical questions about dharma and fine points of *madhyamika* philosophy; the Chinese wanted to know, "Which meditation do I use to shrink a tumor?" When the teachings ended, most took bodhisattva vows—formal pledges to follow a path of kindness to others. I watched them repeat the vows in unison and pour small Dixie cups of water over their heads. The sentiment appealed to me, but I drew back from the baptism.

Back home, I studied the Dalai Lama's teaching text, Shantideva's *A Guide to the Bodhisattva's Way of Life.*[2] Shantideva is very tough on anger. Eons of spiritual development, in life after life, can be erased with one angry outburst. By that reckoning, I had thousands of lifetimes just to get back to square one. To help me, I posted on my office wall a Buddhist poem that praises people I formerly called jerks, and other more pungent names. From the Buddhist point of view, these folks are "patience teachers," sent to give me pop quizzes on forbearance, quizzes I usually failed. I wondered if I could ever reach the sublime spiritual stage of the bodhisattva, who happily embraces such walking nettles as beloved teachers?

The Jew behind the I also needled me. While observing the mind, I also observed Shabbat, attended synagogue (probably not as often as my rabbi would have liked), sent my kids to Sunday school, and otherwise functioned as a normative heterodox Jew, in a town where Jews are as rare as they are on the planet—about one in three thousand. For about a year, I enjoyed the contradiction. I was very happy to sit in meditation; I was very happy to chant *kiddush* with my dear wife and two daughters on Friday nights. But after a time, I felt a growing inner tension. The more attracted I was to Buddhist teaching, the more I searched for Jewish equivalents. This may be an essential difference between those Jews who continue on the Buddhist path and me. I sought parallels.

But I felt the draw of Buddhism and understood the inner debate of friends like Dr. Marc Lieberman, the Bay Area ophthalmologist who fathered the formal Jewish Buddhist dialogue. He wrestled for years, pulled between loyalty to family and the benefits of Buddhist practice. To his credit, he lives the contradiction openly, with a mezuzah on his door and a large brass Buddha in his meditation hall. Approaching bar mitzvah age, his son once asked, "Dad, are we Jewish or are we Buddhist?" He answered, "I have Jewish roots and Buddhist wings."

This mixed metaphor bespeaks a sublime tension. (Later he amended it to "Jewish roots and Buddhist fruits"!) Another Jewish Buddhist, Arnie Kotler, a close associate of the Vietnamese teacher Thich Nhat Hanh, also had a vision of trees. After an initial week of Zen meditation, he intended a quiet walk in the woods. But his mind stayed noisy and busy. He was convinced that every tree he passed on that quiet walk was definitely either Jewish or Gentile.

Kotler's vision of *goyishe* elms and *yiddishe* oaks is only an extreme example of what the Jewish theologian Arthur Green calls the "drama of distinctions," the warring dualisms of Jewishness. Jew and Gentile, kosher and treif, forbidden and permitted—

Jews, no matter how far from their roots, feel that drama in their marrow. After all, these distinctions wove the pattern for Jewish communal life for two millennia, warp and woof for the fabric of law, and the tapestry of custom that grew around it. By now they are deep habits of thought, a basic matrix of the Jewish mind, secular or religious. They aren't so easy to forget, even after hundreds of hours of sitting on a meditation pillow.

But in my shabby Buddhist practice I glimpsed a different realm, where such distinctions loosen. Labels become relative: at the deepest layers of the mind, they lose their stickum. In meditation I was neither Jew nor Gentile, male nor female, I was not even I—at least for brief happy moments. It was refreshing, and then that refreshment challenged me: was I being disloyal as a Jew if I practiced sitting meditation?

Years later, my friend and teacher Rabbi Arthur Waskow taught me a *derash* that would have comforted me those days of Buddhist sitting and Jewish fretting. In the Friday-night *kiddush*, we read the account of the seventh day of creation, when God finished his work—and rested.

And how does the bodiless Being of the Rambam rest? Exodus 31:17 reads: "On the seventh day, God *rested and was refreshed.*" *Shavat va-yinafash.*

The Hebrew *yinafash* means at root "to take a breath."[3] So I follow an alternate interpretation:

God paused—and watched his breath.

○　◑　●　◐　○　◑　●

After a year of spiritual shuttling, I wanted to integrate. My inner and my outer. My spiritual practice and my worldly identity as a Jew. The pieces didn't fit: I had a Buddhist piece for the inside and a Jewish face on the outside. Based on Buddhist practice, cultivation of equanimity seemed a key spiritual aspiration. But as a Jew in Louisiana opposing David Duke, struggle and even anger also felt very genuine and real. Reb Zalman gave me a mission: to find God in reality. But which real was more real?

I have worlds within me, we all do, and at first it sounded confusing when Rabbi Zalman Schachter offered four more. In a JFK Airport lounge on the way back from Dharamsala in 1990, we were waiting for planes to take us home—Reb Zalman to Philadelphia, where he then served as spiritual leader of P'nai Or, and I to Louisiana. I'd picked up some mala beads in the Tibetan market—meditation beads carved from human skull and embedded with Himalayan turquoise and coral. The beads were old and smooth and smelled of salt: some Tibetan Buddhist monk might have used them to count one hundred thousand recitations of *om mani padme hum,* "the jewel in the lotus," a preliminary for further instruction. Now as I nervously fingered the beads, Reb Zalman took them and showed me a "four-worlds mantra."

> I am holy.
> All is clear.
> You are loved.
> It is perfect.

I gave the mantra a few cycles, clicking my beads like a mad jet-lagged monk, and then Reb Zalman took them back and explained that each line is a letter: *Yod. Heh. Vov. Heh.* So I was in effect praying God's nameless name. But what about these "four worlds"—interplanetary travel?

No, he explained patiently, each letter is an *olam,* a world or realm. Of awareness. Going in backward order, the lower *heh,* ה ("It is perfect"), corresponds to *assiyah,* the world of action. In *assiyah* our bodies sat in the airport lounge, blue industrial carpet, fluorescent lights overhead, tan nubby cushions. It didn't look perfect to me. But that was from my limited view as a body that had just logged twenty hours flying from Delhi to New York. From the divine perspective, it is perfect.

In general, the meditation searches out spaciousness. The *vov,* ו, gives the view from *yetzirah* ["formation"], or feeling, where the divine dial tone is "You are loved." The upper *heh,* ה, is *beriyah,* which is creation, but also knowledge. All is clear. And *yod,* י, opens the realm of spirit, or pure intuitional knowledge, known as *atzilut* [literally, "nearness"]. I am holy.

## Four Worlds

| I am holy. | י | yod | atzilut | "nearness" | spirit |
|---|---|---|---|---|---|
| All is clear. | ה | heh | beriyah | "creation" | knowledge |
| You are loved. | ו | vov | yetzirah | "formation" | feeling |
| It is perfect. | ה | heh | assiyah | "doing" | action |

Reb Zalman explained this in about ten minutes and then caught a plane, leaving me and the beads sitting in *assiyah.* But now I know what he was up to: he wanted to plant a Jewish seed.

The four-worlds mantra follows a declension immediately appealing to my nervous system. After a time, I thought of the phrases as continuous broadcasts on the divine frequency of the true state of things, broadcasts on four channels: soul intuition, mind knowledge, heart feeling, and body sense. At a completely deep level, that I'd understand better after studying with Rabbi

Jonathan Omer-Man, the four worlds represent the great cosmic moments of creation and creativity, the slide show of God's inwardness that mystics describe as beginning in an emptiness— the *Ein Sof*—beyond all descriptors, and then extending through the four events of spirit, thought, feeling, and doing that bring an action from on high into this world. Here. Now. And every here and now from now on and ever. During the following year, I cycled the mantra through my nervous system, calm germ of a tiny practice in Jewish meditation.

The next opening came in summer 1991, when Reb Zalman invited me to teach a poetry workshop at the biannual P'nai Or national gathering. He plucked me up and plunged me into his postmodern feminist rock'n'roll kabbalistic neo-hasidic quadruple worlds of Jewish renewal. These worlds brimmed with interesting energies and contradictions that also mirror Reb Zalman's personal history.

O

Rabbi Zalman Meshullam Schachter-Shalomi was born in Poland in 1924 and raised in Vienna. (Shalomi [peace] he added in later years to take the edge off Schachter—Yiddish for butcher.) He comes, indeed, from a family of hasidic butchers; his grandfather shechted meat for the Belzer rebbe. His father straddled secular and religious worlds, but greatly loved davening. Zalman remembers his father crying during prayer. "Does it hurt to talk to God?" the young boy asked him.

Young Zalman straddled, too: he studied in Orthodox yeshivot and a secular high school and joined both socialist and religious Zionist groups. As a teenager, he crossed the narrow— burning—bridge of the Holocaust with his family and escaped via a French internment camp, where he first encountered Lubavitch hasidism in the person of Menahem Mendel Schneerson, who later became the well-known seventh Lubavitcher rebbe. Zalman's family made its way to the United States a week before

Passover 1940. He entered the Lubavitcher Yeshiva in Brooklyn, earning *semikhah*, rabbinic ordination, in 1947. Zalman's rebbe was Rabbi Joseph Schneersohn (1880–1950). For a time, under the rebbe's direction, he toured the college circuit with the great spirited singer and composer Rabbi Shlomo Carlebach. He also worked as a furrier and, like his grandfather, as a kosher butcher.

Starting in 1956, Reb Zalman served as Hillel director and later professor and department head of Jewish Studies at the University of Manitoba. Inspired to broader views, in part by academic studies in the psychology of religion at Boston University, he became increasingly dissatisfied with the limits of Chabad Orthodoxy. In 1966, he "graduated Chabad," as he puts it now. In plain English, he was kicked out after an article appeared in *Commentary* in which Reb Zalman praised the sacramental potential of lysergic acid.

The break caused him enormous pain. For various reasons, he hoped for the rebbe's blessing for his explorations. Reb Zalman saw in the sixties' drug experimentation a spiritual search. He thought he had a useful language in the kabbalah. Though he felt himself within the fold of Chabad, Zalman's adventures, and misadventures, brought him to the border between a Jewish mysticism confined within a strict Orthodox community and a more universal mysticism, promulgated profligately, sloppily, and widely in the late-sixties age of Aquarius.[1]

But after the Holocaust, the surviving sects of Hasidism hardened their defenses. Nazi brutality and general indifference to Jewish suffering confirmed their fear of the Gentile other. Judaism is both universalist and particularist, a paradox that annoys some outsiders. Some strains of Orthodoxy—not all—shut the door to the wider world, interpret a straightforward phrase like *kol ha-adam*, "every human," in the narrow sense of "every Jew." Fear closes the valves of the heart; and then interpretation squints. One untotted damage of the Holocaust lies here: the mystical tradition of Judaism hid itself in enclaves forbidding to outsiders and in the process made outsiders of many contemporary Jews. Seventeenth-century fur hats, black garments, patriarchal family patterns, and deeply conservative politics became barriers to more secular Jews. At the same time, many secular and liberal Jews, out of arrogance or contempt, failed to detect that beneath the black garments, the great mystical heart of Judaism was beating.

While Chabad, under the dynamic leadership of Menahem Mendel Schneerson (1902–1994), emphasized outreach to all Jews, the organization seemingly could not tolerate Zalman's forays into the America of the sixties, into psychedelics and non-Jewish mysticism.

True, Reb Zalman had moved into uncharted territory. But he moved in the company of a whole generation of Jewish seekers. A sabbatical leave to Brandeis in 1969 placed him at the birth of the havurah movement, when Rabbi Arthur Green was forming Havurat Shalom in Boston. Zalman also strongly influenced the Aquarian Minyan in Berkeley. From his Chabad yeshivah training came intensity of davening, a real-life knowledge of kabbalah, and an appreciation of the importance of *yeḥidut*, one-on-one spiritual counseling.

Meeting in small prayer circles (havurot), the havurah movement tended to be egalitarian, politically active, and eventually feminist. By 1973, the huge success of *The First Jewish Catalog*—the *Whole Earth Catalog* of Judaism—spread the news nationally, and carried with it Zalman's influential guide to Jewish prayer, "The First Step." Two years later, after Zalman moved to Philadelphia to teach at Temple University, he helped his followers integrate the feminism, ecological awareness, progressive politics, and egalitarianism of the havurah movement with a universalized hasidic mysticism. The movement called itself Jewish renewal. In the extraordinary community of P'nai Or—these days called Aleph—I took my first footsteps on a Jewish spiritual path.

In the early sixties Zalman dreamed of a commune of Jewish meditators, B'nai Or—"sons of light." As women's voices emerged, *b'nai or* became *p'nai or*, "faces of light." The light spread through a series of biannual national gatherings, or kallahs, each more widely attended than the last. By 1996 twenty-six Jewish renewal communities had sprouted in fifteen states, with seven more in Canada, England, Israel, Switzerland, and Brazil.

At the 1991 *kallah*, on the Bryn Mawr College campus in Philadelphia, I fell in love with Jewish renewal. I was immediately taken with the creative energy of these people, among them artists, dancers, singers, poets, and rock musicians.

Reb Zalman's work with prayer was astonishing. *Or Chadash* (New Light), the P'nai Or siddur, revised the God language[2] that had previously blocked my view. Every prayer was offered in gender column A and column B. *At* alternated with *Atah*—You (feminine) with You (masculine). Shekhinah (the feminine divine presence) was invoked often as a God term. A peculiarity of renewal is reading *Yah* for YHVH; to most in the renewal movement, *Adonai*, or Lord, revisits all the woes of patriarchy.

*Yah* in the *Shema* shocked me, and might have shocked the Rambam. But the changes in gender respond to his philosophy. Why make a fetish of male-only images, when the One has no gender? Such editing reflects renewal's great contribution to contemporary Jewish life, giving breathing room for Jewish women to find their full voices.

Great-spirited singers Hannah Tiferet Siegel, Linda Hirschhorn, and Shefa Gold invented new music for our prayers, dancer Miriam Minkoff brought art to our gestures, and Jewish renewal rabbi Marcia Prager led us on prayer journeys of story and dance. A fusion of rock 'n' roll and Jewish prayer raised a Dionysian joy absent from much synagogue worship. It was the joy of actual participation, not rote recitation—a joy that women led.

Traditionally, decorum never belonged to Jewish prayer. Yet, apart from hasidic and Jewish renewal circles, extreme joy in prayer seems foreign to urbane Jews raised to stand-up-sit-down pew worship. Too many Jewish congregations become audiences: the service is performed at them, with prayers recast in the high aesthetic of Romantic choral music, or in folksier Peter, Paul, and Mary–style tunes—"Judaism's greatest hits." Reb Zalman's four-worlds approach to prayer moved people out of their seats: Jewish renewal liturgy led us through the body, heart, and mind to the spirit.

At the *kallah*, we woke early, before seven, and trooped over to various classrooms at Bryn Mawr to pray, barefoot and in shorts, our bodies stiff, yawning, sleep still in our eyes. Men and women wore tallisim, and many wore tefillin (prayer amulets). Some in the back tai-chi'd; others, fresh from the men's movement, beat cowhide drums. Was this Jewish? I wondered. It was a fleeting thought, the old drama of distinctions. I wasn't a policeman on border patrol for Jewish authenticity. If a woman next to me wanted to wear tefillin, that was fine. If the guy across from me stood on his head to get his body into prayer, that was fine too. We were humming and chanting, moving through new space. The Hebrew words took on new dimensions of meaning. They became about now. When we prayed, "Blessed are You, Yah, living Spirit who opens the eyes of the blind," our eyes opened wide. Then—"who straightens the bent"—we stretched and touched our toes.

A hundred years ago, from sheer embarrassment, American Reform Judaism threw out many fine prayers, such as "Blessed is the Lord who brings life to the dead." To contemporary ears, perhaps, resurrection also sounds outlandish. But in that early-morning light, with my body slowly waking from the death of sleep, "life to the dead" took on an imminent meaning. There's a lot of resurrection in a cup of coffee.

In his introduction to *Or Chadash*, Reb Zalman argues that the basic "function, language, relevance" of the prayer book remained unrevised since the second century C.E. In medieval times, Judaism, awakening to philosophy, developed a sophisticated theology. In the same way, Reb Zalman proposes a davennology for today so that Jews can deepen their understanding of how prayer—in plain Yiddish, *davennen*—transforms consciousness.

Davennology is psychologically shrewd: Reb Zalman helped inhibited, frozen Jews warm up their hearts. In one powerful exercise, I recited a psalm line by line, back and forth with a partner, addressing the words addressed to God to the You sitting in front of me. The words gained a tremendous presence and depth they'd never found for me in a group recitation. By the end of the psalm, our eyes were brimming with tears.

Under Reb Zalman's influence, Jewish renewal settings became laboratories doing "R and D work in davennology." At my first *kallah*, some experiments looked pretty far out: one morning some folks in tallises davened knee-deep in the swimming pool for water prayer; another morning, clay smeared on my face, I prayed earth—I slept through fire.

But these experiments responded to the diversity of our individual paths. I came to Jewish renewal after contact with Buddhist teachings; my fellow *kallah*-niks had sojourned in Zen temples, Hindu ashrams, Sufi dancing circles, and Native American sweat lodges or nourished themselves with Jungian psychology, psychosynthesis, Gurdjieff, and New Age philosophers. To the *kallah* came teachers and social workers, doctors and lawyers, professors of humanities and research biologists, and rabbinical students from every denomination. Also people who channeled angels, told fortunes with palm and crystals, who thought they were psychics or healers and maybe were. Just as sentimentality offers a necessary edge to feeling, belief space includes a wide swath of credulity. We all needed each other.

That lesson got danced into my body one morning when Zalman arrayed ten of us into a praying machine, positioned according to the ten holy *sefirot*. The *sefirot* provide a more detailed map of the inner workings of the four worlds. These divine potentialities operate in all the worlds, including our own.

The sefirotic world is the great theosophical centerpiece of kabbalah, the mystic's answer to the chief perplexity of the Rambam's theology. After all, if God can be described only in negatives, how does one pray to a negative? What image can replace no image? It's fine to say God is not a king, and not a queen, and not a man and not a woman, and not a thing, but human beings have a hard time imagining not this.

The *sefirot* build an imaginative bridge. All I knew at first were their names and that they could be arranged on the human body, which means we carry around with us a very handy map of God's relationship with God, and with us. But where exactly is this sefirotic world? I had a nice Jacob's ladder but couldn't see where the feet met the ground. I'd learn more later.

Because Reb Zalman didn't theorize that summer morning at the Bryn Mawr *kallah*. He wanted us to pray. He got busy arranging a minyan of us on the body of Adam Kadmon, Adam the First, the primordial Adam who comes before the four worlds. Zalman asked each of us to pick a *sefirah*. There are ten: *keter* (crown), *ḥokhmah* (wisdom), *binah* (understanding), *ḥesed* (loving-kindness), *gevurah* (strength), *tiferet* (beauty), *netzaḥ* (eternity), *hod* (glory), *yesod* (foundation), *malkhut* (sovereignty).

Of course I didn't know where to stand. So, of all places, Reb Zalman put me in Adam Kadmon's crotch. *Yesod*. Foundation. He told me that as a writer I would be generative and get the news out about Jewish renewal. I raised an eyebrow, but it turned out Zalman was right.

Each *sefirah*, Reb Zalman explained to us, communicates with the others in a flow of energy. This suggested the possibility of group prayer as a dance. From our position among the *sefirot*, he

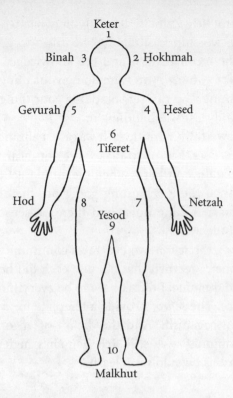

Keter
1

Binah  3        2  Ḥokhmah

Gevurah  5        4  Ḥesed

6
Tiferet

Hod        8        7        Netzaḥ

Yesod
9

10

Malkhut

had us invent gestures, acting out the feeling of *heart* or *strength* or *mercy* as we prayed the morning service. Together we moved the divine energy from the high crown of *keter* through the mind of *wisdom* and *understanding,* the right and left arms of *loving-kindness* and *strength,* the heart of beauty, and all the way down. Here I was, *yesod, foundation,* turning to my friend in *glory* to receive all the energy that had pushed and whirled down from *keter,* then dishing it out with both arms as fast as I could to the last *sefirah,* the open world of *malkhut.* Then in the end, he had us form concentric circles, singing and moving, praying and gesturing, in a loud hubbub of joy. Weird? Yes, but fun too, more fun than sitting in a pew staring at the back of someone's head.

I talked to Reb Zalman later about what we were doing. "That's what worship is all about," he said, "to get us into the sweat and the reconciliation and the knowledge, while we are doing it. There you saw: you were doing your thing, others were doing their thing. You can rely on doing your thing because you knew somebody else was handling it."

"It was powerful," I admitted. "It was a visualization, wasn't it?"

"That was a *we*. I want to make sure you hear that, because that's important everywhere. When the monks get together with the Dalai Lama, there's chanting going on, there is a *we*, and when they start making noise and there's a sensory overload, that's part of the *we*."

Embodying the *sefirot*, we became a community of prayer. A notorious loner, I learned that because each did her part in her place, I could do mine. I didn't have to be everything and everywhere at once. The *sefirot* provide a template for a Jewish community as an organism. And the dream of an organic Jewish renewal community was still Reb Zalman's highest hope and deepest worry, as I would soon learn.

*Moving Under the Tree of Life*

As a young man, Reb Zalman immersed himself in the ascetic life of the Chabad yeshivah, a wonderfully formative exploration. At the yeshivah in Brooklyn he cultivated his inner life through study of the Tanya[1] and other mystical texts, and especially through daily hours of intense davening. Reb Zalman also speaks with affection of his *mashpi'a* (literally, "influencer"), a teacher who guides students day to day on the hasidic path. Oddly, today's liberal rabbinic seminaries offer no such formal guidance in inner development.

The most profound guidance came through *yehidut* with the rebbe. Intimate spiritual counseling, one on one. It's the hasidic version of the guru-student relationship. Aside from bringing to the Jewish world at large the beautiful language of the kabbalah, and the psychological depth of prayer, Zalman Schachter's most important contribution has been his stress on *yehidut*, the personal encounter between seeker and rabbi, between student and teacher. I've met rabbis of all persuasions deeply influenced by Zalman's personal teaching.

As Reb Zalman describes it in *Sparks of Light: Counseling in the Hasidic Tradition*, *yehidut* is a "sacred dialogue in which one person's intuition enters into harmony with the intuition of the other." The hasidic master offers practical advice on career choices, and what we would call today psychological counseling, but goes much deeper. Reb Zalman quotes Nachman of Bratzlav: "In working with people to bring them to themselves, one must work at great depth, a depth scarcely imaginable." The master teaches through every gesture, through silence, and also through stories, such as Rebbe Nachman's tale of hidden gold. *Yeḥidut* may last less than a half hour, yet be deeply affecting; Reb Zalman writes of the momentousness of his first *yeḥidut* with the sixth Lubavitcher rebbe, Rabbi Joseph I. Schneersohn, in 1941. "I felt a connection that defies verbal description. He read my life in sure swift glances, eliciting from me what I needed to see to be able to receive his guidance and blessing."[2] When Reb Zalman later studied the depth psychology of Jung and the human-potential psychology of Maslow, he found new frameworks for appreciating the profundity of hasidic counseling, which is an encounter not just of intellects, but of souls.

But despite such riches, Zalman eventually chafed at the asceticism of yeshivah life. He told us at the '91 *kallah* how as a young man in the yeshivah in Brooklyn, "I used to go and taste the soup, and if the soup needed salt, I'd figure how much salt it needed and put it on the peaches. If you needed salt you'd get salt, but who says you have to get the salt in the soup?" Minor sins were punished severely: masturbation required eighty-four fast days. "The amount of guilt connected with it was enormous.

"So what do you learn?" he said. "If the body is happy—this isn't good. Only when the body is uncomfortable, not too much, because then you won't be able to study Torah. But a little constipation is good, a little pressure, and especially we don't breathe in fully, we just sit like this." He slumped in his chair. "I'm making fun of it, but this was connected with what is a good Jew. A real *tzaddik* [holy righteous person] puts on a *gartel* [a rope belt worn during evening prayers] and separates from all the stuff below, which is pelvic, and not holy."

This extreme drama of distinctions between body and spirit was psychologically unhealthy. Judaism, Zalman concluded, had to get natural, to get in touch with nature, and Jews had to do it as a community. At the '91 *kallah*, Reb Zalman unfolded this issue in an extraordinary Shabbat *shi'ur*, or class.

First the stage setting. Reb Zalman sat on a raised platform in a nice stuffed chair. He invited several hundred of us to sing C–E–G–high C, notes of a major chord. Individual notes jostled, but soon the chord fairly buzzed and rattled in the room. We were attuning to one another. Or as Zalman said, "That was a we." It was.

We lingered in the full chord, then slowly quieted. Reb Zalman dropped in his thought. "All week there's been a throbbing of rhythm in this community. Rhythm is a precondition for mental telepathy. If we could all be in the same rhythm, we would be very transparent to each other.

"The more we get into organic being, the more we fit to the emerging understanding of the cosmos. It's about life, larger than our individual lives. We are like the mitochondria inside cells that help the body to exist. The body is our mother the earth."

Judaism, he affirmed, needs to go natural. But this disturbs some Jews "because they've been drumming in your head since Yehuda Halevi [the great Spanish Jewish medieval philosopher and poet] that what's great about being Jewish is its supernatural teachings. Nature is for the goyim." He cited Arthur Cohen's *Judaism: Natural and Supernatural*, which asks if Judaism is natural, transnatural, or supernatural.

"We're getting into a situation now in which natural gets to be more Jewish. Especially when other parameters of attunement to what's real fail. If traditions are old and don't work anymore, they have to be reformatted."

"We've gone through so much change," Reb Zalman acknowledged. "The best way to adjust is to ask our mother earth to adjust us, so that we live in her rhythms." The Jewish calendar already provides an important tool, since it measures lunar months but adjusts them to a solar year, or as Zalman put it, "Sun and moon are doing their dance together." The careful observance of Jewish new moons and full moons, of spring and autumn festivals, helps us intuit "that God is a being that gives us life, that causes life to unfold."

That is the meaning Reb Zalman found in the prayer formula *Barukh Atah Yah, Eloheinu melekh ha-olam* (Blessed are you, Yah, our God, king of the earth). Though practically written out of the P'nai Or siddur because of its patriarchal implications, *melekh ha-olam* (king of the universe) was reinterpreted by Reb Zalman that afternoon. A cosmic God is too vast for human beings, he said. Even a galactic God is incomprehensible. "Imagine," he said, "for the sun it takes 360 million years to go once around the galaxy, *fershtest du*,* so when you say, 'I am worshiping God on the level on which sun consciousness worships God,' what do I know of that? I don't live in that rhythm, I'm not in that time scale, I've got no notion of what that means." I felt my head expanding: Zalman was taking me on a galactic space trip with Yiddish phrases. Then he brought me back to earth. "The best I can do is feel the *melekh ha-olam,* this world's governing pulse principle, what delights and beats in it."

For Reb Zalman, Jewish prayer is ecological, it attunes with the earth—not because God is limited to earth, but because earthly time and space is our natural human scale of attunement.

From this mystical attunement also comes a deeper respect in Judaism for the truths of contemporary science. Zalman broached the subject provocatively. "If we live on spaceship earth," he asked, "where everything is being recycled, how long is pork treif? I used to ask this question to *noodge* at my colleagues: if you bury a pig in a big flowerpot and in that big flowerpot you plant an apple tree, are the apples that come from the apple tree kosher? You see, I'm not against the notion of kosher and treif, OK. But remember," and here Zalman chanted in the familiar tones of talmudic argument, "as-long-as-I-was-in-the-tree-of-

---

* Yiddish for "Do you get it?"

knowledge-of-good-and-evil,-then-this-was-treif-and-treif-for-ever-and-this-was-kosher-and-kosher-forever. But-now-I'm-mov-ing-into-the-tree-of-life,-everything-is-being-recycled. A corpse five thousand years ago is now a *shtikel glatt kosher shmorah matzah* [a piece of the purest kosher matzah]. The molecules composed of carbon atoms—to what level of organization do you reduce a substance until you can say it is no longer treif? When you start to think in a model of an organic cosmology, a halakhah [Jewish law] has to be rethought in a certain way."

Only Reb Zalman could get *shmorah matzah* and carbon atoms in the same sentence. But I saw what he was trying to do: to integrate body and spirit, nature and soul, science and reli-gion. He was suggesting that the deeply ingrained Jewish drama of distinctions can be loosened into a continuous flow of cy-cling energies. Kosher is not kosher forever and treif not treif forever: at the molecular level, kosher and treif recycle one into the other.

Reb Zalman offered then a midrash on the trees in the garden of Eden. Under the tree of good and evil, which corresponds to our unrefined everyday consciousness, the drama of distinctions governs our lives. "As long as we are under the tree of knowledge of good and evil," Reb Zalman taught, "there's good/bad, kosher/treif, one against the other. Natural versus supernatural. But in the tree of life, the things that look like polarities fuel one another. They keep the rhythm of life going."

Behind this midrash, I could see Zalman resolving the polari-ties of his own experience. In the yeshivah paradigm the body and the body's natural energies and appetites were treif, the mental and spiritual were kosher. But in the organic paradigm, body and soul feed one another.

Whatever Reb Zalman meant by our moving under the tree of life, he did not want renewal to mean simply forgetting the polarities, the old drama of distinctions. Halakhah needs to be reworked, not overturned. He stressed this point because he suspected some of his followers thought that in Jewish renewal, anything goes.

That's why, at the same time that he spoke of the tree of life, Reb Zalman also kept insisting on the importance of Jewish ethical training, or *musar*. He spoke to us of Rabbi Israel Salanter (1810–1883), the saintly founder of the *Musar* movement that arose in the strict yeshivah world of Lithuania partly in reaction to Hasidism. Rabbi Salanter, he told us, died in an inn in Germany, in the presence of a very simple person, a Jew "who doesn't know very much about who is Israel Salanter and about Torah. The students who came to pick up his body asked about his last words. The innkeeper cried, 'He kept reassuring me, "Please, don't be afraid. If I die, it's all right. Nothing terrible will happen. The body is going to be here, that's all. Promise me not to be afraid."'"

This kind of sensitivity to others is the flower of *musar*, but Zalman knew from his own training—the salt on the peaches—that some of *musar*'s fruits were harder to swallow. *Musar* in its extremity connects beauty to sinfulness, and makes the natural desires of the body evil. For Reb Zalman, the question for Jewish renewal is how to extract the ethical sensitivity of *musar* from the outright hatred of the body.

In such matters, Reb Zalman stood between left and right, which has made him subject to attacks from both sides. Reform Judaism and other liberal Judaisms threw out too much tradition. The *haredi**  world preserved the past but refused to acknowledge the possible holiness of our present understanding—for instance, that women's lives need not be defined by traditional roles. But Zalman invoked the paradigm of the mystical Rav Kook, the first chief rabbi of Israel: "What is old will be new,

---

* *Haredi* is Hebrew for "those who tremble" with fear before God. It is the group's preferred term for those whom others call ultra-Orthodox. Cf. *Quakers*.

and what is new will be sacred." As Rabbi Arthur Waskow, who has taken on much of the leadership of Jewish renewal, put it, "Restoration and renewal are responses to the danger of modernity. One response is: this stuff is terrible and disgusting, let's vomit it out and go back to before. That's restoration. The renewal response is to digest modernity, to absorb the truths that are in it. And they are: women are fully spiritual beings, and their spirituality has to transform the traditions that excluded them. Other traditions do bear as much truth as our own; we have to honor and learn from them. We now, on this small planet, bump against each other and discover, God didn't speak at just one Sinai. The earth in danger is a major new step. The renewal movement is saying, 'What do we draw on in the ancient wisdom, without throwing out God's truth in modernity as well?'"

In classes at the '91 *kallah*, I saw the kabbalah of the four worlds mix and bubble with contemporary arts and science. A Berkeley biologist, Dr. Miriam Stampfer, and a mystical rabbi teamed together to teach kabbalah and biochemistry. Others taught kabbalah and music, kabbalah and social action, kabbalah and . . . you name it.

○　　　◑　　　●　　　◐　　　○　　　◑　　　●

I was delighted at first to be a kabbalah tourist. One evening I watched a tall woman with long white hair perform the *otiyot ḥayyot*, the living letters. Yehudit Goldfarb, of the Aquarian Minyan in Berkeley, spelled the Hebrew alphabet in postures that blended t'ai chi and kabbalah. Then magically, silently, her body gracefully prayed the Shema, flowing from letter to letter in a subtle dance. The body is missing from so much of Jewish experience. Here were Hebrew asanas: I saw I could pray with my body, too—not just my mouth.

Four-worlds insights fertilized psychological categories. Renewal people spoke of balancing themselves—their kindness with their strength, their *ḥesed* with their *gevurah*—looking for the place of beauty, *tiferet*, between them. In this way, the body becomes a walking map of the heart, the mind, the spirit.

Others practiced a complex system of prayer based on the *sefirot*, a system with its roots in Tzefat spirituality. One morning at the Havurah Institute, I davened with Mitch Chefits, a Reform rabbi and former commodities trader who leads the Havurot of South Florida. Mitch, a tall, lean man with greying beard, prayed from different parts of his body, leaning right toward *ḥesed*, or shifting back toward glory.

Others adopted the mystical practice of counting the forty-nine days of the Omer, from Passover to Shavuot, using permutations of the seven lower *sefirot*. Each day focuses on a new permutation: the *gevurah* of *ḥesed*, the *tiferet* of *ḥesed*—meditations to refine an emotional disposition. The *sefirot* become wheels within wheels. If *hod*, for instance, represents receptivity, then contemplating the *hod* of *gevurah* (the humility within strength) means learning to curb arrogance in judging others.[1]

But one kabbalist at the '91 *kallah* actually summoned Elijah.

I heard the summons by chance. Greg Burton, a kabbalist and computer wizard who administered the '91 *kallah*, asked me to lead a demonstration of a walking meditation.

A small group assembled outside the dining hall near a cluster of trees. The idea is to become mindful of each footstep as we walked. A man in his forties appeared among us in long hair and beard and a colorful tunic and paisley vest—like an escapee from a Renaissance fair. As I gave instructions—the main one was to keep silent—he moved behind me commenting that if we turned left here and right there, the trees we passed formed the pattern of the *sefirot*: a *yesod* maple, a *gevurah* thornbush. Talk about Gentile and Jewish trees: he couldn't take a walk without bumping into the *sefirot*.

"Who is this guy?" I asked Greg Burton later.

"Joseph Mark Cohen." Greg suggested I check out his late-night kabbalah class. As I walked in around midnight, Joseph was setting up Magic Markers on a table in the tree pattern. I listened in fascination as Joseph bopped musically from note to grace note—a free-form jazz-piano kabbalah. He zipped us all over the universe, then hovered over the crown of a single Hebrew letter. At one point he took *mitzvah* apart—in Hebrew spelled *mem tzadi vov heh*—מצוה. He explained that the letters *tzadi* צ and *vov* ו of *mitzvah* suggest by their shape the skeleton and the spine. The mitzvot seen as commandments are "bony" connections to the divine will—but kabbalists also seek direct, open connections. Which we were about to try.

We never got to the Magic Markers. Anyway, Joseph told me later he considered the strictly psychological interpretation of the *sefirot* an emotional "treadmill." Joseph sailed beyond psychology to mystery.

"We Jews are great thieves and storytellers," he proclaimed.

"Every time a mystery religion is about to bite the dust, we take it with us." He spoke of Abraham in Ur of the Chaldees, Daniel in Persia, Ezra and Nehemia in Babylon. Astrology, hermeticism, gnosticism, Neoplatonism: kabbalah encodes secrets of all the mystery religions.

To the kabbalist, the Torah text is story only at a superficial level. At depth Torah is one continuous name of God, a map of absolute reality. The *sefirot* decode the map. When arrayed on the tree, they create twenty-two pathways, one for each letter of the Hebrew alphabet. Every word hides meanings, every letter buzzes electrically, plus or minus, on the scale from *aleph* (1) to *ayin* (0).[2]

But the vowels supply an inner dimension, and that's where the bone of *mitzvah* can turn into a resonating space, like the inside of a flute. As is well known, the Torah scroll is all consonants; when we read Torah, we supply the vowel sounds. This also has a spiritual meaning: a vowel, Joseph explained, is a *tzinor*, an opening; each vowel opens us to the divine workings, makes a channel for the human spirit.

We "breathe" new life into Torah every time we read; this polysemy is a frequent resource of rabbinic midrash, as is the freedom to make anagrams and gematria. Joseph explained that *tzinor* [צנר, or *tzadi nun reish*] rearranged becomes *ratzon* [רצן, *reish tzadi nun*], which means, in English, "will"—God's will.

In the ecstatic kabbalah of Abraham Abulafia, a thirteenth-century Spanish mystic whose "science of letter combination" greatly influenced later kabbalists of Tzefat, chanting vowels reshapes the body into an instrument of the higher will of the *Ein Sof*, the infinite one. It is a mystical—and musical—attunement.

That midnight, Joseph chanted the vowels in Elijah's Hebrew name, Eliahu, another melodic riff in the throbbing rhythm of the *kallah*. "Ay . . . ee . . . ah . . . ooh," he intoned, inviting us to join him. He gracefully gestured with his hands, associating each vowel with a part of the body: crown, third eye, heart, and navel.

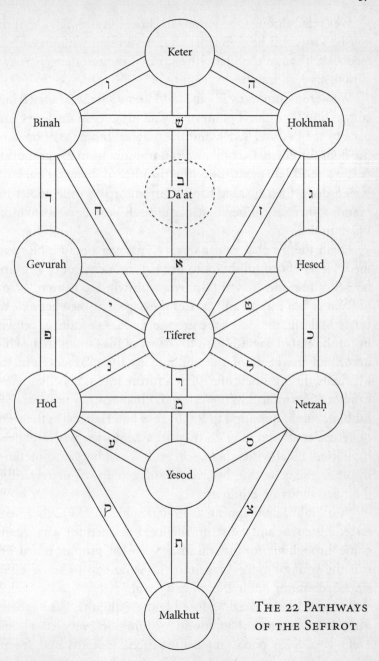

THE 22 PATHWAYS
OF THE SEFIROT

We cycled through the vowels in chorus. *Ay-ee-ah-ooh*. At the *ooh* he kissed his lips, and the sound vibrated with an edge of feedback. Then in the silence he savored the resonance, his eyes closed, his eyelids fluttering slightly.

We were summoning Elijah, and I knew a sense of mysterious connection. The oldest point of Jewish mystery in my heart goes back to the Passover seder, and the magical moment of opening the door for Elijah. Every year, I ran upstairs from my grandparents' paneled basement to let the prophet in, banging back the screen door, then rushing back to monitor the wine goblet my grandmother set on her best plate. Each year I was convinced Elijah took a sip.

Elijah the prophet returns every Passover because he never died. He ascended full-body to heaven in "a chariot of fire, and horses of fire, and . . . went up by a whirlwind to heaven."[3] Now he lives in two realms, and carries messages between heaven and earth. Malachi, the last of the prophets, speaks of him as returning at the end of days to "turn the heart of the fathers to the children, and the heart of the children to their fathers."[4] In the Mishnah, the sages describe Elijah's future role as conciliator and bringer of harmony.[5] In the Talmud, Elijah teaches new Torah to rabbinic sages, appearing to Rabbi Yose ben Ḥalafta[6] in the ruins of Jerusalem.[7] And later through the centuries, wherever Jews have lived, Elijah visits them, sometimes as a beggar, sometimes in other guises, testing ordinary Jews' generosity, or rewarding their acts of loving-kindness.

So, could Elijah appear in Philadelphia in 1991? As Joseph rested his chant and we sat in silence, I listened for what might come through me, for the still small voice the prophet heard. I'm still the young boy peeking into the wine cup to see if Elijah sipped, doubting but half hoping it's real.

Joseph Cohen's dazzling lore blew my circuits. His kabbalah turned text into hypertext, found meanings in every letter—and every tree. Such poetic intensity skirted insanity, and Joseph warned us of the danger of doing kabbalah in languages other than Hebrew. But Joseph's intensity was nicely balanced by his gentleness. I'd misjudged him. Though *sefirot*-obsessed and not the person for a silent walking meditation, Joseph is a witty poet, and brilliant man. His teaching fascinated me, but the simple scheme of the *sefirot* Reb Zalman first taught me had now opened into complexities far beyond what I could work with immediately in my life.

○　　　◑　　　●　　　◐　　　○　　　◑　　　●

Fortunately, as Jewish renewal built a new vehicle for Judaism, some teachers influenced by Reb Zalman created radically simple designs. One such teacher is a forty-three-year-old woman with round blue eyes, a sultry voice, and blond curly hair: Rabbi Shefa Gold.

I first met Shefa at the 1991 *kallah*, where she performed her music, accompanied on guitar and drums. She set Hebrew psalms to frank Gospel rhythms—a distinctly American fusion of Holy Roller and Jewish I never thought possible. Since then I've heard her music everywhere: at Reform Jewish camps and staid synagogues and many Jewish renewal gatherings. Her rousing *birkat hamazon*, the grace after meals—Reb Zalman calls it "Shefa's table banger"—is particularly popular. So is her version of the morning prayers (*Shaharit*).[1]

She basically uses headlines, phrases—not whole prayers—from the sequence of blessings, chanting them over and over. The tunes are both easy and deep; it's not long before you hear them in your head when you wake up in the morning. But they're also ideal for group attunement.

Shefa, like many in Jewish renewal, had opened herself up to a variety of influences, but she'd brought back a winning simplicity.

I had a chance to speak with her about this at the '93 *kallah* in Berkeley. We met in a coffee shop; she came in wearing jeans and a fuchsia chiffon scarf. She has a good eye for colors: she once worked inventing new shades of pigment for a paint company, and giving them names—a good apprentice job for a Jewish mystic. But as a teenager, she couldn't even get to the Torah, much less to kabbalah.

"I had a big fight growing up," she said. "I wanted to participate Jewishly and was excluded. I wanted to read from the Torah, to be at the center of prayer. At this synagogue they still don't count women in the minyan. They said there wasn't really any oppression of women in Judaism, that women are highly respected, and highly regarded, and holier than men. Yet I saw before my eyes something very different. It just made me feel crazy."

Her rabbi wouldn't let her read from Torah for her bat mitzvah, but she found a way around it. She said she would give a bat mitzvah speech on light. "Then I sang in Hebrew the parts from the Torah referring to light. So I snuck it in."

Blessed with that sort of ingenuity, it's not surprising she later took a master's degree in the philosophy of creativity. As a thesis, she wrote a play about Martin Buber and began performing it around the country. When Zalman heard about it, he invited her to the first P'nai Or *kallah*, in 1985. "I met the whole Jewish renewal movement and found out it could be fun to be Jewish, which I hadn't realized before. I thought [being Jewish] was a necessary burden—noble, but not a great joyful gift." She moved from writing plays to songs. "Music opens our hearts," she said. "It's an experience you can't argue with."

She told me about her first breakthrough musical composition. "To open a conference of psychologists, psychics, and scientists on intuition, I wrote a song based on the Shema. That was the heart of it. The basic central command in Judaism is to listen. That's what intuition is, too—a deep listening." Since then, she told me, "my spiritual practice has been moving toward learning how to listen deeper."

Shefa Gold's music, now on several cassettes, shows a Gospel influence, particularly in her renderings of Hebrew psalms. As I suspected already, she acknowledges drawing on a variety of traditions. She told me, "Part of Jewish renewal is a realization that God is not Jewish. Our experience of God is beyond religion. Then we come back into our lives and heritage, history, and culture as Jews to express and explore it as Jews."

"God is not Jewish?" I realized she'd formulated the Rambam's negative in basic English.

"The experiences of God, the glimpses we have of the divine, go beyond any form. So once we have that glimpse we try to express it in whatever forms are part of us. The experience comes first, of what is the essence and the source of life. Then I desire to celebrate and praise it and create from that inspiration."

Shefa and her husband Andy Gold live in inspiration, on a mountain peak outside Las Vegas, New Mexico. Rose Mountain serves as a spiritual retreat center. Andy showed me his natural *mikveh*, a mountain pool; from there you can see sixty miles in any direction, and the aspen leaves quake in the wind. Reb Zalman stressed the idea of a Jewish attunement to nature, and Rose Mountain is a good place for it.

Once, when my family and I were visiting Albuquerque, Andy and Shefa drove down off the mountain to see us. They arrived, laughing, hours late. They'd missed a turnoff and driven fifty miles the wrong way all because of Shefa's "Ma gadlu," which she'd just recorded. It's line 6 of Psalm 92: "How great are your works, *Yah*, how deep are your designs." She chants it in Hebrew hypnotically until the message penetrates the heart. While they listened, a dozen deer darted across the road, leaping in perfect rhythm with the song.

I asked her about her "Shacharis," or morning prayer service, on her cassette *Tzuri (My Rock)*. Where did she get the idea of hypnotically repeating key Hebrew phrases? She learned the technique, she said, "through other traditions that have kept that practice alive" like Hindu mantras and Sufi *dhikr*.[2] "But I do find that when I go back to the Jewish sources, some Jews always knew that the repetition of certain sacred phrases would unlock the experience of the divine for them."

In spring 1996, Gold completed her degree in the rabbinate at the Reconstructionist Rabbinical College. She sees herself researching and developing a whole "medicine bag" of Jewish spiritual practices.

Overall, she's working toward a profound simplicity. She sensed that "some people are turned off to Jewish practices because they are so complicated and cumbersome. They can't find the essence anymore because they find it's 'Do these millions of things' and 'Say these millions of things'—until there's a feeling of being lost in it. Not everybody feels that way. But some who do, maybe those drawn to Buddhist or Sufi practice, want to look for the essence and experience it more deeply rather than saying the whole liturgy."

That's why I thought Marc Lieberman, the father of the Jewish Buddhist dialogue, might get a kick out of Shefa Gold's Kabbalat Shabbat service. So I was pleased when he joined me at the Berkeley *kallah* of '93. But Marc spent most of the service shifting in his seat and riffling through the prayer book while the rest of us swayed and chanted and danced around in our white clothes like angels.

As we walked the streets of Berkeley, I felt overjoyed. He had his reservations.

"What's the matter?" I asked. "Didn't that do something for you?"

He turned to me. "All this Jewish renewal effort to make Judaism attractive and appealing is wonderful. But . . ." He paused. He was wearing a Hindu brocade kippah; it looked like a psychedelic ice cream vendor's hat. "Judaism is like an old Bentley. It's a wonderful vehicle with hand-tooled wood interior and rich leather seats. The only trouble is, you have to stop every few miles and work under the hood to get the engine going again."

I laughed as I often do with my old friend, but his comment stung. Thanks to Reb Zalman's efforts, which now have blossomed and spread through the teachings of Rabbis Shefa Gold, Marcia Prager, and many others, the Jewish renewal movement has revved up the liturgy. It has made worship more fun. But Marc's question made me wonder: why is all the effort needed? If so many parts have to be replaced in the vehicle, might it be better to start over with a new model? These are painful questions to contemplate, and I'm aware that many Jews are answering them with their feet. Our fastest-growing Jewish denomination in America is unaffiliated.

I carried Marc's question around with me to the Havurah Institute much later, where I met Judith Plaskow, a professor of religion at Manhattan College and a major Jewish feminist theologian. I felt she might have a comment about the Bentley. After all, she'd spent a lot of time under the hood. In *Standing Again at Sinai* she teaches how profound and thoroughgoing the patriarchal bias of Judaism is.[3]

Plaskow's early battles, like those of many Jewish feminists, were for equal access: the right of women to read from the Torah, to participate fully in rituals. But a deeper problem emerged. Plaskow writes, "When a woman stands in the pulpit and reads from the Torah that daughters can be sold as slaves (Exod. 21:7–11) she participates in a profound contradiction between the message of her presence and the content of what she learns and teaches. It is this contradiction feminists must address, not simply 'adding' women to a tradition that remains basically unaltered, but transforming Judaism into a religion that women as well as men have a role in shaping."[4]

Judith Plaskow's critique goes beyond substituting feminine words for masculine in Jewish prayers. Rather, she sees in the classical texts of Judaism an exclusion of women's history, women's viewpoints. She notes the scant attention women receive in the Torah, and points out that a major order (division) of the Talmud is *Nashim*, women, but that no order is called *Anashim*, men. It's clear that in rabbinic Judaism men are the norm, women the other.

"Judaism," Plaskow writes, "is a deeply patriarchal tradition. To change it will require a revolution as great as the transition from biblical to rabbinic Judaism precipitated by the destruction of the Second Temple."[5]

That sounds like a daunting task, so I was touched by her willingness to work to change Judaism rather than give up on it altogether. That's why when I met her I thought she might help me with Marc Lieberman's challenging question.

"With Judaism posing so many problems for women," I asked her, "do you ever reach the point where you say, 'We've got to start over, it's too much trouble'?"

"Of course that is the sixty-four-thousand-dollar question," she answered. "I could not convince your friend that he should remain with Judaism. I don't even see it as something that I want to do. Because the response to that question is where we find community in our lives, rather than how many positive things are in the tradition and how many negative—if I wanted to make a list. When I come to the Havurah Institute, and I'm sitting with other liberal Jews who care about spirituality and are working on these issues together, then I feel: this is my community. This is my home. This is where the most parts of my life come together. This is who I am. So it's not a question for me. Yes, you have to crank up the car. But I don't have another car."

As Reb Zalman also had been teaching me ever since I stood in the crotch of Adam Kadmon at my first *kallah*, Jewish renewal is about community.

Marc spoke as a visitor to Jewish renewal. I was, at best, a sojourner. For as long as I was part of a we, I felt inspired. I don't always have Shefa's faith, but I loved being around it; as I was chanting her music, or davened with Reb Zalman, or learned midrash from Arthur Waskow, or shared a Shabbat service with

Marcia Prager or Hannah Siegel, the Bentley raced down the road. But when I left the Jewish renewal community, the engine stalled. I had my doubts, and my doubts are me, too, aren't they?

O

I reached a crisis over doubt a few months after the Berkeley *kallah* when I attended a Jewish Buddhist conference at Marc's invitation.

I looked forward to an encounter between Art Green, the leading theologian of the havurah movement, and Joseph Goldstein, who'd taught me, through his book, simple meditation. Goldstein heads (with Sharon Salzberg) the most successful institution of Buddhist meditation instruction in the country: IMS, the Insight Meditation Society, in Barre, Massachusetts. The conference, in part the brainchild of Rabbi Sheila Weinberg, was held at the nearby Barre Center for Buddhist Studies.

Art Green spoke that first evening with quiet conviction, but Marc found the actual dialogue disappointing, because Art and Joseph slid past each other rather than engage in direct comparison. I believe Marc longed for a direct engagement because by his nature he loves debate and argument.

Afterward, as we discussed the evening's events before retiring, he was emphatic in his dissatisfaction, and very certain of his viewpoint. At one point I asked, "Well, don't you think it's at least possible that there's a God?"

No, he didn't.

Buddhist texts provide artful arguments against Hindu theism, and many Buddhists have armed themselves philosophically against the concept of a divine creator. But I heard a rebuttal in Art Green's presentation.

"In kabbalah," Green said, "we learn that the whole Torah is one long name of God. But we don't know how to read it. God has done us the favor of breaking the divine name up into little words—teachings, commandments, parables—so we'll have something to hold on to and be loyal to. But if we could see with the mind's eye opened, we'd see there's nothing there but the name of God. Yet the name of God is not separate from God: we'd see there's nothing there but God. In the insight of Chabad mysticism—sheer nonsense, but also the greatest truth—nothing but God exists. This is the most profound Jewish mystical teaching. In the words of the *Aleinu*, know this day and settle it in your hearts, that the Lord is God on heaven above and on earth beneath—'*Ein od.*' There is nothing else. Patently nonsensical, yet the only truth. We need to train ourselves to this awareness—that there is no separation between human beings. We must know there is only the One."

In a few strongly worded sentences, Art Green laid out the path I would travel over the next few years. I was impressed that he spoke not as a theologian, but very personally about his spiritual journey. I'd met a knowledgeable teacher I hoped to encounter again. I felt the person behind his ideas—the integrity of someone who admitted the difficulty of the Jewish path, yet affirmed that the language of Judaism brought him closer to the reality of God.

But that night Marc did not find Art Green's language compelling.

That got me thinking, and more than thinking. At least Marc knew his position, whereas, despite Reb Zalman's helpful statement that God is a true God, and all the joys I'd experienced with Jewish renewal, I still floated in a fuzzy agnosticism.

Zalman Schachter speaks of Buddhist nontheism as cleaning out the images of God we may have accumulated. The rigor and clarity of Buddha's teaching appealed to me. The actual practice changed my way of thinking. If I were shopping for a new religion, Buddhism would be high on the list. Yet, as Judith Plaskow suggested, the shopping-list metaphor isn't quite right. Somehow with Buddhism I was in the wrong aisle.

That night I lay awake in the cabin. My head buzzed: the

same old questions. Is there God, or is there simply emptiness? I couldn't sleep.

That night, that moment in the cabin, did I think God real? The way the hasidic masters did, or as Reb Zalman had challenged me in Dharamsala? If there's no place without God, as the *ḥasidim* insisted, why couldn't I get a hint of Her or It in that tiny bedroom on a cool October evening in the Massachusetts woods?

I grew silent. Earlier that evening, describing his own bouts of spiritual "dryness," Art Green paraphrased the Song of Songs: "On my bed I sought the one my soul loves—and found him not."[6] Not. Not and nothing in that deep woods—a few soft snores from Marc in the next room. I put on my jacket and took a walk.

The Massachusetts stars clustered thickly in a black honeycomb sky. I was standing upright, but it is just as correct to say I was hanging upside down with my head thrust into that dark rich and free space. I felt a grounding intuition. Even lacking a definite sense of God in the moment, I could not imagine this beautiful universe or my life in it as *meshugass*—nonsense, meaningless accident.

My own twisting and turning—and Art Green's helpful talk—led me to a basic orientation, one that guided my search in the months and years ahead. I could not imagine a universe without a guiding principle! The Rambam would have approved: the statement is entirely negative.

I am not saying I never came back to doubt. I have come back to it many times, to profound doubts and moments of realization, moments of great joy and openness when of course it seems obvious that the whole earth is full of God's glory. And then a falling away, back to doubt and confusion. And so the roller coaster goes.

Yet the car stopped for a moment at the top and I got a view. In her answer to me, Judith Plaskow had stressed the importance to her of community. But I had my own answer to the Bentley question.

I understood that one chooses a spiritual vehicle not simply for convenience, quality, and road handling. Before all that, one must have an intuition, a ground sense of how things are. In my case, that there is meaning to the world around me and my life in it, even if I don't know what it is.

I was on a search then for a Jewish language for that meaning. Jewish renewal got me off to a good start, by its healthy embrace of the actual world I knew. But I wanted more. I wanted the experience Shefa Gold spoke of, the intuitive experience that precedes all the names and all the words we give to it.

For several years, Rabbi Jonathan Omer-Man had extended an open invitation to study meditation with him in Los Angeles, and to learn more about the community that had grown around his school of Jewish wisdom, Metivta. I was about ready to try it. A telephone conversation with Reb Zalman tipped the balance.

○

That conversation began with a discussion of Jewish mysticism and science. I admired Zalman Schachter's search for the new in the old, in Jewish tradition and in Jewish mysticism; and for the holy in the new: ecology, contemporary science. But how did the two searches fit together?

He astonished me by answering, "I think everyone is a mystic today."

"Oh, I thought everyone was a scientist."

He said, "If you look at the overlap between what science is talking about and what kabbalah is talking about, from the big bang to the black hole—they're covering the same territory. Nowadays if you want to be a well-informed person who is a citizen of the planet, you share those ideas that heretofore only mystics used to have.

"It's mystical—not because its mystifying, or mystagogy. It's mystical in the sense that it looks at reality as other than the reality of our scale of observation."

At the *shi'ur* in '91 Zalman taught that we attune most naturally to our own human scales of time and space—the God of the earth and not the God of the universe. But our contemporary physics moves in realms far beyond our human scales: from subatomic particles to superstrings and the "theory of everything." The language of our physics is literally unimaginable—no images, just abstruse equations. As the social thinker Paul Goodman once argued, this makes most of us ignorant peasants in a world where the doctors of science are the high priests: we accept on authority what we cannot understand.

Our ignorance of the actual basis of science produces a curious dislocation. Our contemporary physics teaches me that the table I drum my fingers on is mostly empty space, and that the permanence and solidity of the table is an illusion. The reality of the table is different from what I can observe at the scale of my senses.

That was precisely Zalman's point. "If you start looking at science," Reb Zalman said, "from quantum mechanics to relativity, we are dealing with material the kabbalists used to deal with. Instead of saying the world is made of electrons, the kabbalists used to say the world is made of divine letters. On both sides, the people who understand really what they are saying will tell you that those things are metaphors. There is no particle that isn't also a wave, no wave that isn't also a particle. When you look at *orot*, *keilim*, or *nitzotzot*,[7] the kabbalah uses the same language: the light and the vessels and the spark."

But if so, why not simply use the more precise language of science and leave it at that?

"The answer is that the language of science does not have enough of the contemplative technology in its hands." Science does not provide spiritual practices such as meditation, prayer,

chanting, contemplation to make insights available and immediate to the heart and soul—practices such as the four-worlds
mantra Reb Zalman had taught me at the JFK Airport, my first
lesson in Jewish meditation.

In Reb Zalman's view, "the mysticism we do today is no less
mystical, except we don't do it by global telepathy: we create a
global network of information sharing. The function is the
same. But today we use the media available to us. We don't use
the psychospiritual media, but the technological media."

"You would include e-mail, faxes?" I asked.

"Yes." I could hear his assent crackling over the phone, his enthusiasm racing through the wires. "That we are talking right
now on the phone is a feat the disciples of the Baal Shem Tov
would have to do spiritually."

"You feel it could be done both ways?"

"Right. Because not everything that I say and that goes
through the wire and that you hear makes for the communication. My background and your background—that we hugged
each other, and were in India together—makes the field from
which you and I communicate. It's also part of the communication, and doesn't go through the wire, and goes beyond the wire."

Much of my communication with Reb Zalman over the years
has gone beyond the wire. His sense of spiritual intimacy, based
on *yehidut*, is profound: he wants Jews to take Judaism personally. He feels people needed to immerse themselves at the *kallot*
or at the Jewish renewal spiritual retreat center, Elat Chayyim.
"You cannot learn how to daven except from a davenner," Reb
Zalman said. "Nonverbal things happen that call for attunement.
Having spiritual intimacy in a group is important."

Certainly I'd learned to appreciate davening most from direct
experience of the *kallot*. And if I were going to get more of the
"contemplative technology" in my hands, I had to study meditation in person, not from a book. So in the spring of 1995, I set off

for Los Angeles and Rabbi Jonathan Omer-Man. On my way, I stopped off to see his teacher, and mine, Reb Zalman, at the time he sat in the Wisdom Chair at the Naropa Institute in Boulder, Colorado.

*Rabbi Zalman Schachter-Shalomi and Eve Ilsen:*
*My Days Are Numbered*
DENVER AND BOULDER
SUNDAY, MARCH 19, 1995; 17 ADAR II 5755

The pilot began his initial approach. As we broke through the clouds, the Rockies emerged, brown and rugged, their crinkles and folds sugared with snow. Young mountains like the Himalayas in whose foothills Reb Zalman and I walked together in our own *yehidut*. Though this teaching did not come in the context of yeshivah training, Zalman's approach with me owed much to his understanding of the sacred encounter, one on one, between teacher and student.

That time in Dharamsala was very brief, perhaps no more than a half hour, and yet the lessons stuck. One lesson, in fact, was about time. Pausing just outside the Tibetan Astro-Medical Institute, he quoted Psalm 90, first in Hebrew, then translating, "Teach us to number our days that we may get a heart of wisdom."

Reb Zalman wears a computerized watch that gives dates in both Jewish and secular reckonings. Following Chabad practice, each day he studies an *aliyah*, or reader's portion, of the coming Torah *parashah*. A special psalm marks each day as well. These practices mark a grid of inner time, and without a grid how can I perceive the rhymes in time known as coincidence?

Judaism, for most of its history a landless religion, has always found the sacred in time more than space. Rabbi Abraham Joshua Heschel speaks of the Sabbath as "a cathedral in time."

Jewish time sings counterpoint to secular time, runs from evening to morning, and moon to moon. This can be joyous music, or excruciating dissonance. My father's father came from hasidic Kamenetz in the Ukraine, chucked the Sabbath when he came to America, and worked seven days a week to support his family. My mother's father, a Talmud scholar from Lithuania, became a barber here. But he refused to cut hair on Shabbat, which made him a poor, proud, and bitter man.

Today the struggle continues. For many Jews the drumbeat of secular time overpowers the fainter ticking of the inner clock. How can we make Shabbat holy when Friday night is date night and weekends are made for Michelob? Yet I've felt the pull of deep Jewish time, especially in Jerusalem, where a new day begins with the setting sun, so that on a Friday afternoon, as the golden light thins, Shabbat settles in.

The months, too, show their rhythm; the darkness of a new moon opens to full light at its middle, when many Jewish festivals begin. Because Jewish months are lunar, the moon shape lights up the date. A full moon was shining three nights before I set off for Denver, marking the fourteenth of Adar II, and the festival of Purim. The next full moon I'd see at home would be a round glowing matzah of Passover. As I crossed time zones from Central to Mountain, and wisdom zones from Purim to Pesach, I kept a picture close to heart: the Passover moon overhead, and my younger daughter reciting the four questions at our family seder.

O

The plane touched down and we taxied a long while to the gate. The architect designed the new airport as an encampment of white tents, an Arabian desert mirage, all clean, pure, and unreal in the distance. I walked a half mile to a train station, zoomed along for several minutes, and made another trek to a prospect of carousels.

None held my bags. Denver had spent millions on a computerized baggage system. For me, the system worked perfectly: it lost my luggage. As passengers waited at their carousels, orphaned bags piled up left and right. I watched other people's baggage whirling by. I was looking for God and couldn't find my suitcase. I saw a fellow passenger speaking to an airline representative and queued up behind him.

"What color is your bag?" the baggage man asked.

"I don't know," the traveler answered.

"Well, can you tell me what it looks like?"

"No I can't."

The baggage handler looked puzzled. Me too. I'd forgotten a lot in my time, but usually could be counted on to remember the color of my suitcase.

Then I saw the traveler's face. His brown eyes were open but unmoving. He was blind. Despite my attempts through meditation to cultivate equanimity, the unkind, reflexive, critical impatient mind still functioned at warp speed, dishing out judgments. It would not be fair—to other Jews—to say it is my Jewish mind. But the impatience I'd learned, the sarcasm, the humor at others' expense were part of my Jewish family's dialogue with one other and had become part of my dialogue with the world and, painfully, with myself.

So the blind man came to remind me: dialogue isn't just two people talking to one another. Dialogue requires an intuition, even before words come out of your mouth, about the person you are speaking with. Without calling upon the world of intuition, the dialogue we do with ourselves is deaf—and the dialogue with others, blind.

We Jews are in a dialogue with a past that is in dialogue with itself, a very complex conversation over millennia of texts and milieus and cultures. In my own way, I would enter that conversation over the next several weeks, with Rabbis Zalman Schachter, Jonathan Omer-Man, and Arthur Green, and their students. But the blind traveler became my first teacher—and omen.

For now, my bags were lost. I called the bellman at my hotel in Denver. I carried a pager so my family could contact me wherever I was. Would he kindly beep me if the bags arrived?

O

I spoke at a Denver bookstore on the Jewish Buddhist dialogue and what I'd learned there. Since the publication of *The Jew in the Lotus*, I'd spoken around the country, at bookstores and synagogues, daylong conferences, Hillels and colleges, departments of religious studies and Jewish studies. The curiosity intrigued me and stimulated me to do more learning and to understand better the meaning of this dialogue.

I'd benefited by spending two years immersed in the minutiae of the exchange between the rabbis and the Dalai Lama. I'd gone over the words and the gestures so often that something stayed with me of the depth of that encounter. I'd learned the conditions that make dialogue possible, or difficult. Often, for instance, when I meet someone different from myself, I am tempted to approach that person through that difference. Then it becomes a barrier rather than a bridge.

Shortly after my return from India, a good friend called to say the Dalai Lama was on TV. I switched on the set, and a small square of light expanded to the Dalai Lama's face in a close-up. The camera panned back, and of all the people on the planet, I saw John McLaughlin, the conservative talk-show host best known for bellowing on TV. McLaughlin turned to his guest, the spiritual leader for millions of the world's Buddhists, and barked, "You don't believe in God, do you?"

That's a pretty good example of how *not* to do dialogue.

Compare that with the Dalai Lama's question when he first wanted to meet with Jews. "Can you tell me," he asked, "the secret of Jewish spiritual survival in exile?" That question came from an intuitive understanding and appreciation of Jewish history and experience. It brought out the best in us.

We Jews are the dialogue people—from Genesis to *I and Thou*. That afternoon, traveling the high dry road from Denver to Boulder, I was thinking about Martin Buber just as a furious-looking spiky tumbleweed rolled across the highway. I burst out laughing, because tumbleweed and Martin Buber just didn't make any sense in the same universe, which is probably why kabbalah mandated at least four.

The deeper level of dialogue, which Martin Buber called the I-Thou encounter, transforms the participants. Buber drew his philosophy in part from his study of Hasidism. Reb Zalman experienced such sacred encounters in the practice of *yehidut*, between rebbe and *hasid*. He brought that experience to his encounter with the Dalai Lama. At one point, after a long conversation stimulated by the Tibetan leader's curiosity about angels, Reb Zalman said, "If we do the dialogue right, the angel of the Jews is speaking through me and the angel of Tibet is listening in you." Saying those words, they became true. "So the dialogue isn't just at one level," Reb Zalman added. Suddenly, it wasn't, because he'd found the most poetic, concise, accurate language to describe every dimension of the encounter.

Many rationalists despise angel talk and other language from kabbalah as *bubbe meises*—fairy tales, superstition. In the name of reason many angels were banished from modern prayer books, though a few lurk prominently, like Isaiah's holy seraphim in the *Kedushah* (sanctification prayer). The Rambam thought belief in angels basic to Jewish faith. Clearly, though, the philosopher didn't mean treacly images of chubby putti with wings, which we've inherited from European painting. Angels are much more interesting language than those images suggest. Reading the Rambam's description of the *sar ha-goy*, or angel of a nation, explicates Zalman's statement to the Dalai Lama. An angel of a nation is that nation's essence. All the anticipation, preparation, difficult travel, Zalman's personal history with the Holocaust and the Dalai Lama's with the Chinese, converged at that moment of encounter. Zalman and Tenzin Gyatso were no longer two men talking: instead the essence of the Jewish and the essence of the Tibetan people were speaking and listening through them.

I met Reb Zalman and Eve Ilsen, his recent bride, at a Himalayan restaurant in Boulder, Colorado. Zalman had been appointed to the Wisdom Chair at the Naropa Institute, a Buddhist teaching center founded by the late Chogyam Trungpa. He'd taught there in the seminal year of 1975.

My rebbe was probably relieved at age seventy-one to be sharing an office with a nice Tibetan lama, far from the day-to-day adventure of the Jewish renewal scene in Philadelphia. In 1987 he retired from Temple University, and since then, at the kallahs, he'd also been announcing his retirement and withdrawal from Jewish renewal. The trouble was, none of his ḥasidim really wanted to believe it.

I know I didn't. There was Reb Zalman with his great smile, waiting with his new bride at a table. He rose and I gave him a big hug, then kissed him on the cheek.

I turned to Eve: in her mid-forties, she has a sensitive and kind face, high forehead, dark hair, and knowing eyes. I felt a bond with her immediately.

Eve had studied with Joseph Campbell, the philosopher of myth, and with the New Age psychologist Jean Houston as well as an extraordinary teacher from Jerusalem, Colette Albouker-Muscat. Eve brought many elements together in her teaching: storytelling, body work, and New Age, Jewish, and feminist strains.

After we ordered vegetarian meals, Zalman and Eve told me a little about their wedding in February. I'd seen a photo of him, dancing, snapping his fingers over his head, eyes closed in ecstatic concentration. The celebration was a Jewish renewal homecoming, but the ceremony more private. Zalman and Eve gathered together some of the children from his previous marriages. The difficult emotional fact was that, as a result of this latest change in their father's life, the children—and Zalman—inevitably felt some pain. He asked for their forgiveness and blessing.

Considering the karma Zalman accumulated with three previous marriages and ten children, who ranged in age from fifty down to eight, the ceremony made sense. Had Zalman invented it for the occasion? No, he explained, he derived it from a talmudic requirement that before a wedding the groom must "see his bride." The simple intent is to get a good look at her face, "so you shouldn't get the wrong bride." But for Reb Zalman, the deeper meaning is, before marriage, you must "see" the other person completely—that is, in the full complexity of his or her past.

Zalman's past is certainly complex, and from time to time he'd scandalized lots of folks in the Jewish world, including me. He'd told me, "Have the wisdom to change your life from where you are." Only later did I understand his own difficulty in following this good advice.

Impulsively, perhaps, but out of real affection, I'd made Reb Zalman my teacher. I learned from him, mistakes and all. Perhaps he had much to account for in his personal life, but so did I, and no one appointed me his accountant. I liked Reb Zalman, he charmed me, and he'd brought me something precious from a world of European Jewry the Nazis had obliterated. Over the past fifty years of teaching, since his ordination by Lubavitch in 1947, he'd done the same for thousands of Jews. I couldn't help but think that his lack of law and order made for part of his appeal to my anarchic generation. But that's also why I found it poignant that at the *kallot* where he was bidding us farewell, Reb Zalman had been meditating so openly on halakhah, *musar* ethics, and the future of Jewish renewal.

The waiter brought over a dish of chapatis, flat Indian bread. Reb Zalman lifted one off the plate, tore it, and murmured the blessing over bread. A smile spread over his lips. He chewed the chapati carefully, taking it in nutrient by nutrient, his tasting also part of the prayer.

The conversation got around to Martin Buber, or rather I got around to him, because of the tumbleweed, and because I'd just written an essay about him. In a 1911 lecture in Prague (which

Franz Kafka attended) Buber spoke of "Jewish renewal." What did Zalman think of Buber as his forerunner?

He closed his eyes for a moment and went into a little meditation, as if pulling this stuff up from the world of imagination. His eyes opened. "At certain moments, the body needs something so much that it's synthesized, like an enzyme."

"What was the enzyme for?"

"To break the surface tension between Jews and Christians. That was very important work."

"Did you ever meet him?"

"No. But I heard recordings of his hasidic tales." Zalman, a deft mimic, instantly intoned a few German phrases in Buber's voice and Buber pulled up a chair at our table. Reb Zalman added, "Jiri Langer told the same stories more casually.[1] Buber's approach was too literary, too gothic."

I said Kafka registered the same criticism.

Reb Zalman smiled. "Buber was in the generation of Lady Gregory. In order to go among the folk, one had to put the literary patina on, and this is what Kafka objected to." Zalman added that Kafka's tale of Gregor Samsa turning into a cockroach, "The Metamorphosis," was based on Jiri Langer's life. After he began to wear hasidic garb, his parents hid him in the back corners of their house.[2]

I said, "It seems to me that story owes a lot as well to the flavor of Rebbe Nachman's tales[3]—which he first read through Buber's translation."

Literary transmission aside, Buber's importance to Jewish renewal derives from his long view of Judaism as a struggle between forces and forms. He was wholly on the side of the forces—the inward spirit. He saw Jewish history repeat this struggle in each phase: prophets versus priests in the era of the Temple, and *ḥasidim* versus *mitnagdim* in the eighteenth century. Buber regarded the exterior forms, the outward observances—halakhah itself—as husk. His rejection of halakhah, the path of Jewish law, was radical and thoroughgoing.

"Buber said something important," Reb Zalman agreed. He reached for the serving bowl of yellow dal and spooned some on his plate. "But he just did not have the immersion in Jewish practice."

"That struck me, too," I said. "To Buber rituals are always ossifying, decaying. But by rejecting Jewish practice, he left us without a vehicle."

A sitarist wandered into the restaurant, sat down in the front of the cash register, and played his heart out, banging and thrumming loudly. I wanted to give him money . . . if he would stop.

Buber rejected all formalism because he wanted to be open to sacred I-Thou encounter wherever and whenever it might occur. But from his Chabad training, Reb Zalman offered the specific practice of *yeḥidut* as a template for such encounters.

Not that Zalman denied the charms of accident. He extends *yeḥidut* from its original formal setting to include chance encounters, like mine in the airport with the blind man. "People with whom we are not usually willing to relate in a vulnerable and open way," he writes, "can engage us in a shattering *yeḥidut*. Once, a stranger confronted me on a busy street. He challenged, 'Are you sure?' and walked away. Another person, drunk and staggering, walked up to me at a bustling intersection and asked me, 'Is there such a thing as real?' He then continued, 'How old are you?' When I, taken aback by his chutzpah, told him, he replied, 'Does it pay to live that long?'"

According to Zalman, "Such figures were Prophet Elijah in disguise, delivering messages that I needed at those moments."[4]

Zalman, raised in the warm hasidic culture of prewar Poland, was friendlier to Orthodoxy than Buber the German intellectual. If anything Zalman encouraged his followers to greater observance by showing how Jewish practice can be reconciled with contemporary thought. That didn't mean he wasn't highly critical of halakhic procedures as practiced in the Orthodox world today. But he saw a possibility Buber rejected: that halakhah might be reformatted.

"Most of the time," Reb Zalman told me once, "halakhah has gone by precedent, which means they've been driving by the rearview mirror. My sense: we have to now go and start looking ahead. I am not interested in what precedent they followed as my primary source. The process by which regular halakhah has been developing is too slow, because it hasn't yet come out and through the industrial revolution, and of our minds coming to the place where we are now building the communications highway. [It has not acknowledged] what we found out in depth psychology."

How can a new halakhah be developed? Zalman proposed the "psycho-halakhic process."

"It says everything we have done in halakhah is important but we have to ask, What function did it fulfill in an earlier time and what's the best way for it to fulfill that function in our current situation?"

I asked him for an example of psycho-halakhah.

"Look at *kashrut*. For a group located in animal husbandry as its main technology—the shofar made from a ram's horn, the tefillin made from the rawhide of the lamb—everything we did then was to say, 'How do we make sacred the technology we were in?' We wanted it to ennoble us, keep it ecologically friendly, so we would share with the other kingdoms in nature a good stewardship of the planet. Today this is best expressed in eco-kosher terms by asking what is the origin of a food, but also by seeking food that comes from good social conditions. Or to ask how much insecticide is being used."

Reb Zalman's psycho-halakhic process is an invigorating proposal, but would require rabbis of great scholarly depth to carry off. But I liked the respect it showed to the Jewish tradition, the assumption of wisdom inherent in halakhah's intent. That seems better than editing halakhah on the basis of personal preference, as in the original theory of American Reform Judaism—something that troubles me, even as I do it, eating vegetarian food in an Indian restaurant and defining that as relatively kosher.

Eve Ilsen asked me about Los Angeles. I explained that I would study with Rabbi Jonathan Omer-Man. I told her I hoped to "find the Jewish practices that will inform my life from moment to moment."

Eve mentioned the *Shema* as such a practice. She said, "You know when people say the *Shema,* they get so caught up in the ritual of it, they don't pay attention anymore to its deeper meaning."

"Well," I said, "that's Buber's point. The language is outmoded, based on ways of life that no longer exist."

"Why do you say that?"

"The *Shema* says to put a mezuzah on the gates of the city.[5] Our cities don't have gates. Yet we still repeat the worn-out phrase. We don't know how to edit."

Eve smiled and pointed to her mouth, her ears, and her eyes. "What we're really saying now is 'Put a mezuzah on the gates of the mouth, on the gates of the ears, on the gates of the eyes.'" She added gently, "Not to read it so literally."

It was a good lesson. Figured outwardly, tradition becomes baggage. But taken inwardly, deeply to heart, each piece can become a treasure.

I asked Eve about her famous teacher, Colette Aboulker-Muscat. I understood that she teaches Jewish visualizations and kabbalah. I planned to be in Jerusalem in the summer. I was interested in learning more about such techniques—an area where Tibetan Buddhist practice is highly developed. I was also interested in learning kabbalah from a woman.

Eve smiled. "Call me before you go and I'll give you her address. But Colette is eighty-seven years old, and I don't think she's taking on any new students."

"Maybe I'd have a chance to visit her anyway?"

"Maybe."

O

As we left the restaurant, Reb Zalman gave the sitarist a big tip. I kept a mezuzah on my mouth, guarding the gates, lest any harmful speech slip out. Now if only I could find a mezuzah for my mind. I'd received no beep from the bellman. Anxiety chattered: had he forgotten? Or were my bags lost?

Reb Zalman and Eve graciously joined me for my evening's lecture at the University of Colorado. I reported a conversation with Geshe Sonam Rinchen, a Tibetan teacher in Dharamsala who spoke of the Holocaust in terms of group karma. This disturbed someone in the audience, who asked Zalman about it. He answered, "There are things that can't be talked about in a large group, but only individually. Because what would be a teaching to one person would be poison to another."

In this reply I saw that "Teach us to number our days" also implies that there's a right time to teach everything. That's how Reb Zalman got to me in Dharamsala. The essence of teaching as transformation is not only speaking the truth, but knowing when the student is ready to hear it.

I said good night to Reb Zalman and to Eve in the parking lot with regret, wishing I could spend more time with them. While waiting for my ride back to Denver, I remembered my baggage.

I was struggling to fish the beeper out of my pocket when a young man I'd seen earlier in the audience touched me on the arm. He looked no more than twenty, tall, with curly hair. In the streetlamp's shine, his face was open and sincere. He rushed out his words as if he feared at any pause I might stop listening.

"I'm starting to get into Judaism," he said, "and I'm thinking I ought to marry a Jewish woman but then people say to me, 'How can you be so narrow in your focus—you shouldn't limit yourself, why can't you just love everybody?' and I'm thinking of going to Israel but how do I know who I should listen to?"

I looked at his face and thought about twenty and what my responsibility would be in our brief encounter. Reb Zalman had changed my life with just a few words . . . but I was no Reb Zalman. How would I do in the last dialogue of the day?

I thought of Shefa Gold saying, "My religion is about listening."

"We all hear lots of voices," I said, struggling for words. "Can you listen for the one inside you? It can be very subtle. So you've got to listen carefully. But if you hear a voice inside you, even faintly—you should trust it. That's what the *Shema* is saying: 'Listen, Israel, listen.'"

He walked away. I thought: suppose that boy goes home tonight and hears a voice saying, 'Kill your girlfriend!' Who the hell am I to give advice? What about the horrible voice I'd heard inside me that dark night in Dharamsala? I looked up: the sky was very black, no stars.

What inner voice do I hearken to, beyond the constant chatter drone of anxiety? And how can I know, or anyone, whether the voice within is angel or demon?

I extracted the pager from my pocket and held it up to the street light. A message waited for me in a line of dim type: OUT OF RANGE.

*Rabbi Jonathan Omer-Man: The Siddur Is a Book of Koans*
Beverly Hills
March 23, 1995; 21 Adar II 5755, three weeks before Passover 5755

My luggage eventually caught up with me. But so did the mood of doubt that overtook me in the parking lot in Boulder. If my beeper was right, how would I get back in range? How distinguish one inner voice from another, or know whether I was getting closer to God or further away?

I decided to clear my mind before my first lesson with Jonathan. I took a stroll near Hollywood and Vine. As a kid, I knew that corner as the epicenter of film glamour, where the great white heat of fame blasted star after star out into the world. Now all the heat has cooled and the stars have landed in dirty squares of concrete. The sidewalk of the stars. Paying my *tzedakah* to a panhandler (I give a little to everyone who asks), I stepped on Marilyn Monroe—then over a homeless man sleeping in the late afternoon sun, curled around William Bendix.

It was Oscar Week 1995, the year of the Gump. The streets of old Hollywood were shabby. I felt depressed wandering through the ruins of lost cinema glory. I wondered if Judaism at the end of the twentieth century isn't like old Hollywood after the studios vacated—full of legendary glamour but past its prime. Despite Reb Zalman's energetic R-and-D work in davening, and Shefa Gold's Sufi-style chanting, have we Jews missed the boat? Is contemporary spirituality exclusively the domain of the East, of gurus and yogis and the wonderfully calm and wry Tibetan masters I'd encountered? I knew that some alienated Jews think so.

From my taste of basic Buddhist meditation, I'd become convinced that a true religious path requires the cultivation of a state of mind free of anger, hostility, and defensiveness. That was difficult in my state: Louisiana.

In 1990, fresh from meeting the Dalai Lama, I'd been plunged into a political struggle against David Duke. I helped form a campus organization called Diversity. One night, working late at an anti-Duke phone bank, I overheard a man in his seventies with a thick accent pleading with a Duke supporter to change his vote. He sounded very upset.

"I noticed your accent," I said after he hung up. "European?"

"Dutch." He had a beautiful, kind face, deeply wrinkled, and white hair.

"Where were you during the war?"

"Dachau."

My eyes filled with tears. Forty-five years since Dachau, did this old man have to stay up nights because of David Duke? I was angry, and the anger felt right.

While a Nazi like Duke offers extreme provocation, I believe many Jews of my postwar generation are haunted by a deep anger. It's a hidden power plant, constantly churning—a generative source of our beloved Jewish electricity, humor, and chutzpah.

The week Zalman and Eve married, I'd spoken in Miami at a conference on Judaism and Buddhism organized by Professor Nathan Katz, one of my Dharamsala colleagues. The program drew Jews of all persuasions and experiences, Orthodox and Chabad, grandmothers who'd survived the Holocaust and dreamy-eyed neo-hippies with beads and bare feet. "Does anyone know the Hebrew word for equanimity?" I asked. A long silence followed. Finally a voice in the back called out, "What's equanimity?"

We all roared—but developing equanimity is no joke. One word used by the Baal Shem Tov is *hishtavut*—"making things equal." But the concept has ancient roots in Jewish thought. The rabbinic sages of the first century also understood that unbridled anger destroys a person's spiritual potential. And the Rambam compares an angry person to an idolator—in classical Jewish terms, about the worst you can say. Yet in my years of synagogue attendance, and Sunday school and Hebrew school, I'd never heard of *hishtavut*, or tasted equanimity through Jewish practices. Simple sitting meditation learned in a T-shirt shop had shown it to me.

Why didn't I stop there? Why not become a Buddhist? David Duke wouldn't let me. Neither would Reb Zalman. He said, "Have the *hokhmah* to change your life from where you are." Where I am is Jewish.

I'd found great spiritual energy in Reb Zalman's company, the fun of Jewish renewal worship, the power of the language of the sefirot and the four worlds. But I had no context, no *mashpi'a* ("influencer"), no rebbe or constant guide.

I did have questions: how could I live this Jewish wisdom day to day? Is equanimity a Jewish value, or is it in fatal conflict with chutzpah? What Jewish meditation practices could I learn and use? That spring of 1995, between Purim and Pesach, I brought such questions and more in a confused heap and dumped them in the lap of Rabbi Jonathan Omer-Man, a sixty-one-year-old English-Israeli-American Jew who at that time in his life—as I discovered—already had more questions than he needed.

○

For one thing, thanks to the publicity following his encounter with the Dalai Lama, business was booming at Jonathan's "Metivta, a school of Jewish wisdom," with classes in meditation and Jewish mysticism led by Jonathan and his associate, Rabbi Judith Halevy. (*Metivta* is Aramaic for "yeshivah"; the reference is to the mystical academy described in the Zohar.)[1]

In addition, Jonathan received letters daily from Jews all over the country anxious to learn with him. Some called frantically on the phone: "Quick—teach me to meditate." A hunger for spirituality was growing in the land even though the depth of that hunger had not fully registered with the Jewish establishment, where for some reason social science had become theology and demographic surveys holy scripture.

The rush on Jonathan began after the Dalai Lama asked him about the Jewish inner life. "What are Jewish techniques to purify afflictive states of mind?" he'd wanted to know. Jonathan, who'd studied several traditions of kabbalah and meditation in Jerusalem, answered: the path of crying out, the path of joy, the path of sovereignty.

The trouble is, such paths were news to most of the rabbis and Jewish scholars in attendance. I wondered if he had made them up on the spot, embarrassed that we Jews had nothing to equal the highly advanced Tibetan systems of meditation.

Since India, I'd visited Jonathan twice. In 1992, we lunched at a nearby noodle place, and then in his garage study he taught me and a friend the week's Torah portion, about the fierce priest Pinchas, one of the more problematic figures in the Torah. Pinchas makes Meir Kahane look like a peace activist. When Zimri embraces a Midianite woman in full view of the Israelite encampment, Pinchas executes both miscreants with a spear through the genitals.

Although the classic medieval Torah commentator Rashi defends Pinchas for this murderous zeal, most contemporary readers find it unpalatable, disgusting—the epitome of religiously self-righteous, judgmental violence, wrath, and fury.

But in his garage study, Jonathan read out a radically different view from the *Mei ha-Shiloah* (Waters of Shiloa) of Rabbi Mordecai Joseph Leiner (1800–1854), the founder of the Izbice dynasty. The Izbicer, who is considered one of the most original hasidic thinkers, describes Zimri and his Midianite mate as two souls ordained by heaven to meet. Because they acted on the heavenly decree despite the danger, Pinchas's summary execution came not as punishment, but reward.

Pinchas is an important figure for Jews to contemplate; his radical zeal inspires certain zealots to violence today. Rabbinic sources are clearly uncomfortable with him. But the Izbicer's mystical reading completely overturns the text in an extraordinary *tikkun*, or repair. He replaces harsh zealotry with the sweetness of love. Perhaps I would have seen more in the interpretation had I known more of Jonathan's personal life.

I have come to think that all Torah is personal and no interpretation is indifferent. For serious Jews the Torah we read reads us. Though I had no intimation from Jonathan at the time of this teaching, shortly after that visit he separated from his wife; they later divorced.

By my second visit, two years later in June 1994, there'd been more changes. Judith Halevy, formerly Judith Fritz, had come to Los Angeles to administer Metivta. In time, they'd fallen in love.

Their personal styles contrasted: Jonathan is phlegmatic and somewhat austere; Judith is a vivacious outgoing woman in her fifties in constant motion. For Shabbas she baked a traditional chicken, then led us in a beautiful "Lekhah Dodi," welcome to the Sabbath bride. Jonathan, pretty jolly for Jonathan, joined in musically with a Tibetan singing bowl he'd picked up in Dharamsala.

Judith had studied over the phone with Jonathan for a number of years, and then after an apprenticeship he had ordained her as a rabbi, a traditional practice rare in recent American Jewish history. Their teaching styles were complementary: Jonathan more subtly introspective; Judith more imaginatively expressive. She'd gathered a good following, especially among women's groups. They added a summer program in her old stomping grounds near Santa Fe, and they were an active couple: whitewater rafting, cruising the gulf of Mexico, teaching meditation in the mountains.

Then some months after my 1994 visit, Jonathan suffered a heart attack and mild stroke that left him temporarily unable to read. I knew he'd fully recovered, but I was glad to see for myself. After my walk in old Hollywood, I found my way to his ground-floor flat just on the cheap side of Beverly Hills.

At the step, I noticed a small fish pond, with thick greenish water. Peering into the murk I detected a flash of gold. The foyer door was unlocked and Jonathan's door ajar, but I knocked. His teenage son answered in oversize grey hip-hop pants, with a shiny chain-metal fob.

Jonathan sat in a red tubular-frame wheelchair, a sleek racing model. As a young man living in Israel, he'd been stricken with polio. In his herringbone tweed jacket, hearing aid, glasses, and dark beret, my meditation teacher looked at first sight like a retired Central Intelligence agent. Well, wasn't I looking for a central intelligence? I touched his hand, happy to see him looking so well.

I had certain expectations about spiritual teachers, but Jonathan didn't fit them. When I spoke with him over the phone, he could be terribly formal, gruff, enigmatic, or mocking. Once when I asked him for a list of Jewish meditation teachers on the East Coast, he told me to look in the yellow pages, under *M* for meditation, or *W* for wisdom. I got his point: such teaching isn't something you shop for casually. His wry humor and the sandy grit in his voice assured me. Jonathan has been tested severely in life, and there is a no-bullshit quality about him. His student Mark Borovitz told me, "Jonathan lives as much as possible what he teaches. There's not a separation for him. He was the first rabbi I ran into who really felt like an old-time rebbe."

But how do freelance rebbes make a living? Jonathan was invited originally by the Los Angeles Hillel council, he said, "to deal with religiously alienated Jews, especially those involved with alternative religions." The program developed into Metivta, which opened its doors with classes in January 1991, not long after his return from Dharamsala. He operated "on a one-on-one basis" before the school started.

"I developed my skills as a religious counselor," he said, "which I picked up in Jerusalem, especially from Shmuel Kraus, who came from the hasidic line of helping people understand their lives in spiritual terms, in Jewish religious terms."

"How?" I asked, thinking this sounded very much like *yehidut.*

"I always tell stories," he said, "fragments of stories, whole stories. Very often it's a way of bypassing an excessively critical intellect. After, the intellect can examine the teaching, but it becomes something very different when it's inside." Shefa Gold uses music in the same way—to bypass that great Jewish specialty, argumentation.

As a privately ordained rabbi, Jonathan felt himself on the fringe of acceptance in the Los Angeles Jewish community. He doesn't have a synagogue, doesn't belong to a denomination. Yet Jonathan's outsider status gives him a certain cachet among other outsiders. He has found a following among the many Jews who have tried other spiritual paths: Buddhism, Sufism, and the esoteric teachings of Gurdjieff.

I gave Jonathan an update on Reb Zalman and Eve, and he mentioned an upcoming trip to Boulder for a meeting of Jewish renewal rabbis who'd taken ordination directly from Zalman Schachter.

Though he tells wonderful stories about Reb Zalman's profound impact on his life, he also has certain reservations. "Zalman," he said to me once, "has the most incredible ability to popularize ideas and touch far more people than any of us can. And mine is much more limited." Yet, he felt, "Zalman's greatness and weakness is that he's instantly seduced by certain new ideas." Moreover, to Jonathan, "kabbalists have to be sought out. The test I give people is: first, they have to be stable. Second, they have to be willing to look hard. Zalman really opens the door. I say they have to knock twice."

Jonathan feels an aesthetic distance from the renewal movement. If they are rock, he is Bach. But at that point, Jonathan's quiet ways suited me fine.

I had quiet questions, born of private practice of Jewish prayer. After our living-room chat, Jonathan directed me to his dining-room table, where, over sodas and coffee, a beautiful conversation opened about Torah, meditation, kabbalah—and Passover. We began with the nature of prayer.

O

Strangely enough, a Buddhist teacher, Sylvia Boorstein, first started me with private Jewish prayer. I found it difficult to come down from Jewish renewal highs, sit in an ordinary synagogue, and listen to "Please rise, and turn to page 387." I needed a more regular daily practice to thoroughly ground myself as a Jew.

Sylvia teaches *vipassana* meditation at the Spirit Rock Center, in Marin County, about a half hour's drive from San Francisco. She also speaks of herself as a *bubbe*, a Jewish grandmother. She's explored both traditions and crosses back and forth with seeming ease. Probably it's her native sweetness and light touch. She tells a story of meeting a rabbi who asked her what she does. "I teach meditation," she said. "Do you daven?" the rabbi asked. "Yes." "With *kavvanah*?" he added—that is, with mindful intention. "Yes," she answered. There was a pause. "Can you show me how?" he asked.

It's a touching story about the problems even knowledgeable Jews have with prayer. Though prayer is one of the three pillars of Jewish spiritual practice, I know I sat for hundreds of hours of synagogue as a child, and it rarely crossed my mind that the words being sung, often quite beautifully, were actually being addressed to God.

Sylvia and I were teaching a class at the Open Center in New York City for a group of Jews, Buddhists, and Jewish Buddhists.

A Jewish Zen practitioner commented that after the silence of Zen meditation, he found Jewish prayer too wordy. I'd heard that before: the siddur, the Jewish prayer book, can seem distant and opaque. So Sylvia surprised me when she mentioned her own Jewish morning prayer practice.

"What are you thinking when you say these prayers?" I asked her bluntly, in front of the class. I suppose I could have waited, but I wanted to know. "What does the Jewish language about God mean to you as a Buddhist?"

She paused and said, "Koans."

The Zen koan is a mind breaker, a spiritual riddle with no logical answer that frustrates the rational circuitry and can lead to instant enlightenment: what is the sound of one hand clapping?

But thanks to Sylvia's hint I could now see the Hebrew prayers as spiritual riddles, mysterious language emanating from an ancient world with meanings I need neither accept nor reject, but can use as the starting point for my own inner wrestling. That helped. I was already friendly to parts of the prayers because of Shefa Gold's tape.

Many Jews feel alienated from prayer, which they associate exclusively with formal public group recitation in a synagogue. Across the land, congregations mumble transliterated words they don't understand, or repeat high-flown poetic translations carefully rephrased to block discomfort. But I know my own squeamishness. Secretly I too believe every prayer is a pledge of allegiance. How can I recite words I don't believe? Words that call for the revival of animal sacrifice in the Temple, or that heap curses on my enemies?

Maybe the synagogue isn't always the place for a Jew to begin. I feel more latitude, less embarrassment, praying at home. I find that my language deficiencies can be an asset more than a barrier. My Hebrew is good enough that I can still delight in discovering fresh meanings in these phrases.

First thing each morning, I swing my feet to the floor and re-cite (in Hebrew) the following koan: "I thank you, living and eternal King. You have placed the soul in me with compassion. Great is your faith."[2]

I don't assume I understand what these words mean. Be-cause my Hebrew is nicely rudimentary, I have the pleasure of memorizing the phrases and sucking the meaning from them, word by word.

This simple prayer restores each morning a sense of wonder, and even gratitude, about waking up, a process I previously took for granted. It's not a bad way to start each day, saying "*Modeh ani . . .*"—I'm grateful! Thanks! Hey I'm alive. (A woman would say, "*Modah ani.*") ". . . *le-fanekha*"—I'm standing before You. Immediately I am in the presence of a being far greater than I, figured in this language as living and eternal king (*melekh ḥai ve-kayam*). Although I understand the feminist objection to fixing God exclusively as male, I wanted, for a time, to work with the given language. To me, *king* means whatever lives, endures, and reigns in being. (It's like Zalman's sense of *melekh ha-olam* as the ground rhythm of life, the ruling pulse of the world.)

Each morning, such a regnant force returns my life to me. Why? *Be-ḥemlah*. Out of total compassion. *Ḥemlah*, compassion, puts me here, into my day.

Then: *rabbah emunatekha*. "Great is your faithfulness." Which at first didn't sound right. Shouldn't it be "Great is my faith in you"? No, the koan suggests, great is your faith in me. I take comfort in that.

I run cold water over my hands and recite another piece, "The beginning of wisdom is fear of the Lord,"[3] followed by the blessing for washing the hands.[4] Then I go through the morning prayers: blessings for the Oral Torah, and Written Torah, the mitzvot without measure, the mitzvot whose reward is now and in the world to come.

These mitzvot extend my prayers into my life; they are a good place to begin Jewish practice, for they touch on everyday events and can be performed often. Many speak to the third of the Jewish pillars of faith: *gemilut ḥasadim*, acts of loving-kindness. Kindness is a general concept, but these are specific ways of remembering to live kindly: hospitality to guests, visiting the sick, attending the dead, bringing peace between friends and acquaintances. Others focus on inner development: praying with depth, studying with care and discipline. Perhaps it can be argued that good people might do these things naturally. But I find it powerful to understand that welcoming a guest into my home, or mediating a dispute, also connects me to a divine order of living.[5]

Then come the blessings for the breath and all the morning blessings that follow. Over a period of time, a different phrase rises to my attention for special focus. I stop and consider and work with it, or let it work on me, until it settles into my mind and we have a comfortable relationship. Of course I struggled. Much I cannot immediately accept in its literal sense; some I still cannot take close to me. But much, very much, became part of my morning, and in that way part of my day, part of my life.

The words and images proposed themselves to me, at first, as objects to be contemplated, not as beliefs. I was free to disbelieve, could figure the whole thing on some days as a wholesome mental exercise if I liked, a Jewish mantra. I was also free to believe, and on the mornings when that was given to me, I did.

The whole question of belief being prior to practice is fascinating. Many Jews tell me they find the entrance into Buddhist practice appealing because it doesn't seem to require subscribing to a belief. I've come to wonder whether that's precisely true, but certainly in regard to Jewish practice, many Jews feel: how can I possibly pray to a God I'm not sure I believe in?

At one point, early in our conversation, Jonathan told me, "I see my lack of belief as a constriction. On the personal level it isn't a matter of belief or unbelief. Many years ago I was sharing a platform with an Orthodox rabbi, a Conservative rabbi, and Zalman Shachter. I was talking to Zalman about feeling uncomfortable sharing a platform with an Orthodox rabbi since I don't believe in three-quarters of the articles of faith. Zalman said, 'Jonathan, that's not true. Three-quarters of you doesn't believe.'

"I've now really come to accept that I'm about twenty percent fundamentalist and eighty percent skeptic. I live pretty comfortably with this. I don't try to play one off against the other: I move from one modality into the other quite freely. In some places the skeptic shouts aloud, like when it comes to the historicity of parts of the Bible. Most times it doesn't. I can read the kabbalistic accounts of the Garden of Eden like a fundamentalist. I'm not a fundamentalist when I go to park my car. The last thing I try to do is have debating societies within my head."

Not me. After nine months of private prayer practice, the debating societies held regular meetings. I was troubled by my shuttling from faith to doubt. I wanted to understand the basis of prayer: what is the historical link with Torah and with the ancient Temple? What is the connection between private and synagogue prayer? What is the Jewish mystical approach? That first afternoon and evening together we launched into it.

*Prayer: The World Is Wrong Names*
BEVERLY HILLS
EARLY EVENING, MARCH 23, 1995; 21 ADAR II 5755, THREE WEEKS
BEFORE PASSOVER 5775

Most Jews associate prayer with synagogue, but I found more of an opening to it at home. Wherever performed, Jewish prayer as we know it developed from animal sacrifice. But what connects recitation of Hebrew with the slaughter of lambs and goats, the evisceration of fowl, and the sprinkling of blood?

I began our first conversation by asking Jonathan a Torah question based on a portion I'd studied with my local study group. "If prayer is a more profound way of worship than animal sacrifice, why does the opening of Leviticus give such elaborate instructions about sprinkling blood and burning lambs?"

In *The Guide of the Perplexed*, the Rambam answers this question by describing God as a gracious teacher.[1] God understands the exact level of development of the students, the freed Hebrew slaves. They equate worship with what they've seen in Egyptian temples—namely, animal sacrifice. The ex-slaves are not yet ready for the verbal prayer of the synagogue. That will require a long period of development.

The Rambam's view sounds like Zalman's psycho-halakhic process in action. A new mode of worship develops in time from the old by paying attention not to the outward form, but to the inner meaning.

But Jonathan looked for the inner meaning in a different location. He struck the table and announced, "Nachmanides said, 'Maimonides, you are wrong!'"

Jonathan explained that to a mystic like the thirteenth-century Spanish kabbalist Nachmanides, "animal sacrifice is a higher form. Prayer is just a cheap modern substitute. It's one of the most fascinating debates. He didn't see slaughtering lambs as the messy business we do."

Jonathan looked at me as I thought of stowing my tallis and sacrificing chickens on my doorstep, like the back-street voodoo of New Orleans. Jonathan, I thought, *you* are wrong! Animal sacrifice is messy, verbal prayer more inward and subtle.

"Do you believe in the superiority of the ancients or the superiority of the moderns?" Jonathan asked. "They are both quite arbitrary positions to take." Then he flummoxed me. "The highest form of human being was Adam, and the highest form of worship he ever did was calling things by their names, and this was a form of sacrifice. The next stage down was actual sacrifice. Since then we've been gradually losing it."

Calling things by their names? How is this a "form" of sacrifice? Jonathan explained that in Hebrew, sacrifice is *korban*, from the root *korav*—to bring close. "When Adam called things by their names he called them by their right names, their names in the divine light."

"Names in the divine light" struck me as beautiful and eerie. I recalled that Jonathan had not always been called Jonathan, or Omer-Man. "An adopted name," he'd said once, "mystical, from the Zohar, something I feel I have to do—and not talk about."

"Liturgical prayer substitutes for sacrifice," Jonathan insisted. "But I like to jump all the way back to Adam to discover the true name, the true essence. It's finding the sustaining divine essence flowing into the world in every object, every person, and every thing. That's the object of meditation, contemplation, and prayer."

The sustaining divine essence—some call it the Everflow, or, in Hebrew, *shefa*.* Others call it emanation. The worlds operate on a trickle-down system. The light that fills the vessels—or

---

* As in Shefa Gold, or as in the magazine of that title that Jonathan once edited for Rabbi Adin Steinsaltz.

if you like, the energy that flows from the *sefirot*—begins in an initial burst of light that is itself only a tiny fraction of the light of the *Ein Sof*. That momentary burst is also all of time as we know it; it's been compared to a single burst of light from the electron gun of a TV tube that nevertheless activates the images on the screen. We are still living in the implications and reverberations of that first burst of light.*

This continual outflow of energy makes its way through the sefirotic circuits from one world down to the next. It's also a movement from potential to actual: the *sefirot* are closest to unified in the higher worlds and increasingly distinct in the lower. Although all the *sefirot* exist in all the worlds (there are four plus Adam Kadmon), different *sefirot* dominate different worlds. One might say it's a matter of emphasis. The *sefirot* form a continuous daisy chain: in the Chabad system, the *malkhut* of *atzilut* is also the *keter* of the next world down, *beriyah*, and so forth.

Our world would completely fall apart from one moment to the next were it not for God's continuing output of creative energy. Which comes out of pure compassion: *be-hemlah.*

Each moment is a bead strung on the invisible wire of God's grace. One lapse of divine attention and the beads would tumble and scatter.

I took this vision of *shefa* in, along with the shadows on Jonathan's smooth-shaven face, the slow change of the light from the kitchen windows heading toward evening, the sounds of the city traffic on this fringe of Beverly Hills at the edge of Pico Boulevard. A year before, I had tried a meditational exercise taught by S. Z. Stern with, he said, the blessing of the Lubavitch establishment.†

---

* A fascinating parallel is the echo of the big bang, which was detected by Arno Penzias and Robert Wilson in the form of microwave radiation—an effort that won them the Nobel Prize.

† The technique is called *hisbonenus* (or contemplation) in Chabad. Stern also calls it "co-creational" meditation.

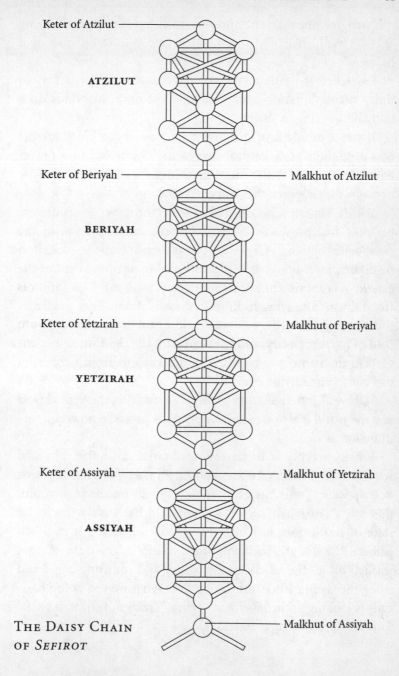

Keter of Atzilut

**ATZILUT**

Keter of Beriyah — Malkhut of Atzilut

**BERIYAH**

Keter of Yetzirah — Malkhut of Beriyah

**YETZIRAH**

Keter of Assiyah — Malkhut of Yetzirah

**ASSIYAH**

THE DAISY CHAIN
OF *SEFIROT*

Malkhut of Assiyah

"Imagine the current moment continuously materializing anew," I was instructed, "and then feel God as the force making it happen."

I watched the tape recorder slowly unwind little packets of time, quanta bursting open one after the other like buds on a branch flowering in slow motion.

It was a moment of discovery; I'd missed the point for the past nine months. True prayer is not saying words in a prayer book. True prayer is the moment things appear with their true names—that is, when they appear as they are.

Yes, the experiences could be one and the same, one could experience true prayer in the midst of prayer, surely, and in the synagogue, but the essence of the prayer is not the recitation from the prayer book, or the beautiful singing of the cantor; the essence was a moment of real seeing, real listening. I felt I understood my own nagging feelings of dissatisfaction. True prayer, as Jonathan described it, was much closer to an entirely different field of my life: poetry, and the search for the right words.

"Do the names we have for things keep us from perceiving this continuing divine essence?"

"Oh yes," Jonathan answered. "The world is the veil of God and the world is also wrong names." That proved a powerful formulation as well.

Jonathan explained that the northern and southern hasidic schools he'd studied, Lubavitch and Bratzlav, offer competing descriptions of this basic situation. Zalman once put it to him this way: "Lubavitch says that the world has nearly reached a state of restitution. Just one more piece will bring it back together. But Bratzlav believes there's been a great storm that washed off all the labels in the pantry and someone came and stuck the wrong labels on the bottles. What we are doing basically is looking at the label and saying, 'That's not sugar, it's salt.' This act of relabeling is *tikkun*.

"We've come into a world in which the labels are wrong. And we people who are part of the esoteric must defend our knowledge that the labels are wrong. What you're calling prayer isn't prayer, and what you're calling salt isn't salt." He paused and sighed. "Of course you can only go so far with this before they declare you schizophrenic. But when an entire civilization—the Jewish civilization, and much of the Christian civilization—basically calls things by their wrong names in ways that obfuscate ... that's a nice word . . ."—he paused to savor it—"to obfuscate knowledge . . ." He stopped. "Look, the true knowledge of something depends on the right name, or at least the wrong name blocks knowledge."

"For instance?"

"Well," he said, "let's start with the G word."

"God?"

"God. It isn't a magical godfather. It isn't even necessarily a hierarchical top principle. It isn't the source of ethics. It might be a demanding and commanding presence. It certainly isn't the guy who's on my side so that when I have a terrible fight with my best friend I can't call on God—'Help me'—because it's the same on both sides. God is . . ." He paused. "There are about . . ." He paused again for a long time, bent his head, closed his eyes as if searching into his chest for the heart of the matter. He wears a brace around his lower sternum for support. His upper chest is quite large and he has strong arms. Finally he lifted his head. "God is used to describe things that are not God, and therefore there's the wrong name on the bottle. Therefore, if you want to find God, don't go and listen to a sermon, don't go to the experts."

I had a new understanding of the mission Reb Zalman had started me on: to find "true God" was a search for a better language, an inner language. To find God's real name. Which isn't *God*.

○

I connected "the world is wrong names" with the Rambam's strong assertion that we can know God only through negatives, that nothing positive may be asserted of God. I wondered where that left the *sefirot*. No names, no attributes, and therefore, assuredly, no *sefirot*?

The Rambam (1135–1204) does not address the *sefirot* as such—though he is harshly critical in the *Guide* of what we call the practical kabbalah—that is, those who use *shemot*, or names, in magical amulets. Yet the Spanish kabbalists of the next century who formulated the *sefirot*, Joseph Gikatilla (b. 1248) and Moses of Leon (b. 1240), considered themselves his devoted students.

When the Rambam addresses the *middot*, or attributes, he explains them as the effects of God's actions. Strictly speaking, and the Rambam is nothing if not a strict speaker, God's mercy, or God's justice, is a nonsensical expression.

The philosopher argues that it is "not that God possesses *middot* (moral qualities), but that He performs actions resembling the actions that in us proceed from *middot* (moral qualities)—I mean from aptitudes of the soul."[2] For instance, in the case of great calamities, such as earthquakes, floods, deaths of many people, the Rambam writes, "Many of these actions would proceed from one of us in reference to another only because of a violent anger or a great hatred or a desire for vengeance. With reference to these actions He is called jealous and avenging and keeping anger and wrathful."[3] But in fact God cannot suffer from such defects as wrath and anger.

In the same way, we tend to interpret positive events, like the miraculous cure of an illness, or the birth of a healthy child, as a divine act of kindness or mercy. But in truth, kindness and mercy are only our human names for God's effects.

Whenever we ascribe attributes to God, or even use the G word as if we know what it means, we are only reformulating in human terms what is actually incomparable. The Rambam catches us in the act of giving the world wrong names. Jonathan was showing me how much a search for God is also a search for finer language. I was seeing a hint of why the *sefirot* need to be handled very delicately.

○

The pauses in our conversation were sometimes for deeper reflection. But once or twice Jonathan excused himself for five or ten minutes to lie down. I wondered if he was still somewhat depressed, or exhausted because of a funeral he and Judith had attended a week before. Their student Rob Hershman, a producer of documentaries for CBS News, died at age forty-one from the effects of AIDS. Hershman himself was a powerful spirit who wrote movingly in the Metivta newsletter of the suffering of other people with AIDS that he'd witnessed: "There have been times when it has seemed utterly impossible, even a kind of blasphemy, to praise God for creating a body so treacherous, so helpless, so open to pain." Yet he found a path to wholeness, even acceptance, within Jewish wisdom: "I struggle to understand God's will, knowing that I cannot know, but also that within this struggle is much of the meaning of my life." [4]

Jonathan and Judith accompanied Rob's body to Cleveland for the funeral, flying round-trip within twenty-four hours. It had been emotionally difficult for both of them.

Jonathan described his relationship to Hershman as "half spiritual, half literary. We moved between the two realms wonderfully. My last words to him were, 'Good night, sweet prince, and flights of angels sing you to your rest.' That was truth, and a more religious truth than any *yisgadal ve-yiskadash sh'mei rabbah*."* He spoke fiercely, as if to defy any nonesoteric Jew who might be listening.

---

* The Aramaic words opening the Kaddish.

"Can English then become a holy language for Jews?" I asked him.

"You know, to quote Zalman's phrase about Buber"—I'd told him of our conversation—"'the surface tension, between the languages has been lessened. There's an incredible flow between the languages.

"To the extent that the Jewish tradition defined itself as existing solely within the Hebrew idiom, a membrane held it very very firmly. When that membrane loosens, then Jewish tradition can move into French, or Russian, Spanish, and certainly into English. And back, too. It's always been the case. Whenever Judaism has been creative it's been influenced by other forces and languages. Maimonides wrote *The Guide of the Perplexed* in Arabic."

With the Rambam, our conversation had come full circle. But Jonathan wanted to add a point: "You are asking maybe where is Jewish spiritual creativity going to burst forth? It's clear—though we don't like it—a lot is taking place in the *ba'al teshuvah*\* and the Orthodox and ultra-Orthodox movements. In some ways more renewal is going on there than out here where we are. Then there's the problematic area of the brand-name Jewish renewal . . ."

Jonathan is skeptical about the Jewish renewal movement. He agreed with me that Jewish renewal had great value. "It has broken many bad vessels. It's really taken the goldfish out of the murky, almost toxic pond and put them in a different pond, if you like. Unfortunately Jewish renewal is too dependent on the aesthetic, without good taste, especially the taste of the eternal. It is so much based on the pop, on the current, on the ephemeral as an aesthetic mode, and some of the taste is just appalling." He added, "As I once told you, we have to move from fun to joy. Fun is not the essence."

---

\* The movement since the late sixties of Jews turning or returning to Orthodox observance.

It's a subtle but important distinction. To Jonathan the legacy of Hasidism, which he and Reb Zalman bring into non-Orthodox circles, is both fun and joy. The fun part is the communal spirit, the prelude to group attunement. The joy is something more subtle, and I wondered if it is even possible for a group. Jonathan called it an "integrated way of knowing, an ecstatic knowledge with all parts of one's being" and added, "It doesn't have to be in a time of fun or a time of pleasure."

"But," I said, "isn't it a task of Jewish renewal to essentialize? To ask, 'Out of this vast storehouse of prayers and ideas and books and concepts we call Judaism, what is most important to focus on now?' People are confused. They don't know what's essential anymore." That's why I thought Shefa Gold's work on the morning service was important. There was a long pause.

"What is essential to you?" Jonathan asked quietly.

"Shabbas."

"Essential prayers?"

"*Shema.*"

"Whatever *it* means."

We sat thinking. Then he added, "Maybe you have to start by distinguishing prayer in the heart and liturgical prayer. Liturgical prayer may not be meaningful, may be boring, but it's a spiritual practice. Here I have difficulty with Jewish renewal: they can't stand boredom. But there is no such thing as a spiritual practice without boredom."

"Well," I said, "in our culture boredom doesn't get many votes."

"But liturgical prayer is a discipline. Just to be able to stay in the same place, the same thing repeated every day three times a day for forty, fifty, sixty years. That's a practice, a spiritual practice."

So what he'd taken away before, he'd given back now: my daily prayer practice did have a value. Later in our conversations, Jonathan would return to this point. He distinguished between *kavvanah* and *keva. Kavvanah* is the development of inwardness, of the careful marshaling of intention in prayer, of devotionalism. But Jonathan also emphasized *keva* קבע, regularity. Sheer discipline. They were both aspects of liturgical prayer.

But there is also "another part of prayer"—he said it with great emphasis—"and for me it is like the psalms: the direct prayer to God. When you have that, liturgical prayer falls into place."

"How does personal prayer work for you?" I asked.

"When you have the ability to say: 'Thank you, God, for that rose,' 'Help me, God, I'm lost'—that's essential prayer. I don't know if we know how to create anywhere, apart from very, very small groups, the ability to cultivate this kind of prayer. Liturgical and personal prayer are completely different. According to traditional Judaism you can't have one without the other, you must have both. And for me—"

The doorbell rang. Jonathan called out, "Pizza!" and his son returned with the delivery.

"How much is it?

"Eleven something."

"So we need some more money." Jonathan took some bills out of his wallet, which his son whisked away. Jonathan called out, too late, "Bring me back my change."

We'd been talking about forms and forces, and I was thinking that, just as the form of *avodah*, divine service basic to the Jewish path, had changed from sacrifice to prayer after the fall of the Second Temple, the form of a mystical teacher today may not be what we expect either. Jonathan taught me in his living room, dining room, over coffee and sodas and slices of pizza. He taught me in intervals of a constantly ringing phone, amid the roar and machine gun of his teenage son's video games, in the ordinary household chaos of dishes and glasses. He taught me not only through his strength but also through his weakness, his difficulties. In its own way, this form of teaching reflects a timeless quality of Jewish wisdom. The rabbi—unlike the monk or priest—must remain immersed in daily life.

His son did not come back with the money. "That's how kids get rich," I said. "But I'm going to ask you more about prayer from the heart."

Jonathan held up his palms and smiled. Our conversation was over for the time being. But at least we'd touched on prayer of the heart. And I had a new language for my experience of beeper out of range. "The world is wrong names," Jonathan said. The grammar jarred slightly, but the concept stuck.

And where were the right names?

*Torah and the Strange Fire*
Los Angeles
March 25, 1995; 23 Adar II 5755, Parshat Shemini (the third of
four special Shabbats before Passover—Shabbat Parah)
Quarter moon waning

The classical description of the Jewish path comes from the
Pirkei Avot 1:2. "Shimon the Righteous was one of the last of the
Men of the Great Assembly. He used to say: the world stands on
three things—on the Torah, on divine service, and deeds of
kindness."

We'd discussed prayer as divine service. Now we took a look
at Torah.

Jonathan led a Shabbat morning service a few days after our
first discussions. He was subbing for Rabbi Mordecai Finley at
Ohr Hatorah, in concrete reality a Korean Protestant church on
the west side. Jonathan explained he'd last been before this congregation at Purim (nine days earlier, on 14 Adar II), when he'd
presented the jester side of himself. But there wasn't much to jest
about in the week's Torah, a very tough portion for anyone who
identified spirituality with sweetness and light.

In the morning prayer sequence is a prayer for the Oral
Torah, the *divrei Torah*. This blessing gives thanks for the mitzvah of "*la-asok be-divrei Torah*," engrossing oneself in the Oral
Torah, which Rabbi Arthur Waskow translates nicely as "soaking
ourselves in words of Torah." The blessing distinguishes "words
of Torah," Oral Torah, from the Written Torah. We pray that God
will "sweeten the Torah in our mouths and in the mouths of our
children." I've often thought of this when reading a particularly
difficult, bitter passage—like the story of Pinchas. Somehow, by

our own words of Torah, we may sweeten what appears bitter in the text and make pleasant what appears difficult, challenging, even violent. Certainly, the main *parashah* that morning, Shemini (Lev. 9:1–11:47), cried out for sweetening.[1]

The *parashah* describes the dedication of the *mishkan*, or tabernacle. In Hebrew, *mishkan* means the place of the *Shekhinah*, the indwelling presence of God. The *mishkan* becomes the model, later, for the construction of the Temple of Solomon.

In the *mishkan* the high energies of the upper worlds meet with the lower, frailer human realm. The meeting is problematic from the start. Nehemia Polen, an Orthodox rabbi and author of *The Holy Fire*, once asked me about my favorite book of the Torah. I said Genesis, because of its stories of individual spiritual encounter. He answered with Leviticus.

For Rabbi Polen, living in an observant community, the *mishkan* is a paradigm for the problem of contemporary Jews: how do we as a community engage holiness? What forms and ritual do we need in order to construct a proper meeting place between the secular and the sacred?

Yet the portion of Leviticus that Jonathan chanted that morning seems, in this context, particularly disturbing. The Parashat Shemini falls at the exact center of—the heart of—the Torah. Here the *mishkan* or tabernacle, first described seven weeks earlier in Terumah (Exodus 25), is dedicated. One would expect a triumphant, glorious inauguration; instead, the dedication ceremony is a disaster.

In Everett Fox's translation: "Now Aharon's sons, Nadav and Avihu, took each man his pan, and placing fire in them, put smoking incense on it, and brought near, before the presence of YHVH, outside fire, such as he had not commanded them. And fire went out from the presence of YHVH and consumed them, so that they died. . . . Aharon was silent" (Lev. 10:1).

Silent also was Jonathan's temporary congregation, at least for a while.

Jonathan is very self-conscious and shy about congregational gigs for which he's not terribly well suited in some ways. Some congregants prefer their rabbis slick; Jonathan, despite his best efforts, is rumpled. That morning, he wore his herringbone tweed jacket and corduroy pants, black Rockport jogging shoes, and a black beret with a little pip on the end.

Rabbi Finley, a young, fiercely intellectual redheaded ex-Marine, originally built his following among young families at the Stephen S. Wise synagogue, a Reform landmark institution in Los Angeles, where he served as one of the assistant rabbis. He'd succeeded in part through his own version of *yehidut*, one-on-one spiritual counseling, as had Jonathan and Judith.

Rabbi Finley considered Jonathan one of his mentors, but Finley had many teachers: he'd studied widely and broadly at yeshivot in Israel, at Hebrew University as well as the Reform seminary in Los Angeles. He co-officiates at another synagogue in the area with Rabbi David Cooper, a student of Reb Zalman's and expert in Jewish meditation.

That Sabbath morning, the third of four special Shabbats preceding Passover, everything looked in flux and temporary in Rabbi Finley's breakaway shul. A long blue banner with a Jewish star covered the cross. In the corner I saw a wooden chest inscribed HE WILL COME, words that seemed, in context, not reassuring. The Torah scrolls were carried in a portable wooden chest, reinforcing a certain nomadic quality that went well with that week's portion.

I saw no prayer books, just a photocopied collation from the Reform siddur with handy transliterations for the songs. No Bibles either, except the church's King James, which Jonathan jokingly referred to as *Melekh Yankel*.

Standing at the *bimah*, Jonathan leaned forward on his crutches to give the *devar Torah* (Torah teaching), his lower back pitched at what looked a painful angle. He initiated a Socratic dialogue with the group, pausing for their questions, hoping to tease out their responses.

Jonathan considered the story of Aaron's sons "one of the most difficult passages in the entire Torah." He pointed out that the traditional rabbinic interpretation supports a certain complacency—and that's exactly what's wrong with it. "The rabbis of the Talmud . . . conclude that the two were drunk! Another, similar interpretation is that they were disrespectful of their elders."[2]

Jonathan felt that such interpretation was "blaming the victims," and so "truly obnoxious." It illustrates the whole danger of naive Torah, found in many Jewish circles—and in my own heart, where it often accompanies a self-affirming pride that somehow the Bible must be perfect because it's a Jewish book.

Naive Torah assumes that merely reading Torah automatically makes you a better person. This is certainly a widespread belief in the Jewish world. But I believe it's not an automatic process. Important inner work has to be done first for the Jewish path to work. If you have an angry mind, you will read out an angry Torah. You will pray angry prayer. You will feel that acts of violence can be affirmed. Just a year earlier, Purim 1994, Baruch Goldstein, a student of Torah, who prayed daily, nevertheless massacred men, women, and children in a mosque in Hebron. Some communities of so-called Torah scholars still justify and even praise this act of murder, as others later praised and justified the assassination of Yitzhak Rabin.

Reading the Torah is a powerful spiritual practice, but only if it reads us as well, jars us out of our complacency.

That Shabbat morning, despite Jonathan's prodding, the congregation seemed to accept the death of Aaron's sons until one man in the front row gave Jonathan an opening. He said quietly that the young men's deaths might not have been a punishment. "After all," he said, "only the good die young."

Jonathan could now lead the discussion to an alternate view. Nadav and Avihu were not sinners or delinquent. "The mystical rabbis," Jonathan later wrote, "following subtle textual leads, conclude that they were souls who had reached the highest possible level of purity. They make their offering out of great, possibly excessive love of God, not insobriety or impudence." Through a long line of mystical interpretation "we learn that what Nadav and Avihu did was a perfect act of worship; that they had reached a level of complete alignment with the Divine. Their death was not a punishment—it was a fulfillment."[3]

Is this even the same Torah? I knew Jonathan was thinking about Rob Hershman, and later he dedicated his midrash movingly as "an offering, mine, in memory of friends who died young."

"Each and every one of these deaths," he wrote, "was an outrage against what we feel is right, the way the world should work."

The mystic's complete reversal of the rabbinic view forced the debating societies in my head into extra session. But Jonathan was really calling for adjournment. Ultimately, he put forth a more difficult—and humbling—view. Namely, that some Torah is truly inexplicable.

○

We got into this after services when we returned to his place for lunch: smoked turkey breast on good sweet challah, and leftover salad from the night before.

I proposed to Jonathan that the congregation's relative silence—which weirdly echoed Aaron's—showed the power of the "basic myth of Judaism, that everything good and true is in the Torah."

He countered that Western civilization also has a myth: "that everything has an explanation. You just look hard enough and you will understand and control it. That's basically what I object to. The fact is, everything might well be in Torah. That doesn't mean you can always reach it, but it's all there. But the idea that you can understand everything is pernicious."

I felt that the Torah's authority had been diminished by the higher criticism of the Bible that culminated with the work of the late-nineteenth-century German theologian Julius Wellhausen. The documentary hypothesis analyzes the five books of Moses into historical layers of composition—J, E, P, and D—distinguished in part by the different names of divinity used in each layer. The thesis that the Torah is not a unitary composition but was written by many hands in various historical periods is widely accepted by scholars today. It has strongly dominated the approach to Torah in the Conservative and Reform rabbinical seminaries in the United States and, through them, generations of American rabbis.

At my mention of Wellhausen, Jonathan sputtered impatiently and pointed to his sandwich.

"Vell vat?" he mocked me, with a fake German accent. "Vas ist das?"

"Wellhausen," I said.

He lifted his sandwich. "I don't relate to that stuff any more than to the chemicals in the smoked turkey. For me it's still a piece of turkey. It's like the information you receive in psychotherapy: much of it is true, but very little of it is important."

"Why irrelevant?" I asked, a little stung. "You know its true. You can't pretend you're living in 1790; you're living in 1995 or somewhere around there."

Jonathan peered at his watch until I laughed. He was checking the date.

"Let me go back to the image of psychotherapy," he said. "You can spend fifteen years of your life exploring your earliest memories only to discover they didn't cause the present, they just reflect it. They're a projection and therefore absolutely meaningless, a nice picture you've drawn. You think you're explaining who you are, but you're not."

Though Jonathan teaches a class for therapists, he is convinced that inner work is best done in the present.

"Well," I said, "the mystical texts you love, and even Rashi's Torah commentary, grew from an environment of great faith.*

---

* Rashi, or R. Shlomo Yitzhaki (1040–1105), of Troyes, France, is the most important Jewish Torah commentator.

These rabbis did not have to deal with a postmodern sensibility. We know a myth is a myth. That's a tremendous difference. Rashi did not think he was making myth when he invested every missing letter in the Torah with deeply intended meaning. We know it's easier to suppose that there are errors in transcription. We may deepen our appreciation through his explanations, but we can't avoid feeling false."

"Do you think it bothered Homer?"

"Homer?"

Jonathan put his sandwich down on his plate. "When Homer described the celestial origins of the Trojan War. Do you think it bothered him that it was poetic hogwash? This postmodern sensibility is vastly overrated. We're trying to make ourselves much smarter than the premoderns. People have always been wise. Levi Yitzhak of Berditchev, the hasidic master, can say, 'You have to be a fool to believe in God and an idiot not to believe in God.' And Rabbi Nachman of Bratzlav says, 'Atheism is the place from which faith springs.'"

"In a way, listening to your sermon—" I began.

"I don't like that word," Jonathan said.

"Okay, your *darshan*."* Jonathan smiled and I went on: "The congregation took God's role quite blithely. I wonder, if a local judge burned two young boys for a minor infraction, would they accept this as easily?"

"It happened in Los Angeles, two weeks ago."

"What do you mean?"

"Some out-of-work actor shot two people painting graffiti."

"That's true. And the public cheered."

"Yes."

"That's even scarier. Where's the sense of justice?"

"Look, you have to put that group in context. Part is the incredibly obnoxious way of the Jewish world in which you argue

---

* In Sanskrit, the *darshana* is the illuminating glance from the master. In Hebrew a *darshan* is a public preacher or expounder.

the whole time. You always set yourself up as smarter than God and smarter than the Torah. This is a very welcome move away from that attitude."

"You mean they're becoming more accepting?"

"Yes—accepting of the authority of Torah."

"In your hands, that's not dangerous, but what about religious zealots?"

"Reform Jews can't do that much harm if they take the Torah seriously. Reform Jews didn't shoot up the mosque in Hebron, it was the other kind. I have the feeling—" Jonathan leaned forward and whispered conspiratorially, "there are quite a few Republicans in that shul."

I laughed. "God, a scandalous comment. So they like law and order?"

"No, but they accept authority too willingly. They're also upbeat yuppies who have a certain picture of the world. If there is gross injustice there must be a reason for it . . ." Jonathan paused, "that can't be solved by raising taxes."

Jonathan was having his fun. I knew he didn't share Rabbi Finley's conservative political views. But I had other concerns. "Do you think," I asked, "when people go to synagogues and fail to make any real connection between their lives and what's in the Torah—" The phone rang in midsentence.

"I'm sorry," Jonathan said. "This is going to happen."

Wedged in, he had to back up against the wall and turn outward to answer the phone. Little rubber skid marks striped the wainscot. A few minutes later he came back, rolling his wheelchair into its tight spot, then tucking it up to the edge of the table.

Jonathan's every move tested his equanimity. He had courage and grace moment to moment in a way I could not imagine for myself in the same situation.

He returned to the synagogue question. "Many people completely separate between their spiritual lives and their synagogue lives. The synagogue life expresses a social and ethnic identity. Often—unless you are part of the working poor—that expression is upbeat. There's no real place for looking at the darkness or looking at the shadow. But one of the primary teachings of every religion, especially mystical religions, is that God is in the shadow. If you try to have a picture that has no shadow . . ." he hesitated.

"You can't see much."

"You can't see much. You can have a nice morning."

"Have a nice morning?"

"Have a nice morning," he said again, making it sound like a cash-register greeting.

"Have a nice day," I answered back. Now we were both in a Wal-Mart. We broke out laughing.

"Have a *very* nice day," Jonathan added.

"So you think the upbeat approach, 'God is good, God is positive'—that's presenting God without shadow?"

"No," Jonathan said. "They look at life. But these groups need to be upbeat and optimistic. I'm not saying the shul should be a meeting place for the brokenhearted—but there must be room for the broken heart, room for the sadness."

The Torah portion suggested the shadow: God could shatter the heart of a parent, as he'd done to Aaron, and take away his children. "And Aaron remained silent." I had lost a child, and this silence seemed terrible to me.

A few months earlier, at a meeting of Jewish-studies scholars, several discussed the theologian David Blumenthal's challenging book, *Facing the Abusing God*. Citing the experience of Holocaust victims and victims of parental sexual abuse, Blumenthal does not avoid the shadow, but wrestles in it. He compares God to an abusive parent.

"You see," Jonathan said, "kabbalah created a kind of glue, a setting, a matrix in which the manifest truth of paganism could be held together within a coherent, fairly monotheistic system. Within this matrix there's clearly a place for an abusing god. The Greeks knew that perfectly well. An abusive god was responsible to nobody. When Zeus was mad he didn't have to say, 'I have a covenant.' He was just mad . . ."

". . . and some poor slob turned into a donkey."

Jonathan smiled. "There's incredible validity to the Greek pagan vision of the world. Kabbalah has a way of saying yes, but adds that 'really, these are just different faces. Here is the structure to help you understand them.'"

"But," Jonathan said, "all the faces [of God] really only come from our perception. If we were willing to let go of our perception, our sense of outrage at the moment, then we could see that yes, one face of God can be abusive, but that's only one face. There are many. You can spin the die." He twirled his thumb past his forefinger.

And some poor slob loses his child, I thought. Or ends up in a wheelchair.

"But let's assume," Jonathan continued, "the Torah is a poem and not a theological statement. As a poem there's no consistency in its truths; it piles the images one on top of the other, and when we get the larger picture we see unexpected correlations between different sets of imagery. You're asking me to look at the grammar of the word processor when you start off with Wellhausen and the critical studies."

The kabbalah of fourteenth-century Spain describes the Torah as having four levels of inquiry, from the plain to the suggestive and homiletical to the mystical. In Hebrew: *peshat* (plain), *remez* (hint), *derash* (homily), and *sod* (secret); the letters spell *pardes*, or paradise. One reads Torah to enter paradise, to see the divine light. Yet judging from the sermons in some synagogues, which range from advice from Ann Landers to an ersatz *Newsweek* guest column, you'd hardly know it.

How we read Torah depends on our preoccupations. Among many Jews, an exclusively intellectual approach to Torah leads at best to sophisticated *peshat*. I've sat in on discussions where every line generates an erudite comment about Sumerian mythology, Akkadian grammar, contemporary archaeology, carbon dating—all of which amounts to elaborate color commentary, but misses the point of the game. How do we make reading Torah a transformative experience? It's far easier to atomize a text than make it cohere.

Most Jews want the Torah to mean something, are conditioned from an early age to hope it might. But how to make Torah mean is an art. Jonathan practiced it through teasing, joking, and sly suggestion.

The first step for many is to move the reader out of Torah innocence. I told Jonathan how I had gotten into an e-mail debate with a logical, tough-minded Buddhist scholar who pointed out some unpalatable, bellicose passages in the Prophets and Psalms. My shock told me I'd been conditioned from an early age to gloss over them, to regard the Torah as perfect and holy. It goes back to childhood. The ceremonies in synagogue of removing the Torah from the ark, lovingly dressing it with silver ornaments, kissing the Torah, holding it in the air, proclaiming, "*Zot ha-Torah!*"—This is the Torah!—all left a deep impression.

"He was a Bible hater as much as I am a Bible lover," I told Jonathan, "and ultimately I had no answer for him."

"Of course," Jonathan said. "Except no holy scripture can withstand such analysis. Look at the first part of the Bhagavad Gita: incredible battles, people killing people, especially in the *Mahabharata*. Even the New Testament can be incredibly violent, depending on what you want to do with it. I relate to the Torah as a poem—one of the best I know, but not the only one. For me it explains some parts of reality no other poem I know can explain. Those parts are so precious that I'm not willing to reject the Torah because of some of the bad poetry in it.

"When we're talking about Torah we're talking about all levels of Torah up to Torah being produced to this day." He meant both the Written and Oral Torah.

"Torah attempts to explain the relationship of the mysterious to the divine, attempts to define a path. How not to get in your own way. How when you do fall flat on your face to get up. How to live with nobility and grace in this world. It does it through archetypal stories, visions, poems within the poem. It does so by refusing to define itself. Torah resists any attempt at definition. The Torah moves the whole time. The Torah is alive. It's organic. It's alive."

He added, "People have a tendency to worship it. But Torah can only be known after the loss of innocence. Before then it has no taste. An innocent can't distinguish between '*Zot ha-Torah*' and Isaiah, chapter one."

Jonathan excused himself, saying he felt tired and wanted to lie down. It was my own innocence we were dealing with. The Torah has violent passages in it and shocking material; God can seem abusive and mean. And in my inner life I'd felt torn between the equanimity and calm of meditation and my rage for identity as a Jew. Jonathan was suggesting that these conflicts were necessary if I were going to move beyond a bland, self-satisfied, feel-good Judaism onto a Jewish path.

○

I took a brief walk down Pico, passing several large families walking back from shul. I thought about Jonathan's power as a teacher. I was conscious of the discomfort he was feeling; at intervals he seemed to wilt. He apologized several times in our discussions for lack of focus, though I hadn't detected it. I didn't know whether he was just tired after that grueling trip to Cleveland, or whether something else was afoot, but I appreciated his generous efforts with me. I came to understood his "rebbeness," how his teaching was not just sharing information, but a far more personal sharing of himself. He had a knack of framing his response to me, using analogies to literature, speaking my language of poetry, just as he would speak to others—therapists, teachers, actors, ex-felons—in terms of who they are.

Realizing his own physical difficulties, as well as the hints of emotional struggle in his life, I wanted to thank him. When I came back, I said, "I can see where Jews, with ears attuned to biblical language and to those stories deep within them, would come and hear you. Through your Torah, they're entering a Jewish path of transformation. There are no prerequisites except possibly their suffering and their willingness to admit that their suffering can be explicable in terms that resonate from very deep within because they go back so far in their own childhood. Is that what's happening? Do you see that in your work?"

Jonathan nodded. "Except for that last sentence about going deep back into their childhood. I don't really work with deep-rooted psychology, I work with the present."

"What kinds of people are entering with you on a Jewish path?"

"They are people for whom my poems work. And they're not my poems, they're the poems I've received. I have certain skills in doing this in a way that creates meaning for a certain number of people." He paused for a long time. "I have skills," he finally went on. "I've received this Jewish poem. I can tell the stories in a way that people can not only hear them—they can also see what they've done for me. That way it's a kind of witnessing."

"You say 'what they've done for me,' meaning you, Jonathan?"

"Yeah." He paused again and I saw him. "There's something very personal. It's why I'm more a rebbe than a rabbi . . . In the text, they see what strength—*they think*—I've received from it."

"They think? Why do you make . . . What's the distinction there?"

He looked away into near space, wistfully. "Sometimes they see me as strong on days that I don't feel strong at all. But then that's an image"—from the Psalms—"of the different kinds of trees. The cedar that can't move at all, as opposed to the willow that can bend over. I feel myself sometimes very much more like a willow than a sturdy cedar—as sometimes they see me. I reveal self sparingly and deliberately in this context so people can really do what they want, and it clearly is mysterious.

"It started about ten years ago in my study. Somebody said to me, 'Jonathan, I get it. You're blessed. If you're blessed, I can be blessed too.' How did I reach *that point*," he asked with emphasis, hitting the table with his finger, "feeling like a cursed chipmunk for much of my life? How did I suddenly reach the point where people can say, 'You're blessed and therefore you're a source of blessing for me'?"

"This move from feeling cursed to feeling blessed," I asked, "how long did that take in real time?"

He refused the premise of the question.

"It's moving. It's like a train that goes in tunnel, out of tunnel, in tunnel, out of tunnel, and so to say where . . ."

I understood. Being blessed isn't a final state of being that he had attained at a given moment.

"You know," he went on, "when I'm out of the tunnel, I'm truly out of the tunnel. When I go into the tunnel I sometimes think it's going to last forever and there's never going to be any light again, but so far there always has been."

*The Jewish Path*

I was touched by Jonathan's vulnerability, and by the fitful nature of the Jewish spiritual path. The difficulty of true prayer: getting past all the wrong names. The difficulty of true Torah: wrestling past pat meanings and naive assumptions. I saw the Rambam in a new light. Getting closer to God means working with the negative: God is in the not.

When I'd first encountered the Tibetan Buddhists, I'd been impressed by their *lam rim*, or "graded path to enlightenment." Imagine that there is such a thing! I spent time wondering why Judaism didn't offer it. Certainly, many Jews today find complete spiritual fulfillment in the traditional path, following the guidelines of halakhah, which after all means a path or way. The mitzvot I had taken on increasingly in the past few years also seemed to me wonderful guidelines for spiritual growth, though I was not yet willing to take on all of them—to take on, as it's traditionally put, "the yoke of Torah." I was tasting the mitzvot one by one, but not signing on to the whole meal plan.

Enlightenment is not a Jewish term, but transformation could be understood by Jews as *teshuvah*. As Jonathan had mentioned, in the past two decades the *ba'al teshuvah* movement had grown in strength. I'd read accounts, and heard testimonies from *ba'alei teshuvah*, Jews with backgrounds like mine, who'd joined the *haredi*, or so-called ultra-Orthodox, world.*

---

* *Teshuvah* is a Hebrew word meaning "return" or "repentance." A *ba'al teshuvah* is, literally, "one who repents."

I'd had a curious reaction to their stories. I loved the first half—their wanderings, their stumblings, their pain and suffering. Story loves trouble. But after the total conversion, I often lost interest. All doubt vanishes, and a bland smooth surface of truth made my eyes glaze over. One such teacher told her listeners how her life is much easier with Torah. It's like a toaster oven, she said; it's best if you read the instructions that come on the box. Maybe so, but I didn't think of myself as a toaster oven. What happened to the struggle? Does the struggle to be close to God really vanish once one joins a particular community?

So I took a cue from Jonathan's metaphor: in tunnel, out of tunnel. Transformation is possible, but not permanent. It requires constant maintenance, constant practice. Jonathan compares spiritual development to the work of an artist: if you're a musician, you practice every day; if you're a writer, you write every day.

Jonathan's own life speaks to that process. The new name he'd chosen for himself continually challenges him. *Yonatan omer man.* I heard it for the first time as a Hebrew sentence. *God has given an* omer *of manna.* A measure of manna.

Manna, to the hungry, is a blessing.

That is the plain interpretation, the *peshat*, of his name. It affirms how he moved from "cursed chipmunk" to "a source of blessing." How what looks like a bushel of curse can become a measure of manna. This was the unfolding story of his life.

He was born Derek Orlans, in Portsmouth, England, in 1934. During World War II he was sent away to a school where anti-Semitism and physical punishment were prominent features of the curriculum. "I first taught myself meditation going through a very difficult period at the age of ten. It was what they call today self-hypnosis, a way of overcoming pain. As a physically abused child in an English boarding school, one used to concentrate on tangles in rugs when one was being beaten. It's a very simple technique.

"The school I went to," Jonathan added, "was actually deemed criminal. The headmaster was sent to prison for five years. It was a small English private school." He paused. "Purchased by a pervert for his private pleasure."

Jonathan felt that even at that age, and under those bizarre circumstances, he was developing an inner life.

"But it wasn't rich. It became very much richer when first I discovered literature in my mid- to late twenties. Then later I discovered the world of kabbalah. Both gave me a language to my inner life that permitted it to be a good place to be. It links me with other people's inner lives in a wonderful network.

"Sometimes," he added, "I look at my life as variations on a theme of wholeness and redemption. When I went at the age of twenty-one to Israel I believed in redemption through the land."

In 1955 Jonathan worked as a cowboy on Kibbutz Amiad, "my people forever," in the upper Galilee, near Rosh Pinah. I tried to picture him and saw a preposterous image of an English cowboy on a black horse roping steers. "I was falling in love with the land of Israel," he told me, "with redemption of the Jew on the kibbutz, with socialist society and ideals of justice. I went there for a year and stayed for twenty-six. It was a deeply flawed vision, but extremely well put over. [In our worldview] the Arab refugees did not exist. Even the poor Jews in the neighboring villages did not exist. It was very difficult to give up. I mean, Zionist propaganda in the fifties and sixties was very successful. Some people still hold on to it like crazy."

"When I'd been on the kibbutz for three years—or less—I got polio. A complete turning over in my life. It made the introspective process more creative." He stayed in bed for a year, reading thick Russian novels—Dostoyevsky, Turgenev, Tolstoy. Then, because he was teaching high school English, the kibbutz sent him to study for accreditation at Hebrew University in Jerusalem.

Jonathan studied English literature and discovered "one of the two richest worlds I know. I found coordinates. I was no longer pasty pale Jonathan trying to find his way in the cosmos and bumping up against my passions and other people's passions."

Living in Jerusalem in the early sixties was wonderful, "a time of real passion about everything, which ultimately meant true passion for nothing." After literature, the "next explosion of consciousness" was marijuana, which, he said, "had a profound effect of dissolving artificial divisions. In a way that prepared me for kabbalah."

He first studied at Hebrew University with Gershom Scholem, the great scholarly authority on Jewish mysticism. But he found the academic approach too intellectualized.

"I studied kabbalah in Jerusalem around a kitchen table half this size," he said, tapping his finger on the table, "with three students and a teacher who was a very important kabbalist. It was a Formica-top table, and his little kid was riding around the table the whole time on his tricycle, ringing the bell."

"How did he teach you?"

"Text. Bouncing off the text. Weaving in and out of the text."

"Was it Zohar?"

He nodded. "Zohar. One bounces off the text. A line of text can last for an hour." He said he left the academic kabbalah behind "because at a certain level there was too much Gershom Scholem and Wellhausen, and not enough 'Where's the beef'?

"Almost immediately I found meditation teachers in Meah Shearim [Jerusalem's old *ḥaredi* neighborhood], people who taught me Torah but recognized who I was and started teaching me meditation."

I asked Jonathan what Hebrew term his teachers used for *meditation*.

"*Ta'aseh et zeh*," he said flatly.

"Which means?"

"Do this."

I liked the simplicity.

"Then," he said, "I developed my own rackety practice, rackety because it wasn't easy. I was involved in a relationship with an absolutely secular Israeli woman. She basically said, 'Listen, in my circles, men get drunk. They fuck your best friends. But they do not get religion!'"

Jonathan had bumped up against the great divide in Israel between secular and religious Jews. He was "getting really deeply into it, enough to realize [that Jewish mysticism] is not about bibliography, not about Hebrew University scholars of Zohar who ask you to write papers. But to realize my teacher was in touch with the cosmic energy and you can touch him and be there too."

His outlook changed from secular to religious. Shmuel Kraus, his first teacher, "drew on Bratzlav with Chabad insights: a kind of demanding introspective work." Yet he opened himself to all sorts of spiritual teachers. One was Picasso.

"I started thumbing through *Picasso's Picasso*. I couldn't stop laughing, because I just knew: he was playing with surfaces on different planes, twisting them and turning them in a way that revealed what the *ḥasidim* call the *ḥayyut*, the divine flow. Once a student tried to push me to say Torah is higher than Picasso, and I wouldn't say it. Because Torah is not higher than Picasso and Picasso is not higher than Torah.

"The Tanya, for instance, the book I've been reading most recently, makes a cross section of reality that reveals the other planes." The Tanya is the classic of Chabad mystical philosophy, written by the first Lubavitcher rebbe, Shneur Zalman. It's studied daily by Chabad *ḥasidim*. But Reb Picasso?

"Picasso also shows you what is really going on. And Torah shows you what is really going on: the expansive forces of divine energy and the restrictive forces, their dance and their flow. And how they do this within me."

In all these encounters, Jonathan was learning a language. "It became so clear I wasn't alone. Many, many people shared this vision and could enrich my vision. My inner world was being inundated by life from these other teachers. Nachman of Bratzlav was another one."

Through Nachman's stories and writings, which he read when editing Rabbi Adin Steinsaltz's version of Nachman's tales, Jonathan came to understand the nineteenth-century hasidic master as a "profound meditator who banged up against his own ego and bangs up against yours. But that was only the way to get through the ego."

Meantime, his defiantly secularist Israeli girlfriend considered him a "religious extremist" because "on Yom Kippur Eve when she served the normal pork chops, I said, 'I can do pork chops and I can eat at Yom Kippur, but I can't do pork chops at Yom Kippur. I'm fasting.'"

At that point, Jonathan seemed to be heading for the Orthodox world. Yet one circumstance kept him just outside. He confronted what he called "the hardheadedness of the Orthodox. For instance, they wouldn't let me drive on Shabbas." They would not make an exception for his physical condition. "I was supposed to stay at home, or live next door to a shul. Certainly my social life was completely unimportant." Jonathan paused and contemplated. "Maybe that's a kind of surrender—that were I more saintly, I might have accepted. But at a certain point rabbinic Judaism for many people has just lost it. Maybe they're going to rediscover it sometime."

I found it difficult to pinpoint his attitudes toward Orthodox Judaism. Despite this outburst, he seemed mostly sympathetic to Orthodoxy. Apart from his driving on Shabbat, he seemed very observant. He describes himself at times as "maverick Orthodox."

Yet Jonathan told me he is unorthodox not just by circumstance, but by inner nature. "I'm much too much of an anarchist.

But," he insisted, "I'm of the generation of anarchists who know what they are rebelling against.

"That's one problem with Reform and Renewal," Jonathan said. "I have a great deal in common with Zalman because we both know the Orthodox world we're moving out of—he much more than I. But so many people today are revolting against a world they've never been in."

A new stage came in the early seventies. "It was my first visit to the United States. On the same afternoon I met Zalman and Art Green. The next day I met Larry Kushner." Kushner is a well-known Reform rabbi and author who draws artful contemporary midrash from mystical Jewish texts.

"I'd found a fraternity of people who took the religion extremely seriously and didn't have to define themselves vis-à-vis the Orthodox, which is how, in Israel, I always had to define myself." There the choice is binary: religious or secular. And oddly, both groups agree on one point: only Orthodoxy is real Judaism. "My secular friends there couldn't take my being a religious anarchist.

"I went into Zalman's place on Emlen Drive in Philadelphia. This was the seventies. He said, 'Teach me something.' I said, 'What books do you have here?' I happened to pick up a book that's very unusual and started teaching it to him and he started dancing, the way only Zalman could do. He was dancing to the teaching I was doing. Then he went into his closet, took out a *shtreiml* [fur hat], and put it on my head. He said, 'Reb Yonatan.'" By saying that, Zalman essentially recognized Jonathan as a teacher, a rabbi in his own right.

"Some time after that, I was a guest at the Lama Foundation [a spiritual retreat center] in New Mexico, doing the hermetic exercise of looking at the different gates of my house. I realized Zalman was the first gate. Zalman was the first who really said, 'Those inner voices are true voices. Trust your inner life.' We've quarreled about my inner life ever since, but basically, that was the gift he gave me. He was the first gate. It was the most wonderful gift, an acknowledgment. He wanted to give me *semikhah* [rabbinic ordination] immediately. I didn't accept it for another ten years. I thought it was just inappropriate. But Zalman sees things ahead of time."

I saw how much the right teacher in the right moment can do for another person. Zalman had done so much for me in Dharamsala. I was interested in this essential teaching process, which I related to stories of spiritual transformation in Genesis. "Zalman validated you by saying you can listen to your inner voices. When I hear the Abraham story, *Lekh lekha* is an inner voice that contradicted his whole life. It uprooted him."

"*Lekh lekha* was wonderful," Jonathan answered. "But," he added dryly, "'*Kach na et binkha et yeḥidkha asher ahavta et Yitzḥak* [Take your son, your only son, whom you love, even Isaac]* and kill him' . . . that wasn't so hot."

Jonathan always leaned to caution, to restraint. Listening to inner voices can be dangerous. Like Aaron's sons, you could get burned.

"Clearly," he said, "a balance has to be held between the opening up and encouraging and acknowledgment that these realities do exist, and the getting out of hand in the manner of kindergarten art teachers who say anything you believe is true. Unbridled imagination is a very dangerous faculty, especially when it turns into fancy. Imagination requires an enormous discipline."

I thought, Yes—and taste.

"I mean," Jonathan said, "visions come and can be extremely moving. One should not dismiss them out of hand. But I don't approve of the idea of cultivating them. It's contrary to everything I've ever learned. Ultimately the goal of meditation is to

---

* Genesis 22:2. The phrase that immediately follows is "*ve-lekh lekha*," which may have prompted Jonathan's quotation. The complete translation is: "And he said, Take now your son, your only son Isaac, whom you love, and go to the land of Moriah; and offer him there for a burnt offering upon one of the mountains which I will tell you."

empty oneself, and not to fill oneself with cultivated visions—which are imagination. If an angel speaks to you, it isn't an angel that you've imagined, it's an angel. One does receive voices. But also it is very important to make sure one is not deluding oneself. The *ḥasidim* use some very clear yardsticks."

"Such as?"

"One is, Does it contradict the Torah? Any voice that says 'Reb Rodger, from tomorrow you can have cheeseburgers' is out. Another guideline: is it good for the Jews? Is it good for the Jews and for you both short-term and long-term? Another, from Rabbi Nachman, is a very simple question: where do you come from?"

"Just like that?"

"Yes. Normally you get a pretty good answer." Jonathan smiled. "I was teaching someone on the telephone from Michigan. She said she has angelic presences. I got quite hard-nosed and asked, 'How do you know?' Then we talked. I suggested she ask them, 'Are you angelic presences up there? Or projections of my ego? Where are you from?' And if the answer is 'From the most high, sheltering you under her wings,' then maybe it is. But if the answer is 'I'm from the ego brigade and I want to show that you are the smartest gal on the block,' then . . ." Jonathan shrugged. "I find in my own understanding that the spiritual requires rigor. I try to maintain this rigor with my students at the risk of being a bit of a downer sometimes, enough of a downer to permit something real to emerge."

I wondered if it isn't high risk to teach that there might be voices or that there's a test for knowing them. I thought again of the student in the parking lot in Boulder and the hurried advice I'd given him.

Jonathan answered slowly, with an emphasis that surprised me. I heard how despite his affection for rigor and for *keva*, he was still with Zalman on the wild side of Judaism. "The risk of losing all the voices is even greater. Of being in a place where the voices are denied. My voices were denied for many, many years."

Women's voices have also been denied for a long time. And our Torah discussion of the *mishkan* reminded me of my visit the week before with Rabbi Lynn Gottlieb. I'd stopped off to see her in Albuquerque on my way from Boulder to Los Angeles.

Rabbi Gottlieb, author of *She Who Dwells Within: A Feminist Vision of a Renewed Judaism*, is a pioneer feminist rabbi. She has served Congregation Nahalat Shalom in Albuquerque for the past fifteen years.

I'd first met her in the summer of 1992 at Shavuot. It had been an auspicious day: lightning and thunder over the Sandia Mountains at the edge of Albuquerque, followed by a magnificent rainbow—the exact imagery we find in the Zohar at the giving of the Torah at Mount Sinai, which is what Shavuot, of course, celebrates. So I was already attuned when I came to the home of one of Lynn's congregants. In a large living room with contemporary furniture, Lynn sat in front of the fireplace holding a 350-year-old Czech Torah scroll that she'd wanted to have for some time. She spread it out before us on a tallis. It was a beautiful old scroll with unique calligraphy: "The *pey*s"—she was referring to the Hebrew letter *pey* פ—"curl up in a circle on the bottom," she told me. It had been in part a communal purchase in a very small Jewish community: she'd put out a can at a citywide Chanukah festival to collect the last money she needed.

From the way she held it, she was clearly moved to have her own personal Torah. From what I knew of Lynn's personal story, the giving of the Torah to women has come with difficulty.

As Rabbi Ellen Umansky tells it, "It is all too easy to forget how revolutionary it seemed twenty years ago when Lynn Gottlieb announced her intention to become a rabbi." Although the Reform movement ordained Sally Preisand in 1972, Lynn encountered a new barrier when "she found the Conservative movement's Jewish Theological Seminary unwilling to admit her or any other woman into its rabbinical program. Undaunted, Lynn found a number of Orthodox, Conservative and Reform rabbis and scholars who were willing to teach her."[1] At various times, Lynn studied with Rabbis Zalman Schachter and Yitz Greenberg, and with the late Rabbi Aryeh Kaplan. Meanwhile, she became a cause célèbre in the Jewish world, featured on the cover of the Jewish feminist magazine *Lilith* in 1977 wearing a tallis and kippah, and in an article in the same issue titled "Why Is the Jewish Theological Seminary Afraid of This Woman?" In the end she was ordained privately in 1980 by Reb Zalman and Rabbi Everett Gendler.

That Shavuot in the summer of 1992, as we sat in a circle around her Torah, Lynn performed a special ceremony to commemorate the moment of giving the Torah at Sinai. She calls it Torah-tarot. She looked at each of us carefully, then pointed at random to a word on the scroll. Together, we meditated on the possible meaning of that word in the context of our lives. For me this exercise also had the sense that the Torah is given to each of us. Each letter in the Torah corresponds to the soul of each Jew: each Jew has special access to some part of Torah, if only he or she will make the effort to realize it. Perhaps, though, for many women, the effort to see themselves in words of the Torah—or to hear their voices reflected in it—is very great.

When I visited in 1995 on my way to Los Angeles, Lynn told me a little about her career. It was clear that Reb Zalman and others saw her in the early days as the Jackie Robinson of rabbis, breaking the gender barrier while taking full possession of the richness of the tradition, including kabbalah. As a young woman, she explained, she had access to many teachers: "The Shekhinah kept opening doors." Yet she was also "devastated" when one Orthodox rabbi dropped her as a private student because he feared repercussions in his community.

I asked her later about the origins of that living-room ceremony, the one she called Torah-tarot. "It's an old tradition," she said, "from the Talmud. You open up the Torah, have a child point a finger at word, and the word is prophetic. You use it this way to interpret a situation. I was struck by the oracular nature of what they were doing, and developed that technique. I first used it with the Aquarian Minyan—a good place to try it out. I recently used the same technique with a Modesto, California, Conservative synagogue women's group. I saw it as an attempt to bring them to the Torah, give them a word, help them process some of the experiences they'd had that afternoon. Which were profound. I found, in working with that group, the synagogue experience had not allowed them to share deep and intimate moments in their lives.

"I led a silent meditation. We were supposed to be looking at biblical women. But every single woman saw her grandmother, and her grandmother had something to say to her. They started crying. I said, 'There must be many things in your lives you wish you could ritualize in a deeper way. Let's go back up to the bimah and do it, and make the prayers for those occasions that you didn't get to celebrate.' We went back to the bimah, opened a small Holocaust Torah. The woman who donated it had never held it! It was a Conservative congregation; they only let them take the Torah out once a year. So we used that Torah. I opened it up to the *Shema*. I know it's one phrase everybody can read." Each came up to read from the Torah. "Women who had converted but never felt received, women recovering from illnesses, women who named their daughters but had not felt blessed or honored or acknowledged, and so on. So we called them up, and people spoke about their experiences. I asked them to say a prayer, what's on their hearts and minds. They read from the Torah and said a blessing. After, there was so much emotion. I did a Torah-tarot. I combined the meaning of their name with a word in the Torah. It was all done intuitively. It was an opportunity to reflect back to them and empower them with a blessing."

Lynn is not at all shy about creating such ceremonies. She told me that in her work as a rabbi, she considered herself a "ceremonial artist" rather than a "social worker." For instance, in her book *She Who Dwells Within*, she gives detailed instructions for building a woman's *mishkan*. Inspired in part by the passages in Torah describing the *mishkan*, and in part by the corn-dance ceremonies of the Cochiti Pueblo Indians, Lynn created a women's healing ceremony. Here is a whole new response to the difficulties of the Torah text Jonathan and I read. Rabbi Gottleib's approach is literally constructive: a woman builds her personal shrine, using a tent or other enclosure to create a meeting place for the sacred and the deeply felt personal experience.

Only seventy-five years ago, the Reconstructionist leader Rabbi Mordecai Kaplan instituted the first bat mitzvah (of his daughter), but since then the bat mitzvah has become routine in all parts of the Jewish world and has proven a powerful way of acknowledging the transition young women make into adulthood. But there are other important transitions in a woman's life. Inspired in part by the model of the bat mitzvah, many Jewish women are feeling the need for more specific ceremonies to acknowledge divorce, miscarriage, menarche, and menopause.[2]

In *The Jew in the Lotus*, I'd suggested that kabbalah, with its feminine imagery, might provide a resource for such reconstruction. But when I saw her in 1995, Rabbi Gottlieb argued emphatically against that notion.

Despite the feminine imagery in Zohar, or the importance of the Shekhinah in mystical thought, she argued, kabbalah has the defect of being entirely written from a male point of view. In *She Who Dwells Within*, Lynn writes:

> Many Jews seeking new avenues of Jewish spirituality turn to the study of the kabbala. New Age Jewish teachers, who are often Orthodox men, teach 'kabbalistic practices' supposedly based on authentic sources. . . . I find the active male, receptive female notion of divine union on which this material rests an inhibiting proposition, especially given the victim status of the Shekinah as a ravaged woman unable to save herself. Moreover, the kabbala is based on medieval and Neoplatonic ideas of a ten dimensional cosmos divided between the spiritual and material worlds, men and women, and true believers and heretics. Medieval teachers of kabbala fostered a trend away from the midrashic imagination of the classical period toward a very intellectualized system of divine life. And with a few brave exceptions, women were excluded from participating in kabbalistic circles of learning.[3]

Rabbi Gottlieb sought different avenues for Jewish women's spiritual expression, such as her creation of a *mishkan* ceremony. "The Mishkan ceremony," she writes, "can be a source of kabbala for women by directing them to work toward a wholeness of spirit based on the receptive and active principles of feminine spirituality, which is lacking in traditional kabbala" (p. 125).

She takes her authority to create such ceremonies from her understanding of Shekhinah, the divine presence, as "the being who connects all life, as the longing for wholeness, and as the call to justice" (p. 7). This sense of connection, of longing, and ultimately of justice for women as religious equals animates the activities of Rabbi Lynn Gottlieb, and others as well.

It's not that Lynn entirely rejects the old kabbalah. In fact, she told me, "I love the old language, it's very inspiring to me. In some ways I read it the way I read fairy tales. As a storyteller you find these wonderful stories, but as you look at the generation of the girls sitting in front of you, you know the princess has to be involved with her own redemption. So it changes the way you tell the fairy tale. The narrative is beautiful, but a storyteller depends on the knowledge of the audience to fill in the gaps.

"People take it"—kabbalah—"so seriously, they confuse narrative for the truth. They forget the idea it's a *livush*, a dress, a coating, and that the deeper truths are somewhat unknown and changing and mysterious. They take the descriptive language as reality. And that freezes the process. It has to be living and transforming, the narrative has to be alive.

"I don't have to feel nostalgic for it, because I can read it. I'm not yearning for a past that's not there. I wouldn't want to live in the Middle Ages. That whole period is so difficult. Kabbalah grew out of the time when Jewish people's desire for otherworldly salvation was so intense because the reality of the Spanish-Portuguese experience was terrible."

Lynn felt that all along, there was both a men's and a women's kabbalah. "Women's kabbalah is based on healing with herbs . . . on a relationship between spiritual healing and the physical body. In male kabbalah it's much more of a head trip, but women's kabbalah is more related to a practical end as well as a spiritual end, well-being both physical and spiritual."

But Lynn saw another source of possible change to worship from what women had already accomplished as Jews. It came up after she told me about her Torah-tarot ceremony in Modesto, the impact on these women of touching and reading from the Torah, in some cases for the first time.

"I realized," she said, "the structure of synagogue actually prevents people from having a spiritual experience. It's a tragedy." Women, she argued, have contributed to the rabbinate, and lay women immensely to Jewish culture. But there's "such a separation between public and the private that even when we moved egalitarianism into the synagogue, we did not move the notion of the ceremonial life as an extended family occasion."

Lynn lamented, "We based the liturgy on the male experience in the synagogue, the Friday-night service became a Protestantized, hierarchical situation, with no room for participation. Women bring in concern for the experience of the children and for themselves. And that brings along men who don't feel moved by just a liturgical experience. So that is a shift happening."

She spoke of "coming back to a deepening realization that there existed two cultures, Jewish women's and Jewish men's. And Jewish women's culture often had a concern with healing physical ailments and keeping family relations in a harmonious situation; one might call it 'baleboostism.'* With the Jewish healing movement and the desire for spirituality in synagogue . . . as a feminist, I would interpret it as women demanding a place for their spirituality. I hope women don't lose sight of, do become more aware of and value, the ways they have a spiritual culture based on food symbols, recipes and eating and family meals, and setting the table, and getting everyone together and dealing with the children, and with life-cycle transitions. As part of the spiritual journey."

A little flag went up when I heard this, as she went on to speak of the traditional preparations women brought to certain celebrations: "Every holiday has a magnificent altar. On Tu Bishvat [the New Year of the Trees] people brought baskets of fruit, figs, apples, olives. It was sumptuous, beautiful, with candles and linen tablecloths and everything. That's the crossover, the sensitivity to create a really beautiful environment for worship; it comes in part, for me personally, from the way my grandmother set the table."

The flag was that I was surprised to hear Lynn praising baleboostism, because I knew many women found such roles oppressive.

But as I understand it, Lynn is in a sense saying something different. In the midst of our current burst of creativity—mani-

---

* *Baleboosta* is the Yiddish term for the traditional Jewish housewife.

fested in new women's prayer, women's ceremonies, women's midrash—women should not forget what they have created already. They need to understand how women have always been the bearers of tradition.

The writer and editor Aviva Cantor, in her discussion of the *baleboosta* role, points out that in the context of survival, it "went far beyond the traditional female role under patriarchy of responsibility for running the household. The home was one of the major support systems on which Jewish life rested" and "the locus for so many ritual observances and ceremonies, from those of kashrut to those of Shabbat and major holidays such as Passover." She cites testimony of the crucial significance of home facilitating, that "the mother is responsible for the physical aspect of [the home's] *Yiddishkeit* (Jewishness, Jewish values and their expression), by which is meant the total way of life of the real Jew." She goes on to cite specific examples, such as the preservation of Jewish spiritual life by women during the centuries of the Inquisition, and in the ghettos and death camps of the Holocaust.[4]

I told Lynn I'd met some rabbis in New York who had attended a conference on "making the synagogue a sacred space." I'd been amused at the idea. Isn't that what a synagogue is supposed to be in the first place?

Lynn answered, "When people are saying they want to make the synagogue a sacred place, it's a skill rabbis need—to open up the ceremonial life so it resembles more closely an extended family experience."

At another time of crisis, the fall of the Second Temple, Judaism moved the Temple into the home. Now, Lynn was saying, let's move the home into the synagogue.

"Take Passover," she answered. "Rather than having one person read a Haggadah, many families have a very creative experience. Different people take parts, there's a little theater—the drama of opening the door for Elijah, the game of looking for the *afikoman*.* There's many voices, children have a part. Why isn't that a model for what happens in synagogue in general?"

It was a good question, one I would turn over again in Jonathan Omer-Man's Passover class, where I would also learn the power of what he calls uprooting questions.

---

* The *afikoman*, a small piece of matzah, is hidden, and children try to find it.

## The Door of Pain

METIVTA, WILSHIRE BOULEVARD
MARCH 27, 1995; 25 ADAR II 5755, 9 A.M.

Monday morning, I was sitting on a gray sagging couch at Metivta listening to talk about Passover and cycles of seasons, and worrying about getting a parking ticket. Doors opened and closed, students were coming in late, carrying cappuccino-to-go in paper cups, and I had a headache.

During my trip west, I'd felt like a hurricane's eye. I was calm, but every time I touched down to visit friends, they were being whipped and lashed at a hundred miles an hour. On the way to L.A., I'd visited friends splitting up after ten years of marriage. I met the wife packing boxes into her car. I gave her a big hug and she shuddered with tears. I felt useless.

Then just that morning several people I worked closely with were fired in one stroke. I spoke to an editor who'd been in the business for twenty years. In a day she would have to clean out her desk. "What are you going to do?" "I'll just drive up the coast for a while and think."

The door creaked open again, and one of Jonathan's students, a well-known screenwriter, tipped his head in, then followed with the rest of his body, slipping into the small space formed by the sofa and a circle of chairs. The door slammed shut. It reminded me that my mission, which I thought was to learn about Jewish meditation, was changing.

During my visit to Los Angeles, I gave a talk at UCLA sponsored by the Hillel director, Rabbi Chaim Seidler-Feller, and the Buddhist chaplain, Heidi Singh. I passed through the lounge and noticed a tall man in his early thirties with a wayward stare. During my talk, he sat a few rows back. Definitely a little off, I thought. Something about how his eyes wandered about, like he wasn't sure what to look at. During the Q and A, he raised his hand, and I skipped him, calling on people behind him, beside him. A friend told me that every time I pointed and said, "You," he answered softly, "Me?" Then his hand slowly wilted and he smiled wanly.

Finally I let him speak, and he told an extraordinary story. On a visit to India, "just to annoy" his Jewish parents he took up residence in an ashram. There he realized he was going blind. He was diagnosed with MS, multiple sclerosis.

He returned to the United States and through a girlfriend attended a Passover seder. Something about that experience got him engaged with Judaism. He studied and practiced for years and came to a basic conclusion: the essence of Jewish spirituality is silence.

That surprised me. With all the prayers and texts of Judaism—the essence is silence? Professor Danny Matt, a translator and scholar of the Zohar, once remarked that the Jews are the only people in the world who on their holiest day of the year—Yom Kippur—read a six-hundred-page book out loud.

But the speaker—his name was Mark Lerner—cited a midrash on Exodus. Only the first two commandments are heard by the Jewish people; the rest are given to Moses. Franz Rosenzweig, the great Jewish philosopher, suggests that only "*anokhi*" was heard. *Anokhi* means "I." At Sinai, the total revelation is the manifestation of the presence of God, through the "*anokhi*." An obscure hasidic midrash goes further. Only the first syllable of *anokhi* was heard, the aleph. And aleph is a silent letter.[1]

I felt the beauty of Lerner's teaching. The law, he was saying, follows after revelation, as words after a great silence.[2]

Psalm 65:2, set to music by Shefa Gold,[3] suggests the same thing: *Lekha dumiya tehilah*—To You, silence is praise.

At the end of the talk, someone asked about my own path. I felt humbled that in the space of a week I'd encountered two blind men and overlooked them both. If I bumped into Elijah on the road, would I miss him too?

"I've been thinking about the Sufi poet Rumi," I said. "Instead of writing 'Dear So and So,' his letters would begin, 'God opens doors'. . . Based on what I've been hearing, including what we've heard from our friend here with MS, very often the door that opens is a door of pain . . ."

Marc Lerner raised his hand, and this time I recognized him. He added, "Yes, but remember that in Hebrew, MS means truth." *Emes.*

"Door of pain" had first come up on Saturday in my conversations with Jonathan about "facing an abusive God."

"You come to a door of pain," I had said, "when something happens that removes the foundation your life. Exactly at that point comes an opening to God that wasn't there before."

"Yeah," Jonathan had said, answering softly. "Provided you take it to religion and not to therapy."

Before the Passover class Jonathan suggested I might want to talk to several of his students who had passed through such a door, including Mark Borovitz and Paul Wolff. He'd already suggested I needed to speak in depth with Rabbi Judith Halevy; I would see her later that same afternoon. I would learn more from their stories, as I learned from Mark Lerner's, about this door of pain. I became a student of Jonathan's students and, through them, understood better the real meaning and scope of his teaching, which went far beyond the cultivation of mind states.

Remarkably, his students of meditation became very outwardly directed, doing good deeds. Cultivating an inner life creates an impulse to change the lives of others around you.

○

But for the time being I was a student in Passover class—which also, in fact, proved quite relevant. Jonathan spoke first that morning of how, in the general decline of Jewish observance,

Passover is "one of the two or three festivals a disappearing Jew honors." He added, mordantly, that "last festivals tend to become minimalized. Pesach is often experienced as purely a family or a social event—quite problematic. In fact," he declared, "Passover is one of the most spiritual of all Jewish festivals. Those of us who really want to go into it and discover its inner meaning often find that in the public or family seders we go to there's no space for it."

Jonathan had a point, and yet, as Lynn Gottlieb had suggested, there is also a spiritual power in the home family seder. I am grateful to my grandmother especially for the extended family seder of my childhood, visited not only by Elijah, but by four pairs of aunts and uncles, and fourteen cousins. In many ways, my deepest connections to Judaism were formed there because of the love she expressed through her prodigious cooking and her loving presence. She was a super-*baleboosta* of the old school, who held our family together so tightly in her nuclear embrace that she attracted to the center of the family orbit second and third cousins, and even former boarders and tenants. Through her cooking—blintzes, *perugin*, pickled rockfish, brisket, roasted potatoes—she created an "inner Judaism" in a whole different sense!

In my grandparents' paneled basement in Baltimore at a very long table, my grandfather sat at one end in a padded armchair, intoning swift Hebrew, while my grandmother shushed us cousins fooling around at the far end, sneaking sweet Manischewitz and getting tipsy. Every seder that followed built on those sweet memories of wine and heaping platters of delicious food. In my twenties I attended a series of "orphan seders" with childhood friends in Baltimore. I played the wise guy then, who probably frustrated others who would have gladly shushed me if they'd known how. Later, in Louisiana, I got my just punishment in a new series of seders Moira and I hosted in the early eighties. Every year the same argument would break out about Israel and the PLO. The seder became a place for secular, nonreligious Jews living in deep *galut* to dump all their frustrations and antagonisms about Jewish identity, Israeli politics, and Jewish life—questions they kept bottled up for this once-a-year foray into Jewish ritual.

Why had the questions at my seders in those years so often led to arguments and bad feeling? Jonathan gave one answer when he read us the opening passage of the Breslov Haggadah.[4]

"Rabbi Nachman of Bratzlav* tended to be very cautious about asking questions," Jonathan warned us. "One can become utterly lost in discussing paradoxes that aren't real. When we come into seder we look at the nature of our questions. We all know questioning is the absolute essence of Passover. We start with the children asking questions. But we have to be very cautious that some questions are wrong questions."

Jonathan explained that before he first started teaching Jewishly in Los Angeles, his mentor Rabbi Adin Steinsaltz told him, "Let's in all our arrogance claim that we have all the answers, that our answers exist in Torah. Our job, Jonathan, is to lead people to the questions for which our answers are the right ones. Our job is to purify and clarify the questions."

According to Jonathan, that's also the special task at Pesach. "Some questions come from show-and-tell," he said, "from idle curiosity. They tend to be paradoxes—some sophomoric and some more advanced—that are never resolved and never can be. You lose your life worrying about them."

But the right questions uproot our assumptions. "Don't ask, 'Why keep Shabbas?' Ask, 'What is the question for which keeping Shabbas is the answer?' Don't ask, 'Why do it? Why do a seder night?' Ask, 'What is the question for which doing the seder is the answer?' This completely turns it around."

---

* "Bratzlav" and "Breslov" are alternate spellings.

Jonathan paused and looked at us. "If you ask, 'Why are we keeping seder?' we will spend the evening talking about Jewish survival, or Jewish continuity. If we ask, 'What is the question in my life for which the seder is the answer?' we might come to examine how we are slaves, where we are incomplete, where we have real spiritual work to do."

I remembered all the seders that circled for hours around Jewish identity and never came in for a landing.

"The questions get bigger," Jonathan added. "'What is the question for which my life is the answer?' 'What is the question for which my suffering is the answer?' Then come the real biggies: 'What is the question for which my death is the answer?' Those really big questions are spiritually creative, as opposed to ones that come purely from the head . . ."

So I understood: pain becomes a door, but only when our suffering goes beyond the personal frame of reference and opens into an uprooting question. But how do we make the move?

I remembered a face from my last visit to L.A. Jonathan and I spoke about our trip to Dharamsala at the UCLA Hillel. I enjoyed that evening, mostly for the pleasure of teaming up with Jonathan on the same platform, because I respect him so much as a teacher and appreciated his wit—and presence. Only a few months before, a devastating earthquake had shaken L.A. While Jonathan spoke, a wave passed through the room. He broke set and asked the audience to meditate silently. He was dealing with the real fear in that room, because every time a tremor passed, people relived the panic of the previous quake. By turning that collective fear inward for a moment, he brought us back to the present. That was Jonathan's gift.

But I felt another tremor in the room, during the question period, along an identity fault line. The story of the Jewish-Buddhist dialogue brings out fascinating people: Jews who want to know what the fuss is about, since "everything is already in

Judaism," and Jewish Buddhists who have spent many years away from Judaism and are hoping there's something they've missed. The "continuity" crisis is not just statistics, but a personally felt anguish. A tremor is running through the Jewish world right now, and a sense that maybe when the wave has passed, not much will be left standing. That was personified by a very anguished man in his late forties who came up to me while I was signing books that evening. He started talking right into my face. He'd already delivered a lengthy speech to the group about his spiritual explorations of Eastern religions, as well as the lack of content he'd found in Judaism. Now he came back for the personal touch.

"Why be Jewish?" he screamed one inch from my lip. "Why be Jewish?" he repeated. He handed me his card, which read "Ashoka Goldstein."* First name Hindu and last pure Jerusalem.

"I'm sorry," I said, as calmly as I could, "but 'Why be Jewish?' has never really been my question. I've just assumed that since I was born Jewish, it's my karma to be Jewish and that I would work with that."

It was a quick answer, but too easy. I wasn't so much responding to his anguish as fending it off. Now, a year later, I could see Ashoka's face before me in Jonathan's class. I could also hear a new answer.

"Why be Jewish?" is a circular question. To ask it is already to step outside of being Jewish to the point where the question can no longer be answered. An uprooting question might be: "Given that I am Jewish, what am I to do about it? What will I make of it?"

○

I'd scribbled notes from Jonathan's class: "Passover: questioning. Shavuot: revelation. Sukkot: fulfillment." Passover: questioning again. The Jewish calendar is a reality map of a continuously un-

---

* I have changed the name.

folding, spiritual journey. The journey continues in a helix, one hopes at higher levels each year, as we accumulate wisdom. "Teach us to number our days . . ." In the rhythms of the Jewish calendar, days form a weekly cycle ending in Shabbas, and Shabbases join in seasonal cycles punctuated by the three great festivals of ancient Israel, inscribed for millennia in the traditional Jewish year. I was, quite aptly, on a journey to Passover—the time of opening up, escaping constrictions, asking questions.

I often despaired of arriving anywhere. But I was encouraged by one comment Jonathan tossed off. A student asked him, "How do we get enlightened and stay enlightened?" Jonathan flatly denied the possibility: "We don't do it in the Jewish religion. We don't know how to do it."

But my teacher didn't want to sound too discouraging. "Let me put it differently. The hasidic tradition that I follow warns us not to compare our spiritual progress with those of completely enlightened human beings." The Tanya of Chabad, for instance, is addressed to the *beinoni*, the person of middle spiritual attainment, not to the *tzaddik*, or wholly righteous person.

"Yes," Jonathan said, "some perfectly enlightened human beings are in the world; the chances are there can't be more than seven or eight in this room . . ." He paused, and someone took the bait.

"Seven or eight?"

Jonathan laughed. "None of us are there." He warned again, "Don't let us compare our spiritual growth to the enlightened person's. Our tradition has wonderful tools to move toward enlightenment. But it isn't a linear path. We have cycles. The cycles are part of greater cycles. The festivals help us move the rhythms of our life into greater rhythms." The same held at the weekly level: "We can't do Shabbat whenever we feel like it."

Obedience to rhythms outside ourselves enlarges our scope, and takes us beyond egotistical concerns. That was only part of what I would learn from my time with Rabbi Judith Halevy.

*Rabbi Judith Halevy: Cycles of Jewish Time*
METIVTA, WILSHIRE BOULEVARD
MONDAY, MARCH 27, 1995; 25 ADAR II 5755, 2 P.M.

"The whole question of women really needs to be looked at," Rabbi Judith Halevy told me Monday afternoon, between appointments in her tiny Metivta office. "I don't have any answers on it, but . . ."—she trailed off—"the crunch is the crunch of a woman's life."

From our first encounter a year before, I'd been impressed by Rabbi Judith's energy. At fifty-two, she balanced multiple roles: freshly minted rabbi, teacher, spiritual counselor, actor-student of Torah and of the tales of Rebbe Nachman, administrator at Metivta, and, in her personal life, partner, homemaker, mother, stepmother, cook. Charming, vivacious, she dramatized in her own life the complexity of Jewish women's time.

"You saw me," she went on, and I nodded. "Are we going to get the chicken on the table? Are we going to take care of the kid and make sure she has face cream? And are we going to prepare midrash at six o'clock in the morning?"

"I was getting tired just watching you," I said.

Midrash at 6 A.M. I'd seen for myself. Friday morning, Judith had been up at dawn preparing her class. When I showed up for a breakfast session with Jonathan, I saw a strip of paper she'd left on the table. In bold black Hebrew letters, Rashi's commentary on the opening verses of the Song of the Sea (Exod. 15:2): "A maidservant at the Sea saw that which prophets did not see."[1]

From a Torah many contemporary women find difficult she'd plucked out an inspiring passage for her women's midrash class. Yet even on this hopeful strip of paper, the poetry—the aggadah—is problematic. It's clearly based on a hierarchy in which a maidservant is the lowest of the low. Sexist categorizing is a very real part of the "drama of distinctions" that define Jewish tradition and make it, for many women, a confinement. In my conversation with Jonathan on Shabbat, we'd touched on my own difficulty with some of the "bad poetry" in Torah. Much of that bad poetry is about women.

Judith tackles this issue with energy and will, and through her teaching inspires other women to do the same. If women's stories are skimpy in the Torah, the blanks themselves become the openings, as Joseph Cohen taught—the openings for creative spirit. The feminist content may be novel, but the process is ancient: midrash always rushes toward the holes in the story. Judith Halevy belongs to a generation of women creating new midrash. Her particular style owes much to her background in theater. Indeed, in a crucial way, theater brought her back to a Jewish path.

○

Rabbi Judith is fairly tall, with short blond hair and fine features. She wore a trim purple suit, the same color as Jonathan's letterhead logo; for kabbalistic reasons I didn't understand, dark purple is the Metivta team color. She's a newcomer as a rabbi, and showed a newcomer's enthusiasm. Her personal path to Jewish spirituality is an Israeli-American *On the Road*, passing from Zionism and Sufism, Mexican villages and the Taos Pueblo, to the harmonic convergence, and, finally, Jonathan Omer-Man.

We talked between spiritual counseling sessions, the buzzing of her phone, and the beeping of her computer. Referring to her last appointment, she told me how she does Torah with women, "chewing our lives" before biting into the text. She'd just spent most of the last hour and a half with her student debriefing each other's weekends. Noticing they hadn't gotten to the week's Torah, the student said, "You know, this is about being women, our need to put things in context. First, to look at our lives, and then to nail our lives into the text, because the text will always be a reflection of your life."

"I do counseling," Rabbi Judith told me, "by Torah study, Torah in a very broad sense."

The road to that Torah began in Lakewood, New Jersey, the home of the Yeshivah Gedolah—the big yeshivah. "But I was a member of a Reform synagogue where, I have to say, the rabbi did credit his heart attack to me directly.

"What really got me into the Jewish world was that my parents were desperate because I was dating Italian boys—we're talking serious desperation here—and without asking a lot of questions shipped me off as a slave, to a Zionist youth camp."

After college, she married an Israeli. "We both performed. He was the director and, um, the last thing I did in Israel was to be in *Hair* for a year. Which I know fluently in Hebrew."

"Which part did you play?"

"I played Jeanie, the pregnant one. The irony is, I stopped because I was pregnant with my daughter."

When her husband left Israel to tour Latin America, she joined him. Eventually they ended up working in a Jewish center in Mexico City, where she had a second child. Then, as she told me, "my life fell apart."

Her husband left, and she found herself alone with two babies in a summer house in Tepotzlan, a village outside Mexico's capital. "There's an expatriate community around it, filled with interesting people. Some of those interesting people are world-class spiritual teachers. I walked into a whole new door."

She became a student of a Sufi teacher, an English author, Rashad Feild.

"What did you learn there?" I asked.

"That the universe in front of us is hardly the universe we're looking at."

For the first time, through Sufism, she found an opening to spirituality. Her turn back to Judaism began with a play. Directing *The Dybbuk*, S. A. Ansky's Yiddish classic based on hasidic sources, she encountered a moving excerpt from a Rebbe Nachman tale about the heart of the world yearning for the spring of the world. It's a tale about feeling disconnected from the *mekor hayim*, the source of life, figured as a spring pouring from the rock of a mountain.[2] *The Dybbuk*, after all, is subtitled *Between Two Worlds*, and as an American-Israeli Jew in Mexico practicing Sufism, Judith was clearly there: Rebbe Nachman's tale affected her deeply.

"I would question myself: 'Can I sit here and do these Muslim prayers?' Because the longing for God, the longing for union, is the same. 'There must be Jewish words that go with this.' I started reading everything I could get my hands on about kabbalah and matching it to the Sufi tradition."

After four years, Judith left the community in Mexico and gravitated to Taos, New Mexico. She taught in the public schools and ran a community theater. Soon she involved herself with the small Jewish community. "I led holidays and became a para-rabbi, out on an edge."

She met the spiritual "characters who came floating in," including Zalman Schachter and Shlomo Carlebach. Then, in 1987, with the harmonic convergence, Jonathan Omer-Man popped into her life.

A friend called from Santa Fe. "'You've got to come.' I said, 'I can't, it's seventy miles, over a bad road, and I'm busy.' I get off the phone and I say, 'OK, if we believe this harmonic convergence crap, maybe I need to get in the car.'"

She ran a sweat lodge at dawn, drove to Santa Fe, walked in just in time to hear Jonathan telling another Rebbe Nachman tale, the story of the lost princess. "I've been working with this story forever," she said, and the coincidence overwhelmed her. "I cry, I can't catch my breath, I go through this 'I'm—you're—really—' I can't talk to him. He says to come back the next day. Next day? This is like seventy miles one way, seventy miles back, plus I have a whole bevy of activities I'm supposed to be involved in. I come back. I bring Jonathan to Taos. I make this connection and at the end I say, 'Will you be my teacher?'"

Rebbe Nachman's tales provide a gold mine of kabbalistic symbols, and as you work with them, they work on you. They are stories full of mysterious strangers, beggars who are teachers, princes disguised as peasants, bizarre coincidences that teach that every accidental encounter might have a hidden meaning. I told her I thought such coincidences as her meeting with Jonathan happen all the time, but we don't pay attention to them. I was thinking of the blind man in the airport.

"Absolutely. The messages are always out here. You are given all the guidance you need. We're just stubborn, and I couldn't ignore this one. After a couple of months I came to L.A. for a weekend and it was *davka*, as they say—a celebration of Jonathan's ordination. There was a big party for him. That's when we said, 'We'll study once a week over the phone.'"

Jonathan proved a demanding teacher.

"I'm directing three shows a year and doing my kids and I'm in the middle of a marriage—it's just life out there, honey—and I start studying and just add it in by getting up a little early and my Hebrew skills are not all that hot, I mean I can read but not these texts, I painfully put it back together." I nodded, taking a breath for myself. Judith talks, not exactly in sentences, but in big unpunctuated bursts of words and gesture, a demonstrative rush of energy and many voices. "Jonathan gave me very difficult work," she went on, "and waited for me to rise to the occasion."

"What kind of work?"

"Oh," she said, "complicated hasidic texts like the college-board questions. To do one little paragraph you have to look up the midrash that goes with it, know which psalm this refers to, know the Hebrew skills to get there, you have to read Rashi script. So for every hour with Jonathan was probably fifteen or twenty hours a week without him."

In time, Jonathan persuaded her that she needed to leave Taos for a larger community with "a real synagogue." Her two children were now out of the house, her marriage had broken up. She moved to Santa Fe.

Jonathan's directives soon bore fruit. She led a Conservative minyan in the Reform synagogue. "I had a real-life synagogue to play with, an apprenticeship, and I could call Jonathan and discuss it with him on the phone."

At one point some in the synagogue wanted to hire her as a full-time rabbi, but she didn't feel ready then. Jonathan offered her a job as an administrator. She came to L.A. in December 1992.

It was a difficult move. For her, L.A. "is a desert, you have to create community by little tiny pieces and work against the norm—which is alienation, fragmentation.

"I never asked to have *semikhah* [rabbinic ordination]. I just wanted to learn. One day sitting here talking to Jonathan I said, 'I think I'm studying to become a rabbi,' and he said, 'I thought you'd never ask.' Jonathan decided after five years it was really time. I had done all this apprenticeship and was deeply into everything and was about to move here." They held a private ordination ceremony in New Mexico, "my spiritual home," with Zalman Schachter and Jonathan officiating.

After such a zigzag journey from America to Israel to Mexico to New Mexico, from Zionist to Sufist to Rabbi Judith—what did she consider the most important aspect of her Jewish spiritual life?

"The most nurturing place for me," she said, "is within the cycle of nature, the holiday seasons. Judaism has a built-in path—like paint-by-numbers. Follow the dots around this circle of time and you will be exposed to every spiritual *middah*— attribute. This is only one gear inside the complex watch of Jewish time."

In the Talmud, a *middah* is a personal character trait, such as equanimity, patience, humility. Perfecting the *middot* (plural) is essential to spiritual growth—as I'd been trying to understand better ever since the Dalai Lama's question about the Jewish inner life.

She was touching on a question I was working with. The *sefirot* are also based on the idea that God has *middot*, or attributes. But attributing qualities to God, such as wisdom, or kindness, violates the Rambam's dictum that God can be known only in negatives. On the other hand, the Rambam could not ignore biblical language and rabbinic interpretations, which attribute to God such positive traits as wisdom, mercy, loving-kindness—and also negative ones such as anger. The Rambam answered this dilemma by asserting that the *middot* are the effects of God's actions upon us.

Rabbi Judith felt the effects. She found that each festival on the Jewish calendar opens a special window on a different *middah* or attribute. "For instance," she said, "when I come to Sukkot, I want to understand about joy. I'm also going to learn about a temporary dwelling, a *mishkan*." Living in the fragile *sukkah*—observant Jews sleep and eat in one for eight days—she reflects on how she relates to others: "What am I under? What is my protection? Who am I, how many barriers do I need for my home? Do I need big walls, do I need little walls?" In this way, personal questions join up in larger cycles of season and religious memory.

"Sometimes," Judith said, "Judaism will actually send you the signals in its ground rules." I could feel her great enthusiasm. "The holidays are special windows. It's like, 'Hi, now we are going to give you twenty-four hours of special access. Guess what, this is Shavuot, you get to access revelation. This is Sukkot, welcome to joy.'"

Here was a particular realization of Zalman's "Teach us to number our days . . ." The traditional Jewish calendar provides us with inner direction, a road map through time. But based on the hints Judith was scattering about how pressed she felt, I wondered, Do men and women have different inner calendars, different ways of responding to the windows Jewish time opens?

Traditional Judaism recognizes men's time and women's time as separate qualities. Women, Orthodox Judaism argues, are free from certain spiritual obligations—such as fixed prayer—because their biological cycles make them naturally more deeply attuned spiritually than men. But from a contemporary perspective, these categories seem more social than biological. The net effect has been to exclude women from equal rights or equal responsibility in Jewish ritual life and to give religious authority and power primarily to men. So that in the 1950s, a young Jewish woman with the spiritual gifts of a Shefa Gold was kept from reading the Torah, in the 1960s a Jewish woman with the nuanced sensibility of a Judith Plaskow could not count in a minyan, and in the 1970s Lynn Gottlieb could not be ordained at the Jewish Theological Seminary.

On the other hand, talking to Rabbi Judith and thinking about other women's lives, I realized that women's time does need special acknowledgment. Lynn Gottlieb had suggested that "baleboostism" is a very powerful expression of women's Judaism, even a women's kabbalah. When I reflected on the power of the Passover seders my grandmother created, I had to agree. But given the limitations of human energy, was it really possible for anyone to play that traditional role *and* the new role of rabbi? So many of Judith's statements to me touched on the theme of time, from her opening remark about the "crunch of a woman's life" to her understanding of the calendar.

She is a relatively late entry to a new generation of women rabbis trying to figure out women's time in the context of Jewish time, drawing on the richness of the tradition while adding the missing woman's point of view.

She felt she had no choice but operate outside of an ultra-Orthodox framework, even though many of her insights clearly were rooted in Chabad and Bratzlav spirituality. "If I had become a *ba'alat teshuvah*," Judith mused, "then you live your whole life from Shabbas to Shabbas and cycle to cycle. It's all nice and neat. But we don't have that, because with that comes taking on other garb that is not mine, this isn't who I am." Still, she wanted to find a way to mesh her personal cycles of emotions and feelings—"of who I am as an unfolding human being"— into the traditional holiday cycle. She wanted to make a space for herself, not in the role of woman as defined by traditional Judaism, but as woman in an entirely active sense.

"So when you lead your life in a Jewish path in this way," she declared, "you're looking for all levels at the same time. I mean, come Pesach, I'm going to have to put a meal on that table and clean my house as well as look for the alchemy [i.e., the deeper meaning] of the seder . . ." She paused as if realizing the next fact. "I'm also truly honestly going to have to kosher my kitchen." During Passover it's necessary to remove all traces of leavening, or *ḥametz*, from the kitchen.

"Wait a minute," I said. "This raises a feminist issue. Why all these roles? Aren't you trying to do too many?"

"Can we table that question? This is very relevant."

We tabled it.

In addition to the holiday and personal cycles, another gear moving inside the watch is the fixed sequence of Torah readings that, she said, "in the meshing of gears, creates sparks. The Torah cycle will give you all the teaching you can possibly absorb at any given time," she asserted. "The Torah is current events."

"Do you find that often?"

"Always."

"Always? Every week it works? Come on."

"OK, OK," Judith said, her blue eyes lighting up and laughing, "here we go. You saw in my very own house—you don't have to doubt me. Eyewitness."

I laughed: she had me. I was at the dining-room table studying with Jonathan when a call came Thursday night from an old friend in Taos who'd joined a search-and-rescue party after a plane crash. It had been horrifying: bodies hanging from trees. Here was the Dalai Lama's question in point: what tools did the Jewish tradition provide for dealing with afflictive states of mind—in this case, profound grief, a feeling of contamination and being overwhelmed? What did Judaism teach about this state of mind? This is a priestly sort of question, and we were in Leviticus, the priest's book.

It's remarkable not only that Judith found an answer, but, as she affirmed, that she found an answer in the "current events" of that week's additional Torah portion, one I'd heard Jonathan chant at Ohr Hatorah Synagogue a day after the call. It deals with the *parah adumah* or red heifer.[3]

As described in Leviticus, this sacrificial animal has unique spiritual properties. The ashes of the red heifer purify those who've been in contact with the dead. But those in a pure state who touch them are made impure.

"We're dealing with purity and impurity," she said, "and how one cleanses oneself from *tumat meit* [contamination of death], from having touched the dead."

"You got the call."

"I got the call. Not only did I get the call, but I've just come back from dealing with Rob Hershman, who I held in my arms while he was dying." Judith shook her head. "*Tumat meit* means you've gone into that world between life and death, but you can't stay. You have to come back into the land of the living." She closed her eyes, remembering last week's trip with Jonathan to Rob Hershman's funeral. "I stood at this grave filled with water and thought, 'Oh, is this the end of where we are?'"

"Filled with water?"

"Yes. Because of the water table, when they opened to bury him, water was in there. Oh my God, it was tough. So *tumat meit*, the impurity of death, is very much on me, personally."

Her study of the *parashah* taught her that after *tumat meit*, you "need to celebrate life and renewal." This gave her the answer for her friend who called from Taos.

"I said to her, 'Go out and celebrate Rosh Hodesh [the new moon].' She said, 'Funny you should mention it, it's in my house this month.'" She was part of a women's Rosh Hodesh group.

Judith laughed and shook her head, knowing she'd proved her point. "It's always current events," she said. "I've rarely seen it fail. It's because Torah holds so much—and it's beyond that. We're given everything we need. We just have to be not afraid to ask the questions."

Here again, Jonathan's point about knowing how to get people to ask the right questions was relevant.

"Sometimes the questions are too big for me," she admitted. "To be told I need to take my own being and turn it into ashes and dust to renew myself . . . I'm feeling particularly pulverized lately." I liked the way she took the metaphor of the heifer into her life; it's how she made it real. I was being persuaded anew to Rabbi Nehemia Polen's opinion, that the book of Leviticus is really important, in providing an answer to the question posed by the Dalai Lama. The priestly rituals manifest concretely our inner psychological states; they are about healing and coming to terms spiritually with pain, and other difficult mind states. What in the priestly terms is called pollution we today call anxiety. Rabbi Judith took these metaphors as ways to understand her inner life.

For Rabbi Judith, and it was clearly true for Jonathan as well, teaching is not just an exchange of information but a transformative process, one with strong effects on teacher as well as student—which is why perhaps she found it so exhausting. In that sense, teaching resembles a priestly sacrifice. Just as a priest must learn how to examine the wounds and sores on the bodies of petitioners in order to determine the necessary form of sacrifice to heal their illness, so a teacher must come in close contact with the open emotional wounds and sores of her student. In Rob

Hershman's case, this was not even a metaphor: Judith told me she'd held him when he was bleeding from the open wounds and sores of his illness.

She tapped the desk that came between her and her private Torah students. "Let's put our own stuff out on this altar," she said. "If in the study of Torah we really ingest and eat Torah, what part do we send up and what is the waste material? If it's not going to go through my body, why did I bother to come to this table?" I'd always considered Leviticus dry reading, but she found another powerful metaphor in the text. She mentioned that when the priests would burn an animal, there would burn as well the *deshen*, the *shmutz*—or waste material. "The ashes have some excrement in it, the *shmutz*, and you've got to burn the *shmutz* with it." She also brought all parts of herself to the teaching, the good and the bad, the pure but also the impure. She didn't have to be perfect, but she had to put all of herself on the line.

She found this intense teaching process exhausting. I'd sensed that already in working with Jonathan, and wondered if that accounted for his frequent requests to rest, to take a nap. Metivta was filling a deep need in the Los Angeles community. How many Jews outside hasidic circles can come to their rabbis in this way? How many Jewish women, in particular, have access to such personal teaching? In larger congregations, rabbis simply can't offer this sort of psychological, spiritual counseling on a regular basis.

"Well, Jonathan did it for me," she said. "And he for others. We all need spiritual *ḥevrusa* [companions]. You can't just read a book, you need to come here and sit and talk to me chapter by chapter. I need to bring where I am as well. Otherwise it doesn't really work."

So where was Judith today? Why was she feeling "pulverized"? This pulverization seemed very much like the door of pain. She was about to open a door that was painful not only for her, but also for me.

"I'm interested in the point in people's lives," I told her, "where—we're always very shy about it—the anguish that ordinarily would drive us nuts for some reason leads to a door. You didn't focus on the pain so much, but I mean it was there, in your story about Mexico, the dissolution."

"Huge," she admitted.

"You're alone in Mexico with two kids and doubly out of context, an American Israeli in Mexico."

"You want to be out on a desert, then you've got it."

"You're really *bemidbar* [in the wilderness] and you're looking at hard time."

"Right. And suddenly the spiritual world jumps out at me."

She paused and reflected. "How do you get to this place? And yeah, pain does push us. In each birthing I feel I've allowed myself to die and be reborn a number of times." Her voice shifted to a softer register.

"They're always hard. I'm going through one now where I am asking, What is my rabbinate? What am I really supposed to be doing? How do I do it as a woman? That is my next question, which brings you back to your supermom question." The one we'd tabled.

"Yeah. Do you have to take on both the traditional Jewish *baleboosta* role and on top of that spiritual leader? This seems like a lot."

"This is probably the pain door where I stand at this moment," she said softly. "This is a place of incredible pain for me personally. I am smart enough to know that is the door I'm standing at: how much do I put into a personal relationship?"

I took that in with its implications. I was surprised, and felt protective of Jonathan, who was after all not only my teacher, but hers.

She spoke of the enormous amounts of energy she put into her one-on-one sessions, her version of *yehidut;* of her preparation for her two classes. She spoke of the completing claims on her time in her roles as woman. "Whether it's taking care of the rabbi, being a lover, being a wife, being a stepmother, being a . . . a . . . I mean, it's Pesach—it's your house. When you're younger you've got more energy, but I'm fifty-two years old. I can see where some of those roles are going to have to go."

I could read between the lines. "Maybe it's OK to send out to dinner," I said, thinking of my wife, who like me is a writer and a teacher as well as full-time parent, and who was juggling all those roles with some difficulty while I was out in L.A. interviewing Judith about her life. "Maybe you don't personally have to do it," I added.

"That's right.

"Maybe it's OK to eat out. Maybe it's OK . . .

". . . to have a meeting here. Maybe it's OK sometimes, even it's OK to live alone and not be a wife."

Well, that was clear enough.

"There's a frightening thought," Judith went on, considering it. She spoke of keeping her focus on work. "But you're a woman—you're supposed to be a wife and a mother. Any of us who dare to become women rabbis need to define these roles for others. My sisters are talking as if 'the face of Judaism has changed forever.' But out on this lonely front line, folks, nobody's got those answers, and every woman rabbi has struggled with these questions."

Judith's life had been quixotic, and I saw more upheaval just ahead for her and Jonathan. I had other thoughts, some of them pretty silly. I was a bit mad at her for this disruption. At an infantile level a student expects his teacher's life to be perfect. Now, of all times for me to come study Jewish meditation, I had picked the week she was dumping Jonathan! But that was my calendar, not theirs.

Although she praised the Jewish calendar, and found its complex winding of gears powerful, there is also an opposite pole, a moment outside of time, a miracle of freedom when the sun stands still or when the ordinary order of things is reversed: when the strong are overthrown (the Egyptians in the sea) and the weak (the Hebrew slaves) have vision. I could see why, in the context of her life, she found promise and vision for herself in this passage she'd jotted down in the early morning while I was still snoring: "A maidservant at the Sea saw that which prophets did not see. . . . The dancing and singing that celebrates the drowning of the Egyptian pursuers is led by Miriam the prophet, and for this moment out of time, women and men are on equal footing spiritually."

Such nourishing Torah for women is precious, and requires a special effort to uncover. Simply taking the biblical stories at face value is not enough: a new midrash is required.

Judith Plaskow, in *Standing Again at Sinai*, points out the short shrift given to women's stories in the Torah: there are mostly only fragments, glimpses. Miriam the prophet, Moses' sister, clearly is one such figure. The hints of her power that peek through the text are so enticing it's clear there's much more we'd like to know about her. As a man, I have a stake in this process as well: not only for my daughters' sake or my wife's sake, but because I feel the lack of wholeness in a Torah that does not give full voice to women. As at the kallahs, I feel the beauty and strength of Jewish expression when women have their full voice.

Judith Halevy told me that when she teaches traditional midrash to women, she always adds an imaginative exercise so the students can fill in what's missing for them.

Often this involves writing new midrash, or acting out scenes from Torah. For instance, the students read in Genesis 34 the story of the rape of Dina by Shechem. Dina basically gets three lines of the story; the rest of the chapter, twenty-eight lines, focuses on the revenge of her brothers. The rabbinic midrash doesn't help much. Dina is much cited in misogynistic midrash as the paradigm of the "gadabout."[4] Another midrash blames Dina's mother, Leah.[5] Some women react to such texts by rejecting the Torah altogether. They have the same difficulty, doubtless in a more deeply felt, personal way, that I had when discussing the *mishkan* passage with Jonathan.

But in Judith's midrash class, the women write new midrash dialogues. She asks them to imagine, What if? What if Dina could talk to her mother, Leah, about the rape? The Torah tells us about her brothers' reactions, her father's reactions to them. What counsel would her mother give her?

She gave another example. "We did Mrs. Noah. What did Mrs. Noah think? Someone wrote this incredible midrash saying, 'Excuse me—my neighbors are floating away, and I'm going to get in the boat with this guy? It's terrible.'" I laughed at her impersonation; she gave it a funny Yiddish intonation.

"So the very absence and sparseness of text creates the need to add so much more?"

"That's also true," Judith said.

"The traditional midrash may not be that big a help given its male point of view?"

"That's right. Every week they say, 'Who wrote this crap?'" She paused and thought a moment. "We have to reinvent the tradition. Yet always tie it back into text, because the last thing you want is people just going off on flights of fancy."

I heard Jonathan's caution in that last remark, but some spreading of wings was necessary if women would bring life to the text. Clearly Judith's end of the Jewish spectrum felt a sense of freedom and entitlement about doing it.

Creative work—like Lynn's Torah tarot, and Judith Halevy's theatrical interpretations of a Rebbe Nachman tale—joins a larger movement of women's midrash. Ellen Frankel, editor in chief of the Jewish Publication Society, recently published an imaginative book of commentary on Torah, *The Five Books of Miriam*, which offers a complete sequence of women's midrash for all the *parashiot*. Often Frankel's midrash counters or supplements the rabbinic tradition—in the name of Sarah and Esther, in the name of "our daughters" and "our bubbes." But similar midrash are created by women every week in havurot Shabbats and renewal gatherings, and elsewhere no doubt. Perhaps the most interesting movement is coming within the Orthodox community: women's prayer groups meet separately, and Orthodox women are receiving higher levels of Jewish education than previously. Dr. Blu Greenberg has long championed the cause of Orthodox feminism, and predicts the day will come when Orthodox women will be ordained as rabbis. Meanwhile, Dr. Avivah Zornberg for one has shown what power Orthodoxy might gain from such a move. She has produced extraordinary midrash, in *Genesis: The Beginnings of Desire*, that blends keen insight with sophisticated literary allusion, while staying within the boundaries of Orthodox belief.

Apart from the Torah, Judith's favorite teaching texts are the tales of Rabbi Nachman, especially the tale of the Seven Beggars. These tales are said by the Bratzlav *hasidim* to have the power of spiritual transformation for any who hear them. In her class, theater techniques help expose their spiritual depths.

One section of Rebbe Nachman's Seven Beggars is called "The Beggar with the Crooked Neck." At one level, it's simply the story of two birds. "The female was lost," Judith told me, "and the male went to look for her. He searched for her and she searched for him. They searched for one another for a very long time, until they got completely lost."

The two birds symbolize many things. They are God and the Shekhinah; the Shekhinah goes into exile with the Jewish people at the time of the destruction of the Second Temple. They are also the two cherubs on the ark of the covenant, the small box or coffer at the heart of the *mishkan* that carries the tablets of the covenant.

Aryeh Kaplan comments that, "As long as the ark with the cherubs stood in the Temple, the relationship between the Holy

One and the Shekhinah was perfect, and prophecy could exist. However, after the Temple was destroyed, and the ark hidden, prophecy ceased. The concept of bringing together the two birds is thus that of reuniting the Holy One and His Shekhinah which is the redemption."[6]

Beautiful—but for me, as for Judith, the question is how to make this reuniting real today.

Judith's way is to show that the words in the Rebbe Nachman tale apply to each and every one of us, and at every moment. To make that connection felt, she uses a theater exercise.

She pairs her students up. "You and I are partners," she tells them. "We're on the ark cover, we're angels. No words. Make a sound and you communicate with your partner. Really get into a bonding place." The students had already been working with sounds for weeks, working with shofars, and with jazz saxophones and with the notion of the "sound beyond sound," with the sound of the shofar as "the sound that's beyond the words that are said in prayer.

"Then I say, 'Turn around, we're now separated. Walk away. How does it feel? You long for that being.'"

A midrash teaches that when the Temple was destroyed, the cherubs on the ark cover turned their backs one on the other. So the students in this exercise enacted, in part, the historical tragedy of the Jewish exile, the loss of the Temple and its deep meaning to every Jew. But they brought as well to their gestures every personal loss, every personal separation. As she described it, I thought of how at the deepest level, the personal and the historical are intimately connected. The pain each feels individually echoes that historical pain every Jew feels somewhere within, the pain of loss, displacement, exile.

She described these broken partners calling to one another.

"Everyone is blindfolded," she said. "I tell them, 'Find your partner in the room by sound.'" The students wander, calling to one another in the welter of competing sounds. "Ach," she said, "incredible longing! At the end there's silence; in that silence the Holy One comes. At moments in this room the holy spirits are here. As that last class ended, for twenty-five minutes, no one spoke, no one moved."

When I'd told Jonathan before his Passover class on Monday about my sense of the door of pain, he mentioned that I should talk to Mark Borovitz. We met briefly that afternoon at Metivta, and agreed to meet again on Friday for a talk.

He joined me for lunch at Merv Griffin's Beverly Hilton. I was staying in unwonted luxury thanks to the odd and fitful munificence of my publisher. I could slide open my cabana doors and walk straight to the edge of a shimmering luxury pool. Waiters circled around with drinks on trays, and attendants bore fluffy white towels. In between classes with Jonathan, I lay on a plastic lounge chair and studied *Tormented Master,* Arthur Green's landmark biography of Rebbe Nachman of Bratzlav. I was having trouble concentrating on Rabbi Nachman's spiritual torments while gorgeous Hollywood walked by in bikinis. Oscar Week 1995: Tom Hanks was Gumping his way to a second golden statue, the O. J. Simpson trial was in prosecution phase, and I was learning about Bratzlaver meditation on a lounge chair.

I met Mark at the valet parking. He was about six feet tall and wore a houndstooth English cap. We walked back to the indoor pub and ordered beer and pizza. But the TV was running Kato Kaelin brushing back his hair on the witness stand. We decided to move out into the light. Mark serves as the prison-visitation and community-outreach coordinator for Beit T'shuvah\* (literally, House of Return), a halfway house for Jewish men

---

\* This is the spelling of *teshuvah* used by the organization.

recovering from addictive behavior. Twenty-five reside there at any given time, and the house is always full, with a waiting list to get in.

"Our program is based on the spiritual and ethical principles of Judaism," he said. It was founded by Harriet Rosetto, a remarkable social worker also in Jonathan and Judith's circle at Metivta, and Mark's wife.

How had he gotten involved?

"I am an ex-felon."

I must have registered shock.

"I was incarcerated twice in the California state prison system and a few times in the county jail. For about twenty years I wrote bad checks and did various types of white-collar fraud."

"That was your way of life?"

"Yeah. I was a thief."

*Thief* struck me as harsh, but he said it with real authority. "What was behind that?" I asked. "Did you . . . was there something behind it? Maybe that's the wrong question." I fumbled, wondering why Jonathan asked me to meet him.

Mark was raised in a Conservative Jewish family in Cleveland. His father died when he was fourteen. "I felt he was working too hard to keep up a middle-class lifestyle. I thought the world owed me something because it had taken my father. I was going to get back and get mine. If I had enough money I would be something. If I didn't I was a *shtik drek*." A piece of shit.

Mark began as a petty thief and shoplifter, moved on to insurance fraud and "a little extortion, a little armed robbery." He fenced stolen goods, sold phony Florida land grants and home improvements, and wrote about two million dollars' worth of bad checks. He served time in county jail and state prison.

According to statistics put out by Beit T'shuvah, about 1.25 percent of America's inmate population are Jews,[1] and the majority of Jewish offenders (85 to 95 percent) are "incarcerated because of an addictive/compulsive disorder." With his gambling addiction, Mark Borovitz fit the bill.

"I was on my way to Las Vegas to bet a ten-team football parlay. I was a fairly good football handicapper in those days. I owed about fifty thousand dollars in bad checks. If I won it would be seventy-five thousand and I was going to pay them off. The officer turned the corner. He had arrested me five years earlier, in 1981, and seen a wanted poster on me from Santa Barbara County about three weeks prior to that. It all clicked for him in a matter of seconds.

"The cop called out, 'Mark, Mark,' and I said hello. It was the most bizarre happening in the world.

"I called the woman I was married to at the time and said, 'Come pick up this money,' because I had about two thousand dollars on me. She said, 'Do you want me to bail you out?' and I said, 'No, the man upstairs is trying to tell me something and I have to sit here to figure it out.'

"So I'm sitting in Van Nuys Jail on a Thursday, and on Monday I was taken up to Santa Barbara County Jail. I got the newspaper, the sports section; all ten of my teams had come in. I realized God has a sense of humor."

Mark was sent to state prison in February 1987 and saw Rabbi Mel Silverman, whom he'd known in '84 and '85 in Chino. "I asked him if he was going to cut me loose too, if he was just disgusted with me, as many people were. He smiled and said, 'You're a Jew, you're one of my own. How could I ever be disgusted with you?' I cried. I knew I had to do something different. The only place for me to turn that I felt comfortable was Judaism."

Mark's sole Jewish practice was remembering his father's *yahrzeit*, the yearly anniversary of his death. To do it properly, he asked his brother, a Reform rabbi, to send a prayer book, and his brother sent him one and a Torah with commentary as well. "It worked out perfectly, because I started to daven each day in prison and read the *parashah*." Transferred to Chino, he became the rabbi's clerk and studied with him. He worked on the *Hilkhot Teshuvah* [Laws of Repentance], Maimonides' tract on *teshuvah*, "on how to turn."

"You were already thinking about this?"

"I knew I had to."

"Why this time and not the last time? What was the difference?"

"Number one, I was tired. Number two, Rabbi Silverman touched me. I don't know whether I would have been able to stay on the path if I hadn't had a guide. Then the people from Beit T'shuvah, the Jewish committee for personal service, visited us in jail, so I got to know about the halfway house."

When he left prison, Mark couldn't find work. "Store owners weren't thrilled about having a thief at the cash register. Beit T'shuvah hired me. I went to work for five dollars and sixty-three cents an hour as a thirty-seven-year-old man. It was humbling."

He attended Jonathan's course on the Pirkei Avot in January 1989. "God was good to me because I found my new guide. Jonathan was talking about essential pain and voluntary suffering."

Mark explained: "I had kept myself in voluntary suffering. I volunteered to be a victim—a poor me. Society didn't treat me right, I didn't have enough money, if only and if only and if only . . . I never wanted to feel the pain of understanding my place, my purpose. God's purpose for me may not be what I think is the best."

"You thought best would be to have a lot of money?"

"Right."

"But that wasn't God's idea?"

"I don't think so. I earned a lot of money but I blew it all. So I started studying with Jonathan. He has guided me in this path and so has my work at Beit T'shuvah—of understanding what repenting is, what turning is, and then new responses to similar situations.

"People think of violent crime as physical violence," he said. "But I perpetrated emotional violence because as a con man I got people's trust and abused it. In some cases that prevented people from trusting others again."

So *teshuvah* to Mark meant turning his persuasive abilities positive. "I talk to the clients about recovery, about not having to do the same things I did. Thank God I've never had to have a relapse."

"Have you been tempted?" I couldn't help but ask.

A long silence, and Mark looked down at his plate.

"Not tempted," he said and paused, adding, "The thought has flashed through my mind."

After one of Jonathan's classes Mark said to him, "I need your help. I don't know how to experience the essential pain that's momentary and how to get out of voluntary suffering. That's been my journey for six years."

Jonathan explained that pain is not necessarily bad. "When a woman gives birth, that very painful experience brings great joy." The Passover story also helped. In Hebrew the word for Egypt is *mitzrayim,* the narrow place. "The journey," Mark said, "from that constricted place I'd been in into openness and freedom is painful, but the end result is joyous."

From Jonathan, Mark learned "how to use this wisdom tradition, to fortify myself and stay out of voluntary suffering." He passes it on now in his own counseling. "I talk to people about 'How long do you want to stay in the narrow place?' We all have to go to the place of pain. We run into narrow places all our lives. We choose how long to stay in them."

Jonathan always asks him to imagine himself being more generous, and taught him the reciprocity of generosity.

"What is it?"

"If I'm generous, even if it's not returned, the generosity rewards me immediately because I'm no longer in a tight place, tense, wound up, crazed. I get out of tunnel vision. It's very freeing."

I wondered if the Jewish path, with its emphasis on study, was difficult for some longtime criminals and addicts. Mark said quietly, "I don't think anymore that spirituality is something difficult."

"You don't?"

"No. Spirituality is being present in the moment. All of us have been searching for something. We have a huge hole inside. Most don't know what it's from, or how to fill it, so we find anything to relieve the pain. But when the hole is filled with *ha-Shem*, with God's work, then it's not painful. It feels good, and we keep that high for a lot longer than any drug or scam. So, when working with addicts and outlaws, it's trying to get them to shift. Jonathan says it best. It's a two percent shift, to where fifty-one percent of me is not going back there. Just two percent, to make it a fifty-one percent so I never cross that line. It doesn't mean I don't get near it, but I don't cross it."

This reminded me of Jonathan's notion about not having debating societies in the mind. His point is that since we are ambivalent about our old ways already, it's not necessary to change one hundred percent—just two. I always have half a mind to change my mind. Speaking of odds, Mark explained that Beit T'shuvah has a fifty percent success rate "as far as staying clean and connecting to Judaism and repairing the damage done with families." By contrast, the general prison system rehabilitates only about fifteen percent of offenders.

Mark mentioned the Friday-night service at Beit T'shuvah. "We just have a ball," he said. "For an hour or two, we create Shabbas: peace, joy, comradery, community. Friday afternoon about four o'clock, no matter who's arguing with you, who doesn't like you, there's a shift.

"The Shekhinah is in that tent. She shows up every Shabbas . . . that house is blessed. It's in a terrible neighborhood, gangs control our street. But if one of the guys in our house tried to buy drugs, they tell him, 'We won't sell you drugs, you live over there.' In an area that is almost all Latino, we have a respect and we give respect. It's an amazing oasis."

I was struck again by the relevance of the Torah passage Jonathan had read. It was just as Rabbi Judith said: the Torah is always current events. The *mishkan* kept turning up in new guises. Lynn Gottlieb built a *mishkan* for women in the New Mexico desert. Mark Borovitz and the men at Beit T'shuvah had built a *mishkan* of their own using a big old tent in one of the tougher neighborhoods in downtown Los Angeles. I had to see it for myself, and asked Mark if he would mind a visitor. "Not at all," he said. "We have people come all the time."

O

On Friday afternoon I took Beverly Boulevard east toward downtown. Past Rampart Street the neighborhood went multi-cultural, Korean on signs, black folks outside the Praise Christian Fellowship Four Square Church, and Hispanics leaving the Rodeo Market holding *tacos al pastor*. I saw just one hint of Jewish: the Brooklyn Bagel announced "Now Open 7 A.M." I turned onto Lake Street, past the Lake Chiropractic Medical Center, parked my car on the slope. Across the street was my next step, Beit T'shuvah.

Up close, the "House of Return" did not look very promising, a three-story Victorian frame-and-stucco house way past its prime: battleship-gray paint faded and peeling, trash on the sidewalk, and some torn-up car seats strewn on the lawn. Four guys sat smoking on the steps, and they looked tough. I was happy to see a big mezuzah on the doorpost.

It reminded me of a meditation Mark Borovitz taught me.

I'd been asking Jonathan all week to teach me meditations, especially to cultivate equanimity—*hishtavut*. He kept putting me off. But Mark told me one he learned from Jonathan. "The most helpful meditation is looking at the doorway," he said. "I look at the doorway, and whether there's a doorway or not, I picture the mezuzah, and I picture the *Shema* there and I'm able to get focused, get centered. I ask, 'What's really important?' If I'm in a counseling session, 'What's the person saying to me? What is he really saying?'"

"So the door is not just a physical door?" I asked. I was beginning to catch on.

"No. It's knowing that I am in a holy space."

I thought about what doors must mean to prisoners. Mark had told me that in two weeks they'd do a big second-night seder in their tent for about 150 Jewish men, women, and children.

"We have a Haggadah written to compare *mitzrayim* to 'a narrow place,' and we are talking about how addiction is our Egypt of today. People tell their own stories of slavery and how they are becoming liberated."

Well, if Rumi is right, and our Jewish morning prayers are right, God is the one who liberates, God opens doors. But now I'd picked up two specific ways to remember that in the course of my life. First, back in Boulder, the mezuzah on the gates of the lips that Eve Ilsen had mentioned. And now Mark Borovitz's meditation.

Before you enter a home, you ask, Why am I coming here, what is this for? The same when you cross a threshold with another person. At a certain moment you are talking, just conversing, and then you see a door opening to a deeper relationship. That is the holy moment, the holy place. Suddenly the clerk at the counter is no longer a clerk, but a person in the image of God. You stop and meditate on that and perhaps you see a mezuzah on a doorpost, with the *Shema* inside, to mark that you are entering the precinct of the Holy One. The mezuzah meditation is one way to hold yourself open to the spiritual depth of another person. Which is a key to stalking Elijah.

It was a good thought to have as I crossed the threshold of Beit T'shuvah and met "Dave," a long-haired voluble man.[2] We stood together in the dim foyer. I was quickly immobilized in the deadly curare of one sentence chained to the next. His darting eyes made it clear that his psyche was as fragile as glass stemware. His face was framed by a whip of black hair streaked by silver, tied back in a ponytail; he had haunted, pockmarked cheeks. While he talked he held a pack of Pall Malls upside down with long slender fingers. They spilled out one by one but he didn't notice, so soon a pile of unsmoked cigarettes accumulated at his feet, measuring our time together.

It was weird: two Jews standing in a doorway shmoozing before Shabbas. Only I was a nervous skeptic looking for faith, while Dave defined himself crisply as a "dope fiend." His career trajectory included petty theft and prostitution. He'd wakened on at least three separate occasions from death due to overdose. He'd stumbled through desperate burglaries. The last time out, the cops found him passed out at the crime scene, a bedroom he'd been rifling. Drool spooled from the side of his mouth, his arms were tracked and bruised. In the ambulance, his heart stopped dead.

Along the way to that nadir, he'd passed through every Twelve-Step program in sight. He ticked them off for me with his shapely fingers, programs with cute names like Impact and ASAP. Programs that didn't work for him. As the list grew longer, my sense of the hopelessness of the whole process increased. What is it like to enter your tenth recovery program? What hope can anyone have for you, or you for yourself? Now he was at Beit T'shuvah, a Jewish place with a big wooden mezuzah on the door. Would Jewish make any difference?

As Dave talked, I kept looking at the door. Looking *for* the door was more like it. Jonathan had twirled his finger past his thumb; the die kept spinning. I was looking at a new face and having trouble with it.

I thought I knew Jews: Jews are by definition upper middle class, successful, intellectual—white. They are doctors, lawyers, pharmacists, professors, business people. They aren't dope fiends or male prostitutes, aren't "Ray," a scrawny dried-up yellow-looking addict nearly fifty who bounced through the door, stepping on Dave's cigarettes, very proud to announce his day's work. He'd walked all the way to Social Security on Wilshire and for his labors received the coveted SSI award. SSI meant that he now had claim to permanent aid to the disabled—a steady check plus MediCal. As Ray explained the deal to Dave and me, his face lit up like he'd won the lottery. I wondered how it felt that a good day's work meant being declared totally disabled. I had all sorts of middle-class judgments to offer, free of charge.

On the wall behind him I read a chart with each resident's name, the stage in the Twelve-Step program he'd reached, the issue he was struggling with, and how he'd resolved to deal with it. In one frame "afraid to commit" was scribbled.

Ray saw my eyes at the chart. "Guess who showed up yesterday?"

I shrugged.

"A judge," he announced with a certain pride. Dave added, "Dope doesn't discriminate."

Dave and Ray withdrew to discuss the SSI coup further in private, so I made my way past the kitchen, through the TV room, and out the back steps. Men were gathering for the service. I'd come for what Mark Borovitz had promised was the best Shabbat in town. I hoped.

The problem of Jewish addiction to alcohol or drugs is often ignored by the Jewish community, probably because of the same middle-class prejudices I was feeling. Yet nationally, as at Beit T'shuvah, there are Jewish movements addressing the problem. Rabbi Abraham Twerski, M.D., of a distinguished hasidic lineage, has been a leader in Jewish Twelve-Step programs. He's the founder and medical director of Gateway Rehabilitation Center in Aliquippa, Pennsylvania, and has worked closely with JACS (Jewish Alcoholics and Chemically Dependent and Significant Others), an organization similar to AA. When asked about the

Christian origins of Twelve-Step programs, Rabbi Dr. Twerski doesn't flinch. "The Twelve Steps have a Christian origin. We as Jews are quite paranoid about that." But, with its stress on *teshuvah*, "the concept of Twelve Steps is compatible with Judaism."[3]

After passing through the TV room of Beit T'shuvah and into the scrubby backyard, I found a seat under an awning tent with clear plastic sheeting for sides. Just outside the perimeter was a weightlifting bench and a rusty barbell set. Ahead of me, a wooden ark with purple velvet curtains sat on a table beside a kitschy Shabbas candleholder with a babushka *bubbe* and a bearded *zadie* coated in melted wax.

The range of faces gathered that evening gave me a sense of the extent of Jewish criminality in the greater Los Angeles area. In the back sat a couple of young handsome guys, clearly middle class, shop owners and businessmen who'd picked up a cocaine habit and ended up embezzling for all they were worth and more. Nearer to the front sat an Israeli who barely spoke English and sported an outlandish brown velvet yarmulke with swirly gold trim. He had sad droopy eyes and a droopy brown mustache, read prayer-book Hebrew perfectly but with the bored intonation of the native speaker for whom the holy tongue is kitchen-table familiar. Many guys under the tent you might see at a Jewish men's-club meeting, but a few were seriously pumped up. One was a double for Hulk Hogan, the TV wrestler, complete with long straight blond Viking hair, muscle builder's T-shirt, and muscles to match. He had obviously done serious time, as had his friend "Lester," whose thinning hair was slicked back with grease and who had three silver earrings punched through one ear. For Shabbas, Lester wore green Crazee pants, a tank top that showed off a particularly artful lizard tattoo on his bulging shoulder— poised to leap. When Lester stood up to lead us in "Mah tovu," the prayer for entering the sanctuary, I knew I was in a very different Jewish space from the fastidious Reform synagogue of my childhood, where the ladies in the polished pews wore furs for Rosh

Hashanah, even in September heat, and a highly dignified rabbi invoked the great ethical heritage of Judaism.

Here the pews were white plastic lawn chairs, and "Mah tovu"—How goodly are thy tents, O Jacob—never sounded better. Mark had talked about shifting two percent, and I was shifting a few points in the odds myself. We sat in a plastic tent opened to the breezes in one of the rougher neighborhoods in L.A. Hanging above us, oddly, was an elaborate multiarmed chandelier.

A tall man in a sports jacket slipped in and sat next to the ark facing the congregation. He would serve as rabbi tonight. We had spoken at length a few days before, and now, to my surprise, I was going to see him in action. A very intense man, with a large rubber face, an actor's face—and eyebrows that slant at an angle, a large wide mouth, receding hairline with hair in wings behind him, a soft, soft shirt, and intense eyes, a beautiful laugh and smile. He spoke like a preacher, what the ḥasidim call a *maggid*.

The *Maggid* started off the service by telling us he'd had a really hard week. He pleaded with the group, "I really need this. It isn't just for you, it's also for me." The men responded, especially when Lester stood up and led us singing in rounds. Of course, given his size and strength, you'd have to be a bit nuts not to sing along if he asked you to. The Friday-night service at Beit T'shuvah mixed standard prayers and blessings with Twelve-Step confessional exercises and some Jewish renewal renderings from the P'nai Or siddur. But for all the liturgical patchwork and informal quality of the service, there was no question that for some of us this prayer was vital.

As we rustled our Xeroxed prayer books, I remembered Mark Borovitz's statistics. Only half the men sitting here would make it to real freedom. The rest would recycle back to the prison house. The stakes, therefore, were higher than at most services I attended.

The *Maggid* asked, "What are you grateful for from the past week?" This question sounded therapeutic and *shabbasdik*.

One man spoke of patching up a misunderstanding with a fellow resident. Another expressed his deep thanks for a ride to the airport so he could work in Arizona. Then "Bobby," a handsome dark-haired man in his late twenties, stood. His eyes shifted back and forth nervously, as if he expected something to leap out at him from an unseen corner.

Gratitude did not come easily to his lips. He was infectiously nervous. He had arrived on Tuesday, caught up in the system for the first time. That same day, the court ordered him back to prison on a technicality. Mark Borovitz ran downtown to court and cut a deal: if Bobby behaved at Beit T'shuvah for thirty days, he could stay out of prison.

Now Bobby spoke quietly from the side of his mouth, gave thanks for Mark's help, the support of his family, and especially for Beit T'shuvah hiring him a lawyer on retainer.

The *Maggid* labored to keep the spirits moving. The Hebrew speaker reminded him, gently, to go back a few pages and do the *Shema*, which he'd inadvertently skipped. But the technical precision of the liturgy, the aesthetics of prayer that in other settings seems so important, seemed less so in the Visqueen tent of Jacob. Something was being born here, and the aesthetics of the delivery were not that important.

Sometimes the *Maggid* sounded more Baptist than Jewish. He had the chutzpah to say, "God really loves you and God wants you to love him." I'd never heard that in a synagogue in my life. I tried to imagine how that would go over in a suburban synagogue somewhere and laughed. I recoiled at the language. That plea sounded as kitschy to me as the *bubbe-zadie* candleholder. I thought, With these men sitting here in desperation, you're going to sell them that old soap? Lester mentioned he'd lived at Beit T'shuvah for four years. Four years halfway living—and what could God do? I looked back at Dave, my ancient mariner. Clean for a year, he'd told me. Could Dave climb the invisible ropes of God?

"God wants us to love him," the *Maggid* said, "he has so much love for us." I fought the language every inch of the way. Look at these men, a few probably buzzing on their paper cups of methadone. But the *Maggid* spoke with great conviction, earnestness, sincerity. I didn't know if they believed it, or if I believe it, but you need to believe it if you're going to find those two percentage points of *teshuvah*.

I knew now why Jonathan had urged me to meet Mark Borowitz and through him the men at Beit T'shuvah. He wanted me to see that for some people, finding a Jewish path is more than a consumer item. It's life or death.

At the end of the service, a big loaf of challah came out of the kitchen, and we passed around paper cups of grape juice. The *Maggid* of Hollywood led the *kiddush*, then the *motzi*, the blessing, over bread. We gathered around, the guys closest in with a hand on the challah, and the rest of us with hands on their shoulders, and another layer with hands on theirs, so we were all woven together around the braids of challah. Then we broke the bread, and passed it around, and started chewing and talking one-on-one. The service was over. I looked at the sky—Erev Rosh Hodesh, a new moon. I noticed for the first time that it had grown quite dark.

The man who led the Friday-night service at Beit T'shuvah was the *Maggid* of Hollywood, another of Jonathan's students. At first I couldn't figure him out. Paul Wolff is a successful Hollywood scriptwriter, and from what I knew of the business, that's no easy achievement. Among his other credits, he'd written for *Little House on the Prairie* and *Home Improvement*, and developed the groundbreaking series *Life Goes On*. So why was he preaching to addicts and volunteering in Jewish old-age homes instead of writing more hit TV shows? We met for lunch by the pool to talk about his spiritual journey, which, to hear him tell it, had a rocky start.

Born in 1946, the *Maggid* grew up in Brooklyn, was raised in a Conservative shul. His first glimmer of spiritual awareness came at age five while sitting in front of a TV. He saw footage of naked bodies being pushed by a bulldozer into a pile, the bodies rolling over one another.

"What was that?" the boy said to his father, who answered, "The Nazis did that to us." And, "Some of your relatives are in those piles."

"It had a powerful effect," the *Maggid* told me. "It started me on my search for meaning. To know what it's all about."

But postwar Judaism gave him no answers. "I became very rebellious. One day I was studying for my bar mitzvah, as the Hebrew teacher followed me in the siddur. You had to have your finger on the spot where you were reading. He came by and asked me, 'Where is the spot?' I didn't know. He took my finger and slammed it into the book." The *Maggid* hit the table hard with his finger. "He almost broke my finger. It was throbbing. I lost my temper, gave him an elbow in the stomach. I doubled him over. I stood up and said, 'Sayonara!' I was like a madman."

The rabbi called his parents. He would have to do his bar mitzvah lessons over the phone. "I was calling the cantor every afternoon," he said, "which I liked, because if I said to him, 'What do the words mean?' he would try to tell me as best as he could." The *Maggid* leaned back in his chair and reflected.

"To me it's all about meaning. Why do any of this? Why bother? Judaism is so vast and fantastic we can get lost in it. What's it about? How to be a human being, to live your life as a servant of God." He told me that's why Jonathan and Zalman had ordained him as a *maggid*, a ceremony that took place February 27, 1994.

In an article describing the ceremony, Jonathan announced that Paul is "acknowledged officially as a Jewish storyteller, a Maggid. He has been filling such a role with marvelous talent for many years. But as a Maggid he now has our approval and permission to do this as a Jewish teacher within the Jewish world.

"Traditionally," Jonathan wrote, "a Maggid is not necessarily a book person, in the way a rabbi is or should be. When a Maggid looks at a Jewish text, he does so with a sense of the immediacy, the urgency of scripture. His task is to awaken people from spiritual sleep."[1]

As we talked, I could see Paul getting caught up in his own preacherly enthusiasm, his *maggid* energy. So I asked him back to his bar mitzvah. He laughed.

"The bar mitzvah was an insane day. There were two other kids. I did my *haftarah*, I was very proud of myself, and at the end of the ceremony the rabbi gets up and calls the first boy. 'Seth Goldman, you did a wonderful job and we'd like to give you your Bible.' Then he picks the other boy and says, 'Joel Grossman, come up, you did a great job, here's your Bible.' Then he looks at me, my family . . . they came from Florida, they came from all over the country. 'But the Wolff boy gets no Bible.' He uses this moment, my bar mitzvah, to nail me for all my transgressions. So my father, may he rest in peace, was a great hothead—goes for him, on the bimah, leaps . . . my grandmother is dragging my father off and I'm egging my father on to deck the rabbi. You can imagine the party afterward. It was like a wake."

The bar mitzvah melee left its mark. "At that point I said, 'I know there's a God. I'm going to find him. This has got to mean something, it can't be a cruel joke. *They* just don't know.' And I instinctively knew they didn't know."

At eighteen Paul started working for United Artists in New York, picking up stars from airports and taking critics out for lobster dinners. "It was an extraordinary job for a young man, but also I felt the emptiness of it." Later he assisted on the production of *The Owl and the Pussycat* with Barbra Streisand. "One producer was reading a book about the Gurdjieff system, *In Search of the Miraculous*. I found it on his desk one day. It just grabbed me by the throat. I found my way into the Gurdjieff foundation. For the first time I was with people who were awake and living with integrity. I stayed as part of the Gurdjieff system for twenty years, until my Jewish *neshamah* [soul] started needing something else."

We ordered lunch—poolside—and the *Maggid* tracked away from the story. I sensed that a profoundly painful event hid in the gap. I mentioned how many people came to Jewish spirituality through a door of pain.

"For all of us, though," he said, quietly.

"I see it in Jonathan," I said.

"Absolutely. I mean, his life is very obvious in a way. His suffering. But all of us . . . no one is getting out clean. This world— I hate to spoil the party—it's basically painful."

"This is why Buddhism is so appealing," I said. "No one can read the first noble truth, that the nature of existence is suffering, and say, 'That's wrong.' It's correct."

"Right. Judaism also has to be a response. What do you do?—that's what people want to know. At Beit T'shuvah I deal with people at the outermost limits of human suffering. You can't bullshit them. Something real has to touch them. Because only God can help them in these situations, let's face it."

"So why did you leave Gurdjieff?"

"I had my own tragedy," he said slowly. "In 1982 I was very successful in Hollywood, a young man in my early thirties. Weekends I was a Gurdjieff group leader and during the week I was Hollywood. I wrote *Little House on the Prairie*. I did a new series for Mary Tyler Moore. I thought I could have it all." He opened his mouth, and a big laugh choked in his throat like pulling an emergency brake.

"Anyway, my wife and I had our first child, a beautiful girl. At ten months she got very, very sick. We didn't know what it was and ran from doctor to doctor. It turned out it was cancer—inoperable, very rare cancer even grown-ups don't get too often, let alone children. At the age of seventeen months, she died. I would have rather died, gladly. But it broke my heart open to suffering."

I looked into his face. I held my own face steady.

"You see, the Gurdjieff work is very much about one's own development. Suddenly here I was in a waiting room of a hospital, of the intensive-care unit, and all of us have children dying there. I had the strangest feeling that the other parents—they were black and Mexican and Oriental—they were praying for my child. You couldn't just pray for your child, you had to pray for all the children. The brotherhood of man, this banal slogan, became an absolute reality. There weren't Jews or Mexicans or Christians in the room. We were just all parents with children who were dying and we were all praying together for our children. We were in a life raft out in the middle of the ocean, and every hour a shark would come and grab one of our kids. It ripped open my heart. I couldn't any longer work just for myself:

everybody suffering on this planet is me. I couldn't turn away anymore. This was God's terrible gift to me."

*Terrible gift.* Not something I would say. He looked at me and I nodded, "Please, tell me more."

"I became Job. I railed against God and I fought him tooth and nail. 'Kill me, you've got the power! I'm not questioning your power, I'm questioning your morality. I'm questioning your goodness. You want us to be good, where is your goodness?'" This passionate questioning comes only from what Jonathan calls essential pain.

"That search, that insane crazed search, led to an answer. It's hard to say, because only an individual with God can say what it is. But just like at the end of Job, Job is OK with it, and I'm OK with it. I understand this isn't the whole picture and that when someone dies, especially the way my little angel died, it was voluntary on her part. I've since learned she was my most important teacher, more important than anyone I've ever had, and she continues to be.

"So yes, while something may look terrible from this corporeal point of view, and it is terrible—I wouldn't wish it on my worst enemy—there's another dimension where another story is being played out and these beings that come in and go out are heroes. They have a mission. Her mission was to give me this sense of compassion. As a species, we have to start seeing each other this way, to start loving each other this way. So that was the turning point.

"After my daughter died, I realized it's one thing to be mindful and walk around and be conscious all the time. It's another to address the abject suffering of life. So my daughter, when she was sick—all right, I could love her, I could hold her. I said, 'My parents are dead, who's going to love me? I want love too. I want to be loved. I want to be loved by God. Does God love me? Is God possible in that, or is it just some distant omnipotent creator who's not concerned with me?' I had to know this, and that's why I had to come back to Judaism. I had to find a relationship with God that was not only cosmic but intensely personal."

I confessed I found a personal God hard to believe, "that the force that created this huge universe, these huge perspectives of time, really knows or cares what happens to me—or any individual." That wasn't my experience.

"It is hard to believe," the *Maggid* said.

"It's *very* hard to believe," I said, and Paul interrupted.

"—which is why we have to give up belief."

I laughed. "What do you mean?"

"We have to give up the rational mind. It has its place, but here it's out of its league. Spirituality is highly irrational, which is why people don't like it. Now I've found that—this is paradoxical—it's irrational, but it's completely sane."

I wondered. People who bluntly express strong beliefs in God make me uneasy. But I trusted the *Maggid* mainly because, in his crisis, he'd turned outward, serving others.

"I started to volunteer," he told me. "When I wasn't writing I'd go into hospitals and work with parents of dying children, and work in old-age homes, meeting suffering head-on. In the Gurdjieff work this is not what they do. They are concerned with this very extraordinary teaching, but they don't go out." He began to feel disconnected from Gurdjieff. "I wanted to pray, which was new to me."

"You had prayed when you talked to God?"

"Yes. But I had no prayer life. Like all of us, when we are in the trenches, we pray . . ."

I saw again the corridors of a certain hospital, and a baby on a respirator with a face like stone. A boy who could not open his eyes or move, his legs spread, heels akimbo—a sign, the doctors said, that he was decerebrate. A baby whose life had been in my hands.

## Directions to the Lake
BEVERLY HILTON
MARCH 29, 1995; 27 ADAR II 5755

This was ten years before, 1985. In those days, the only prayer I knew was in a siddur. So when the baby died, I had already looked up a prayer in an old dark blue prayer book: *Barukh Atah Adonai, Eloheinu Melekh ha-olam, Dayan ha-emet*—Blessed are you, Lord . . . the true judge. The traditional blessing Jews say upon death. In the room where he gave his last breath, I felt no connection to the words in the book. They came out hollow. Yet I very much wanted to say something Jewish to mark that moment, to connect with a tradition, even if it seemed awkward and desiccated. I did not know then how to pray.

A rabbi visited us in the hospital, during the days when the boy lay in the intensive-care unit. When the rabbi heard our story, he burst into tears, and my wife and I had to comfort him. He opened his prayer book and riffled through the pages. It was the eighth day after my son had been born. We couldn't circumcise him, so this was a prayer to say instead. Only, the words of the prayer were no comfort. "That he may grow to study Torah." Study Torah? He couldn't open his eyes.

Yet prayer came to that room—what Jonathan would call essential prayer, prayer from the heart. It came from Reverend Tommy, a Baptist preacher assigned as counselor to the hospital. I never would have thought before then that I would take comfort in the prayer of an evangelical Baptist. But Tommy listened to what was in my heart and Moira's heart, and then he spoke toward God—the only way I can describe it. He spoke toward God—addressed our anguish and turmoil and what was in our hearts, summarized it with his own plea for compassion and guidance, and directed those words toward a being he believed in with great force, even though I, standing beside him, could not believe for one instant that there was a true judge or anything but emptiness in that space where our baby lay without life.

The personal prayer of Tommy shocked me as much as it comforted me. It seemed exotic, *goyishe*. In the starkness of our pain, the emptiness of that room, I could accept it, it worked. But this was not the prayer language I knew as a Jew. As a Jew, I mumbled formulas, *berakhot*, I recited set liturgies, I read silently in English in despair while old men around me raced through Hebrew syllables. Or I stood up and sat down, stood up and sat down while a cantor and a rabbi led us in set readings. These could be strong moments, uplifting moments, comforting moments—but I never once, in all those years, imagined I was saying these syllables to God. As Jews, we did not talk to God, at least not in public. Rarely in private that I knew of. I had never seen my father pray or my mother pray or my grandparents pray, not in that sense. Not like Reb Zalman, who had seen as a child his father pray in tears and asked if it hurt to pray. I had never prayed in that sense, seeking a personal petition, or connection with a divine creator. Whether God existed or not seemed to me a cosmic riddle, not a personal question. I would have thought such prayer outlandish, embarrassing behavior.

At that time, I had no language for it, no behavior for it, no training in it.

The *Maggid* came to Jonathan for the same lesson I did: how to pray Jewish. No matter how many times his finger had been slammed down "on the spot" of the siddur, those lessons had taught him nothing of how to pray, or how the black words in that book might come alive in his heart. But after the death of his daughter, the sense of feeling abandoned by God produced in him a search for prayer.

Paul found an answer in the teaching of Rebbe Nachman. "The pain doesn't exist because God wants to punish us. The pain is so that we'll turn to that place that is not pain. The pain exists so we will go to the healing and through that. . . Look, Jonathan healed himself and look how many other people as well. His suffering didn't just have to do with him. None of our suffering just has to do with us. Actually it's all illusory, there's no us or him, there's just *Adonai ehad* [the Lord is one], that's all that's really going on here. In our delusion we keep seeing ourselves through our biographies, but that's not really what's happening. There's another story being told—a bigger story.

"So," the *Maggid* explained, "I began to do this volunteer work, and I wanted to pray. I read books on prayer." Particularly helpful was a book on living prayer by Archbishop Anthony Bloom, from the Eastern Orthodox Church.

"I read his book and started to experiment with his prayers, but they were Christian. I didn't think I would have a problem because at that point I thought I was a universalist.

"I experimented with these prayers and some had the words Jesus Christ in them. To my amazement, my heart wouldn't do it. My heart said, 'No, I won't say this.' I tried to force it. My heart said, 'Screw you, I'm not going to do it.' I said, 'Well, OK.' I'd learned by that time that you can't push the heart around. I said, 'Let me find some Jewish prayers.'"

The *Maggid* had met Jonathan ten years earlier and been impressed. But he felt too far away from Judaism then to be serious about a Jewish path. Now he called and Jonathan said, "Isn't that odd, I was just thinking about you. I just sent you an invitation to this new school that I'm founding." Metivta.

"When Jonathan came back from India in 1990, from the Dalai Lama, I started to study with him. I thought I was just going to learn some prayers." He smiled because their relationship soon went beyond exchange of information. After a few meetings, "I realized he had something and I wanted to learn from him. I said, 'Should I go sign up for a class?' He said, 'No, the first thing you should do is go to Fairfax Avenue—that's the

Jewish neighborhood in L.A. Just hang around the bakery or the butcher shop, just hang around with Jews.'"

"So step one, when you went to the kabbalistic master he said, 'Go to the bakery and hang out'?"

"Hang out."

"That's very funny."

He shrugged. "He wanted me to get back to the sense of Jewishness and being with my people and having a love for my people, and that's what he gave me, this intense love of Judaism, of Jewishness."

The *Maggid* began studying Torah and kabbalah with Jonathan on a weekly basis. "We would just talk," he said. "He gears his teaching to each student. That period was like a trip to Mount Sinai for me. I was not working, and when I wasn't with Jonathan I sat in a car on top of a mountain and prayed all day. That's all I did. Prayed all day for a whole year. Just prayed and prayed and meditated and prayed, studied with Jonathan, prayed, went to classes, went to shul. That's all."

"This praying on the mountain was not from a prayer book, was it?"

"No. This was *hitbodedut*, talking to God.* Rabbi Nachman's *hitbodedut*, direct prayer, one's own language, one's own heart. I didn't even know what I was going to say before I said it."

Jonathan had spoken about *hitbodedut* to the Dalai Lama. He said it involved screaming, crying out to God with all your might. He said that after a time, "subtle things emerge."

Was the prayer coming from his experience of his daughter's death?

"Oh no, because she died in 1982 and this was already 1990. Of course she's always there, the experience, but the prayer came out of a need to get closer to God and realizing I was in denial."

---

* *Hitbodedut* literally means "seclusion of oneself." Cf. Aryeh Kaplan, *Meditation and the Bible* (York Beach, ME: Samuel Weiser, 1978), pp. 1–4.

"Denial?"

"As a writer you learn that all good characters are interesting because they are in denial. The essence of good drama is denial. Because someone in denial needs to learn something and at the end of it he does. We're all in denial. About who our creator is and what we should be about. The planet is in denial. I was in denial of the fundamental fact of my life. It's not accidental that we're Jews, for instance."

"For instance?"

"I don't know what happens in the upper spheres, but I feel that to negate one's Jewishness and not learn about it and not be part of the community and not identify oneself as a Jew is to be in denial. You are not letting the power that's built into our genes join in your search. A whole part of me was in the wings: my Jewish soul wanted to pray and I never let it. So now I was allowing the Jew to live. *Teshuvah* means 'to come home'—back to Judaism, to be with my people. But it doesn't stop there. The real home is still not that, but something else."

"You mean beyond the label of Judaism?"

"Absolutely. The real home is not the label."

"God is not Jewish." Shefa Gold's words came to mind.

"God is not Jewish. Judaism is our way to God."

But there are so many Jewish ways, and I wondered if that wasn't confusing. The *Maggid* seemed ambivalent about rabbis—not surprising given his bar mitzvah story and his independent streak. The dryness, the lack of spiritual immediacy he found in many synagogues bothered him. "For the intelligent seeking person whose need is large, we can't just say, 'Come on Shabbat, we'll have herring, we'll have bagels.' Judaism in my mind, maybe I'm wrong, but it exists for God. So that God can have a place on earth, that we'll be his people. It doesn't exist for itself.

"An intelligent person will say, 'What tools are you going to offer me? You're telling me come to services on Shabbat? That's the tool? Sorry. I've got to find out how to live this minute by minute, day by day in my life.' Someone needs to systematize a clean halakhah, a new way for us to be holy people without at the same time being Orthodox. Because at this point it's a grab bag. We study this, we do a little Talmud; there's so much to choose from, you cannot get anywhere. A few times a year we follow out a certain intention. During the counting of the Omer and during the High Holy Days, the month of Elul, we actually follow a definite path of work on ourselves and then we get lost, lost."

I asked the *Maggid* if he kept kosher since his return to Judaism, and he explained that he didn't. "I'm not kosher to the law," he said, "but I'm not going to eat treif." I wondered exactly what he meant by that.

"I observe it in the way I'm comfortable observing. I don't see any particular meaning in it, I'm honest with you. I did at the beginning, because it was a struggle not to order the shrimp, so that woke me up. But at this point it does not wake me up anymore, it's just what I order. I feel like I am *proceeding from* Judaism. I'm part of the family, these are the family rules. I'm going to obey the rules. I'm not going to just throw them all out."

It seemed to me that many disaffected Jews had only two rules: one, I will not be Orthodox; two, the only authentic Jews are Orthodox.

"Okay," he said, "you hit it on the head. We have this strange behavior with the Orthodox. We negate what they are doing in our own smug way, saying it's not for us; they're back in the past. At the same time we're always looking over our shoulders. Are they judging us, are we doing it right? We need to be secure and confident in our own relationship with God as Jews and not keep looking over our shoulders at our Orthodox brothers and sisters.

"We were having an endless discussion one day at Ohr Hatorah"—the synagogue where Jonathan had subbed the previous Shabbas—"about these things. Orthodox. Non-Orthodox. Are we doing it right? Are they doing it wrong? It was really upsetting me because my whole question is, Are we awake? Are we alive? Finally, being a *maggid*, a story occurred to me.

"Our ancestors, who were all Orthodox, went on an adventure. They found a pristine, beautiful, endlessly deep lake with the purest sparkling, azure blue water. They mapped out a path to this lake and it was very precise. Turn left here, go right here. They said, 'If you want to reach this lake, follow this map, because we worked on it and we're not bullshitting you—this works.' Then somewhere along the line somebody who wouldn't follow that map found the lake and told the other mapmakers about it. They said, 'You're crazy. You couldn't possibly get there without this map.' They started to argue about it. They argued and argued for centuries—and nobody went swimming. That's what we're doing. Nobody's going into the lake. Go in the lake!" the *Maggid* shouted, laughing. A kid in an orange suit pulled himself out of the pool.

"I say to my Orthodox friends who want to argue with me, 'I tell you what, I'm not going to convince you and you're not going to convince me. Go in the lake. That's the most important thing. That's where you're supposed to be. *Go in the lake.*'" Paul paused and added, "'And if you see me in the lake, don't be too surprised.'"

I laughed. But how do we get to the lake, now?

"[Rabbi] Mordecai Finley was speaking one day in temple," he told me. "He explained how the early synagogues had a carved-out space in the front of the bimah to coincide with the empty space of the Holy of Holies in the Temple. Then somewhere along the line, someone got the idea 'Why don't we take this Torah and put it into that empty space?' That's how we got what we have today.

"But there was an empty space in the Holy of Holies for a definite reason. Real holiness is to empty oneself completely and become an empty space for God's presence. Out of that silence comes real contact.

"We can fill it with adoration of the Torah scroll. We have emotion toward it, like seeing an old friend. But does it get us to that empty space, which is real contact, which is the living Torah? I'm at the service of that, not the book. I mean, the book is beautiful, the book has wisdom, I love it, but it's a scroll. Where's the living Torah? I don't want to study 'What did this rabbi say, what did that rabbi say?' That's why I'm not a rabbi. Yes, they had revelations—but what about mine? I have to have my revelation. You have to individually find this.

"I wish more and more people would do what Rabbi Finley is doing and Rabbi Omer-Man is doing and Zalman has been doing for years, which is, before we pray, before we embark on this journey, let's stop and empty ourselves. On Shabbat we don't care about who's making what for a living, we don't carry our wallets, we're not interested in all that, but let's inwardly do it, let's empty our biography."

"What do you mean *empty*? What does that mean to you?"

"It means to become as if one is listening to a seashell, one is just listening—as we're told to do in the *Shema*. If there are anxieties, getting to them, acknowledging that they are there, and letting them go. I mean, what was the Temple? The Temple was a corporal representation of the possibility that exists inside us. That empty space is in us somewhere."

"Do you know something amazing about that Temple?" I asked. "It was very small."

"Was it?"

"Smaller than that swimming pool."

We looked over to where some girls were splashing around with an inflatable dragon. Paul had touched on events very close to my life. But I had no way to empty them out. What practice was there for me in Judaism when I stood at my own door of pain? Perhaps it was this *hitbodedut*, this calling out, but I didn't know if I could let myself do that.

I let Paul know the pain I'd experienced. But I could not say, as he had, that God brought me a terrible gift. I did not have that certainty or faith. I wondered what he meant, finally, by this process of emptying one's biography. It sounded like amnesia or anodyne. The *Maggid*'s enthusiasm was contagious, but I felt a certain reserve.

And in regard to reserve, he told me several times that he felt Jonathan was "sitting on a secret." He said I had a mission—to bring that secret out into the world. He called this secret "the path of blessing."

The subject came up when I asked Paul about his own spiritual practice, his inner life as a Jew. Because of his Gurdjieffian background, he was looking for a way to experience closeness to God from moment to moment. The Jewish tradition calls this *devekut*, clinging to God.

"I have a prayer life," he told me. "I put on tefillin every morning and I meditate and daven every morning. But I have from Gurdjieff a practice of mindfulness that is now part of my being. I have a technique. I'm not a genius, *I was trained*. I know what to do when I'm on line at the bank and I'm bored. I know how to sanctify that moment without doing anything weird. Part of the problem is that all of our Jewish forms are taken from an Orthodox source. Some of us are not Orthodox, but we're still not off the hook. The demand is on us to find the practices that will keep us centered during the day. Some Orthodox follow the halakhah as an endless Japanese tea ceremony to keep one's attention on the Shekhinah at every moment. But those who are not going to do that, what is our practice to sanctify the moment? That has not arisen yet. Jonathan is beginning to address it now."

"Sanctify the moment?" I asked him. "What does that mean?" Mark Borovitz had said much the same thing—that Jewish spirituality for him meant being in the moment.

"For me it's, What's going on in God's moment? What am I filling it with? Am I filling it with my next stop of the day? The person I'm angry with? The sex I'd like to have, the food I want to eat? What's my inner life, my inner terrain at this moment, and how can I let go of it and just be here? So no one knows what I'm doing. I'm not saying any prayers, I don't have a yarmulke on, I'm just a human being standing in the bank, but I'm here and I'm able to see human beings. I'm able to see what I couldn't see before when I was lost in my own chaos."

"Are you asking for guidance?" I asked. "Are you asking God to tell you what to do next?"

"Well, no. It's meditation in action. For me meditation is emptying oneself and coming into this moment with whatever is in this moment. I accept what's in this moment. It's grounding oneself. I believe our ancestors knew about this practice. Jonathan has redeemed it and found it again in the teaching he calls the blessing teaching. This is a teaching I've been badgering him for five years to give us: what's the Jewish mindfulness."

"We want it in Jewish."

"Right. We want to do authentic Jewish practices. I know they're there because I see it." He spoke of prayers that alluded to mindfulness, such as the *Ve-Ahavta*, the section of the *Shema* from Deuteronomy recited at every service. "'Love God with all your mind, with all your heart, with all your strength.' This isn't metaphor," he said, "it's a recipe for what has to happen physically. There's a physics to spirituality. The physics of being awake. The mind needs to be united with the body, which needs to unite with the heart to attend to this moment, which is the vehicle for the Presence. I see it in our prayers, but no one's teaching it. It's assumed, just do the prayers, say them. But that's not enough. We need specific work, now, as we head into the year 2000."

I'd come to the same conclusion.

"Of all the Jewish teachings I've studied," he went on, "and all the teachers, Orthodox and hasids, I've studied with, this teaching of Jonathan's I believe to be the missing piece."

"Can you give me a hint of what it's about?"

"Look," Paul said, "a Jew is supposed to say one hundred blessings a day. Why? Does God need to be praised that much? He doesn't need the blessing, we need it. To really say a *berakhah*, one needs to stop. It's not just some words one gets out of the way on the way to a meal. It's there so that we'll stop and give up everything that's going on in our minds. We'll give up our plans, we'll give up our schemes, and we'll stop and we'll look and we'll see the holiness. We'll really look at something—a piece of bread, a flower, a human being—and then, and only then, when you're awake enough to see the holiness, you say the *berakhah*. Or one can say it inwardly, quietly, without anyone knowing it, or outwardly if you're in a place where you can do it.

"So that all day we're stopping to wake up. You know the blessing isn't the point; the point is, Am I even aware that I have a soul now? Am I aware that these flowers are from God and were put here?" A pair of lilies leaned in a majolica vase at our table.

I said, "It's funny, because when I asked Jonathan, 'Where do you start with people?' he said, 'I encourage them to say a blessing at every meal.'"

"Again," Paul said, feeling frustrated, "Jonathan is my teacher, he's the rabbi. I'm not the teacher, he is. I'm the gadfly, I'm the *noodge*. I just have to *noodge* everybody. I will say it publicly and I say it to him: he's sitting on the single most important thing that we need. We need a practice. That was the question the other night to you: what's your practice?" After my talk at a Tibetan Buddhist temple in Pacific Palisades, a very sincere meditator had asked me for my practice.

"I hear it everywhere I go, at Ohr Hatorah, every place in the community. I travel around the community quite a bit.

Everywhere I go there's the question. Intelligent, searching Jews are saying, 'Okay I come home from Shabbat, I say the blessing, but what's the practice?'"

"You're saying now that as you go through your day you are searching for these occasions for blessing?"

"I'm saying the blessings are a gift from the tradition, and by the way, Jonathan's approach is esoteric. Jonathan never negates the law, but his approach is inner. You should talk to him personally. I don't want to say too much about it, because it's his teaching he redeemed from Judaism, and I believe it to be the single most important thing." And, the *Maggid* added, laughing, "I'm not given to extravagant statements."

I laughed too. The *Maggid* had a sense of humor about himself even though he is also a very zealous man. It was even inscribed in his Hebrew name, Pinchas, the zealous priest with the spear.

Zalman Schachter had changed that name for him. "When we met," Paul said, "Zalman asked me my Hebrew name. Something didn't feel right about Pinchas. I never liked it anyway because of the way it sounded, but when I found out who he was I liked it less. Still, I see why it's my name. I'm a zealot, there's no way around it. I'm zealous in my search for God. Nothing is more important to me. That made sense."

But Reb Zalman added a name that "has to do with the energy of compassion, of *rachmones*,* for other people." He added *Eliahu*—Elijah.

I smiled to myself.

He had traveled a long way from Paul to Eliahu Pinchas, a circuitous path back to Jewish, from stubbing his finger on a siddur, through *The Owl and the Pussycat*, to the intensive-care unit, to a kosher bakery in Fairfax. He'd become a *maggid*, a man with a mission, and before we parted, he laid a mission on me.

_____
* Yiddish for "compassion."

"Annoy Jonathan," he said, "and insist that he teach you the blessing teachings so you can teach others. Because he's sitting on it and it's the key. You need to do this and other people need to have it. Get it out."

"He hasn't taught it to me."

"Jonathan's training is very Orthodox, he's very traditional, he's giving it the way he's received it. He goes along very slowly. People are hungry; it isn't an idle curiosity. It's coming from 'I want God in my life every day, how am I going to do this?' Give it, give it, give it. Let other people teach it; let it get out."

I looked at the swimming pool again. Without telling him, I made Eliahu Pinchas, the fierce Elijah, a promise. One way or the other, I was going to get wet.

*Learning Meditation: Do This*
LOS ANGELES
MARCH 23–31, 1995; 21–29 ADAR II 5755

But first I had to finish my swimming lessons.

With our other conversations, my lessons in Jewish meditation began at Jonathan's house over his kitchen table, later
moved to his offices at Metivta; some even took place at an outdoor café on Wilshire Boulevard, to the sound of honking horns,
screeching brakes, and interrupting waiters. It was Judaism on
the hoof, meditation on the run.

"Tell me what you know," Jonathan asked me quietly the first
day. "Tell me your practice, what you've done."

I described my experiences in sitting meditation, watching the
breath, observing thoughts, the sources of thoughts, general
mindfulness meditation. I described certain Jewish meditations
I'd learned. Zalman Schachter taught me one from the thirteenth-century Spanish kabbalist Joseph Gikatilla. It involved
mapping the four-letter name of God to four stages of the breath.

However, I was not sure where meditation fit in the scheme
of Jewish practice. In fact, there is some controversy about this.
A *haredi* rabbi in Brooklyn's Boro Park, Rabbi Meir Fund, later
told me he'd never done such practice, nor did he think it necessary. His path was halakhah, doing the mitzvot. It was study and
Torah and prayer, not meditation. He asked me pointedly, "What
is the Hebrew word for meditation?" When I had no immediate
answer he added, "That should tell you something."

At the other end of the spectrum was Paul Wolff's sense of
urgency about finding a Jewish awareness practice, and his absolute conviction that such practices are hidden in Jewish teach-

ings. And Wolff's belief that somehow you could practice this Judaism as a non-Orthodox Jew.

If Jewish meditation is so important, why did so many learned and serious Jews like Rabbi Fund question its provenance? Perhaps the practices were hidden, passed on privately to a very few. But if so, had the time come to bring them more generally to light?

The late Rabbi Aryeh Kaplan argued that there are Hebrew words for meditation. And through his writing and teaching he decided to bring the practice of Jewish meditation out in the open. An Orthodox rabbi from Brooklyn with strong connections to Chabad and Bratzlav, in the sixties he taught kabbalah and meditation in small groups, and published many volumes on Torah, kabbalah, and meditation before his untimely death in 1983 at age forty-eight. In his *Meditation and the Bible* Kaplan identifies several Hebrew terms from the Bible that he believes represent authentic Jewish meditation practices, including *hitbodedut, hitbonenut,* and *suah.*[1] For Kaplan, these practices cultivate a state of mind receptive to *ruah ha-kodesh,* the holy spirit. He felt that these practices led the patriarchs, and later the prophets, to prophecy—an ambition far beyond my scope, or certainly the scope of most of those I encountered in Los Angeles. Kaplan writes, "Many people are initially surprised to discover that meditation plays any role in Biblical teachings. . . . One important reason for this is that such practices have not been in use since the great Hasidic renaissance almost two centuries ago. Where the experience itself is not known, the meaning of words used to describe it also becomes forgotten, and the entire vocabulary is lost."[2]

In his companion book, *Meditation and Kabbalah,* Kaplan traces the later development of Jewish meditation techniques in the Talmud, among the *merkavah* mystics, the kabbalists, and *hasidim.*[3] Academic scholars, notably Gershom Scholem and his successor at Hebrew University, Moshe Idel, support the thesis that meditative experiences underlie the imagery and insights of the Zohar and other kabbalistic texts. They are the matrix of experience from which these texts are born.

As a contemporary teacher, Jonathan spoke more modestly of meditation in general as "a way of changing the way the nervous system works.

"I find it works cumulatively," he told me. "To meditate occasionally just doesn't work. One consequence of meditation is the ability to remain within paradox." For just that reason, he would not recommend that teenagers meditate. "Teenagers thrive on paradox, they become creative and obnoxious and delightful because of their inability to tolerate paradox." Imagine Holden Caulfield meditating: he would lose his sarcastic edge.

Already, my feeble *vipassana* meditation practice had altered my teenage nervous system with its knee-jerk either-or sorting system. Buddhists speak of the reactive mind. "It was a great relief," I told Jonathan, "to find I didn't have to identify with every one of my thoughts. I call that freedom."

At Metivta, Jonathan teaches basic meditation in five-week sessions. In my first lesson, he explained certain preliminaries. "One is to keep a meditation log. Not a diary of the content of their meditations, but a log of the process. Rather like a truck driver's log. Not where he's going, but how the truck is running. I find the log is an essential part of the spiritual work altogether. It helps one to discover the cyclicities of one's life and therefore to ride them. To know where we are on the roller coaster."

I knew about that roller coaster. "What's put in a log?" I asked him.

"'Mind agitated.' 'Very smooth meditation.' 'Meditation for thirteen minutes then had to get up and smoke a cigarette.' 'Couldn't meditate again today.' '492 straight days couldn't meditate—when will this ever end?' Very, very short. A notation of the external, not the internal. A truck driver's log. A truck driver will say, 'Right front wheel vibrates about 55.' Not talk about the views you see through the windows. It helps a person establish her own rhythms and see her own cycles." He paused. "I mean, do you keep a journal?"

"No," I said. "it's unpaid writing." He smiled and I asked him about postures.

"Comfortable. Not to cross hands or legs. This is basically from nothing inherent, just Jewish cruciphobia."

I rather liked this informality. "But didn't the chariot riders— the *merkavah* mystics—sit with the head between the knees?"

"In that position, if you fall asleep, you fall over. It acknowledges that falling asleep is a danger."

Jonathan suggests that a meditator find a buddy to talk over her experiences. Preferably, he said, not a spouse or partner. "A buddy is a wonderful source of common sense. It's also a tiny move toward spiritual community, one with a narrow purpose of encouraging commitment to the spiritual life." To Jonathan, spiritual seeking can be summarized as "keeping better company." "One really needs to hang around people on the same path."

That made sense to me when I considered the effect on me of keeping company with Reb Zalman or Rabbi Yitz Greenberg or Shefa Gold.

"I also ask people to read ethical literature. Abraham Twerski's *Living Each Day*"—a book keyed to the Jewish as well as secular calendar, with teachings from the Torah, Talmud, and *hasidut*. The same Rabbi Twerski so active in the Jewish Twelve-Step movement. "It has a rather nice mixture of profound wisdom and rabbinic bromides," Jonathan added. "But the idea is to have the discipline of reading some ethical literature each day. This is the Baal Shem Tov's very specific advice. Whatever you do, read some spiritual guidance. One page at a time."

"What's the logic?" I asked. "Why an ethical text? Why not a kabbalistic text or a psalm?"

"We have to work on ourselves." He sighed. "You know, Ramakrishna was asked to describe the spiritual work in three words. They were: purification, purification, purification."

Jonathan teaches first the first meditation Shmuel Kraus taught him in Me'ah She'arim. Kraus said, "*Ta'aseh et zeh*"—do this. He broke the *Shema* into three parts on a cycle of breath. *Shema Yisrael*—breathe in; *Adonai Eloheinu*—breathe out; *Adonai ehad*—breathe in. Then *Shema Yisrael* on the outbreath, and so on. I asked him how long is one sitting.

"I don't answer that question."

"Are you supposed to watch the distraction from the performance or the performance itself?"

"Yes."

"You're not going to answer my question?"

"That's always my answer to that question."

Jonathan Omer-Man, I quickly realized, is in many ways a "patience teacher." He evades certain questions, postpones them, mocks them if necessary. He uses humor, timing, just a lift of his eyebrows, but his chief tool is silence. He would sit there while a question of mine hung in the air, until it dropped of its own weight and we laughed. His intentions were deftly to uproot my questions, to display my presumptions. I had many.

Jonathan treated his students' minds as he hoped they would learn to treat their own. Authority is a projection, even the gentle authority of a meditation teacher. A niggling demand for reassurance lurked behind my questions about how long, how much, how to stop, what to do.

"Ultimately," Jonathan stated, "meditation is a refinement of the person, a refinement of who we are. One becomes a more complete human being. The Jewish way is becoming a more complete Jew. As Buddhist meditation will help you to become more complete and whole as a Buddhist." His crucial point: "The nature of meditation is to find one's context."

That last statement intrigued me.

"Is there a meditation before davening?"

"Watching your breath. Watching your breath. Just emptying."

Ancient sources support Jonathan's view. The Talmud describes a group of *ḥasidim*[4]—in this context "pious ones"—who meditated an hour before and after each hour of prayer:[5] "The pious ones of old would be still (*shohin* שׁוֹהִין) one hour prior to each of the [three] prayer services, then pray for one hour and afterward be still again for one hour."[6] The scholar Mark Verman supplies the Rambam's comment: "The explanation of *shohin* is they restrained themselves: that is to say, they restrained themselves for one hour prior to praying in order to settle their minds and quiet their thoughts. Only then would they pray."[7]

This practice of these "first *ḥasidim*" seems precisely what the Dalai Lama was asking about—a Jewish technique for dealing with afflictive states of mind. It would be fascinating to know precisely how the pious ones quieted their thoughts, but meditation on the breath, as Jonathan suggested, would do the trick.

Reuven Hammer, in his excellent introductory guide, *Entering Jewish Prayer*, points out that, over time, the practice of *shohin*, of emptying, was filled up again with words:

Instead of the quiet meditation recommended here [i.e., in the talmudic text], prayers , blessings and readings from the Psalms and other books of the Bible were suggested, all to the same purpose: "Directing the heart" toward God. Eventually some meditations that had been recited informally by individuals became part of the official service and some prayers and blessings that people had recited in their homes were taken over into the synagogue service.

There has always been much controversy over exactly what was to be said, what was actually required and what was not. Different communities added various reading and hymns, so that the first impression is of a haphazard collection of prayers, blessings, and biblical readings.[8]

These include two entire preliminary services, the blessing of the morning and the *Pesukei de zimra*, or verses of song. Although Rabbi Hammer defends these accretions with great vigor, I would tend to read his history as suggesting that the original *shohin* of the pious ones of old has now been overgrown by extensive cultivation. It makes it easier to understand the paradoxical assertion of Marc Lerner that the essence of Judaism is silence—even though our experience of prayer-book Judaism is dense with verbiage. The greatest damage to contemporary Jewish prayer is no doubt that prayer books are bound and printed, suggesting a fixity to the siddur that was not part of Jewish reality in the ancient world.

I find now that if I arrive early to shul, meditating on the breath can be a wonderful preparation and opening to the service. Meditation on the breath is Shabbat on the scale of a minute. When we read the account in Genesis, we think of the six days of creation as constant motion, hubbub, activity: birds are flying, fish are swimming, clouds are moving, man and woman are stirring, God is doing. We think of the holy one as active, as *hei ha-olamim*, the life of all the worlds, who gives life.

But all this activity culminates in nonactivity: On the seventh day, *shavat va-yinafash*—God ceased and watched the breath. The verb root of *Shabbat* is "to cease."

Each of us is also a world, full of business and busyness.

To empty—to cease the mindless activity of the mind, the endless chatter of business and busyness—is how meditation on the breath finds its Jewish context in Shabbat. Because in every cycle of breath comes a moment of Shabbat—a moment of not breathing.

Here then is a specific practice, rooted in Jewish sources, that speaks to Paul Wolff's quest to empty one's biography. In that moment of meditation, one is not one's biography.

I have also found powerful Reb Zalman's meditation drawn from his reading of the thirteenth-century kabbalist Joseph

Gikatilla—as perhaps Gikatilla drew it from earlier sources. Here is how it is practiced: the breath is divided into four stages. Each part corresponds to a letter of the *Shem ha-Meforash*, the four-letter root name: *Yod Heh Vov Heh*.

The moment before breathing, the moment of empty lungs, is the moment of emptiness, nothingness, that we know as pure intuition, pure spirit, the beginning before the beginning, the *aleph* before the *bet* of *bereishit* . . . the world of *atzilut*, of nearness, of spirit. It is the letter *yod*.

Then the first calling of breath, the first intimation in a flash of the whole cycle to come, the expansion of the lower rib cage as the breath begins to be drawn. This represents the moment of knowing and corresponds to the upper *heh* of the divine name, the world of *beriyah*, of first creation, of knowledge. The letter *heh*.

Then the full expansion of the chest, the exfoliation filling the lungs and all the passageways of breath, into the blood system, streaming through the vessels, delivering oxygen, purifying, removing waste and fatigue . . . the upper chest comes in, the spine straightens, and the spine is the shape of the letter *vov* of the root name. This is the world of *yetzirah*, of formation—the imaginative expansion of the initial thought, activated by feeling. The world of *yetzirah* corresponds to the letter *vov*.

Then the exhalation, the giving back to the world of the cycle of breath. This reminds us of doing in the world, of the world of *assiyah*, of action, the lower *heh* of giving back what has been given.

And the cycle begins again as long as we have life, from our first breath to our last, continually reminding us, linking us with the patterns of creation, these four stages, of inspiration, thought, feeling, action.

The mystery of Shabbat is the mystery of the power of *not* doing. Through this meditation one reflects on the moment of no breath, the Shabbat of breath, as the profound moment of transformation between nothing and something, between dust and life. It is the eternal moment when the life of all the worlds breathed the first breath into Adam—or, in Hebrew, "earthling." Then "earthling" lurched into life and entered the continuing life of breath. As we do the meditation, we feel the holiness of that first breath breathed into us.

○

After Jonathan's students work with the three-part *Shema*, they "shatter" it. The Torah commands Jews to say the *Shema* twice a day; this prayer is uttered also at the deathbed. In an Orthodox synagogue, and in Jewish renewal and havurah, I have felt the intensity with which it is prayed, the eyes covered with the hand in profound concentration. Unfortunately, for some Jews the *Shema* becomes no more than a national anthem. Jonathan felt that the words, and the music, need shattering to "get people to break away from the old associations."

"*Shema Yisrael*," I sang in the familiar tune, and Jonathan interrupted to spare his ears.

"I always get the picture," he said, "of porcelain waltzers on a clock that goes round and round. I try to bring the *Shema* to a place of silence" through a group recitation timed with in and out breaths. Then they turn the dimmer down, say it softer and softer, until silence is reached. "Not many people can do it," Jonathan added. "They lose connection with the breath. Some do it for a minute or two and get incredibly bright effects, a different way of understanding *Shema*. It becomes luminous and numinous."

Shmuel Kraus's simple meditation can also bring power to the *Shema*. *Shema Yisrael*—in breath; *Adonai Eloheinu*—out breath; *Adonai eḥad*—in breath; *Shema Yisrael*—out breath . . . and so on for ten, fifteen, twenty minutes. Simple, but not easy. I practiced and saw the difficulties. One is soon exploring all the distractions, all the ways the mind diverts itself away from the *Shema*. And in that very multiplicity of thoughts, feelings, sensations—the sparkling waterfall of mind—the audacity of the *Shema*'s affirmation emerges clearly: that somehow this seething multiplicity has a root in one.

Unlike Freud, Jonathan said, hasidic masters did not concern themselves with the origins of habits. "Ultimately the problem in spiritual practice is breaking habit. How the habit started is probably irrelevant. The point is to get people to be adventurous with their minds."

My personal mind adventure continued at the Metivta office, on Tuesday morning, March 28, after Jonathan's kabbalah class. We sat alone together, he in his rocking chair in the office with a homemade brown quilt on his lap. He showed me a sheet with the names of the first four weekly Torah portions or sedras, chapters from the book of Genesis read in sequence in the synagogue. The names are chapter headings, derived from the first significant Hebrew word in each portion: Bereishit, Noaḥ, Lekh Lekha, Vayera. Bereishit, or Beginning, includes the account of creation and the fall of Adam and Eve; Noaḥ tells the story of Noah and the flood; Lekh Lekha, the story of Abram/Abraham's journeys; and Vayera begins with the birth of Isaac and ends with his *akeidah*, or binding, on the altar at Mount Moriah.

But the stories are not the main point. In his customary manner, Jonathan refused to explain the purpose of the meditation. He simply showed me the printed sheet. "One just lets them go before one's eyes. Bereishit is beginnings, stirrings, something out of nothing, generations. Noaḥ is rest, isolation from the heavy stuff outside. Rest. Lekh Lekha is pilgrimage, moving out, movement. Vayera is manifestation. Just let them go before your eyes one at a time, like a carousel going around and around. Sometimes you spend more time on one than on another."[9]

"Images or words or concepts?" The idiot questioner was on the case.

"Yes," Jonathan answered in his usual gnomic way.

"You alternate?"

"You have to find your own way of doing it."

OK, enough questioning. I closed my eyes and brought up Bereishit, saying it out loud. Bereishit was easy—the creation story in the first chapters of Genesis, something beginning out of nothing, a light appearing out of darkness. Then I moved to Noaḥ, and all I could see was the boat. So I moved to Lekh Lekha, going forth, adventure. Ever since I'd left home for this trip west, I'd been thinking about the moment when Abram hears the voice within that tells him he must "*lekh lekha*"—move out from his familiar environs for the spiritual adventure of his life.

I then tried Vayera. Manifestation. Basically just thinking the word and trying to see what images came up. The line in the Torah is "*Vayera alav YHVH*"—And the Lord appeared unto him. Three angels visit Abram with the news that he will have a child.

After the carousel spun once, Jonathan told me to "do it much faster, at the speed of reading under your breath, around and around and around."

I spent several minutes moving from one to the next. I stopped and said, "The image of Noaḥ I see is the ark. What part of the story are we in? I'm having trouble."

"Just make it rest," Jonathan said. "The word *noaḥ* means 'rest.'"

"It does?"

"It's the opposite of movement. If Lekh Lekha is movement, Noaḥ is rest."

"And what is Bereishit? Stillness?"

"Stirrings."

Obviously I was in the meditation slow lane. "Oh. So before you move, there's a period of rest, then you move, then you manifest. Does this get into the four worlds?" Before I had an experience, I already had a theory.

"No," Jonathan said, firmly.

"Well, you could."

No I couldn't, Jonathan told me with his eyes. And added, "Try it."

"I'm going to work with it," I promised and closed my eyes again.

"When a dancer does a pirouette," Jonathan suggested, "she holds her eye on one thing. Focus in, hold it even though you're moving around. Play with it."

"The one that's giving me trouble is Noaḥ. I can see beginning, doing, manifesting, but . . ."

"Then try another one for it. Play around with the image of Noaḥ."

"As something begins," I said, "you need to let it develop in a state of rest before you go on. In a way that encapsulates the whole meditation." Idiot questioner, move over; idiot explainer at the mike.

Jonathan stayed silent.

"Doesn't it?"

No response.

I was intellectualizing, verbalizing like all get out, and Jonathan tossed me back onto the carousel. It was a good example in action of Reb Zalman's brilliant formulation: "Judaism today is ororverbalized and underexperienced." Could I ever get my mind to quiet down, to shut up? I sat with my eyes closed, heard a car starting up in the background, a soft explosion, a coughing in the metal lung of the engine. Then I settled in, whirling the words past: Bereishit, Noaḥ, Lekh Lekha, Vayera— first slowly, like black print on white index cards, and then faster. Soon images arose for each word, and when I had the images, which I drew from sweet memory, I found I could move even faster. I saw the images as photos, and then mental places I was visiting, touching, places with rich and warm associations. Sometimes the spinning slowed and I lingered on one of the stops; other times they raced by. And I lost time. When I stopped and opened my eyes, Jonathan sat in his rocker, with the same even expression, very patiently eyeing me.

"It's good," I said.

"Some people like that one very much."

"It seems to take you through the creative process."

"If you do it for twenty minutes you discover which places you need to spend more time on. Even though you spend more time on one, you start to do the others quickly. Like a wheel that doesn't stop."

"Where did this come from?"

"Pascal Themanlys in Jerusalem.[10] He's a meditation teacher from North Africa. That wasn't the first he taught me, but it was a major one." In Jerusalem, Pascal Themanlys's group, the *Hugei Argaman*, or Circles of Royal Purple, met weekly for meditation and discussion.[11]

Jonathan left me and told me to "stay with" the meditation for a while longer. I closed my eyes and reentered the calm refreshing circle. Bereishit. My daughter's face at birth, that first look into her face. Pure incipience. Noaḥ. Rest: baby sleeping in her crib. Lekh Lekha: baby crawling. Vayera: my daughter pulls herself up for the first time in her crib. Manifests herself. I soaked the Hebrew words in these powerful images until they glowed and spun in colors. Then I could go much faster, using the words alone.

Jonathan returned. I told him my experiences and asked for suggestions.

"Just do it," he said, like the Nike commercial. "Sometimes I do it for two or three months at a time, then I do it for two or three weeks, see what happens. The word you used—refreshing —is extremely important."

"It should be refreshing."

"Yes."

"I didn't relate to any of the biblical stories. I took them as universal processes of the mind and universal processes of creation."

"The key is time," Jonathan said, skipping over my own comments. "All mystical thought is concerned with time and changing the nature of time."

"How?"

"You change the speed of time. You can make it extremely slow or extremely fast. Just turn it over and over and it acquires its own qualities. Not only refreshing, but also a sweetness. It's probably one of the most Jewish of all the Jewish meditations."

In consensual time, that little baby born, sleeping, standing in her crib, was fifteen. Yet the images were "not only refreshing, but also a sweetness"; I pinned them to the carousel and stepped out of ordinary time.

Pleasant, but had I missed the point? According to *Sh'aar le-Sodot Ha-Hitbonenut* (The Gate of the Secrets of Meditation), a publication of the *Hugei Argaman*, "The order of the *parshiyyot* [sections] of Genesis hint at the levels of spiritual ascension." There are four levels: wisdom, serenity, ascension of the soul, and revelation. Each corresponds to a state of spiritual accomplishment or perfection and each to a *parashah*. Thus Bereishit, the Beginning, corresponds to a person's attaining wisdom; Noah, which means "rest," to a person attaining serenity. Lekh Lekha, or "go forth," corresponds to the actual ascension of the person's soul. Finally Vayera, or "and he appeared," hints at the moment of revelation.

The manual explains why Noah gave me so much trouble. The meditators interpret Noah as "one must rest," and they cite Exodus 14:14: "You shall be silent."[12] The spirit of wisdom cannot manifest itself unless there is first a silence within. A silence my noisy mind lacked.

○　◐　●　◐　○　◐　●

We were ending my meditation lessons, and Jonathan wanted to correct a misunderstanding. I wanted to connect the four *parashiot* of the Bereishit meditation with the four worlds: emanation, creation, formation, and doing.

"Where do you get those things?" he asked.

"Zalmanology." After all, Zalman had introduced me to the four worlds. In the context of the *kallot*, I'd understood them as a map of thoughts and feelings.

"Get them from Steinsaltz," he urged me. "The problem with the way Zalman does it is that they are entirely psychological. It isn't a cosmic principle that's reflected."

He directed me to read Rabbi Adin Steinsaltz's account of the four worlds in chapter 1 of *The Thirteen Petalled Rose*.[1] But I insisted that the psychological language of Jewish renewal is the same as the cosmological language. Jonathan said, "They are more than subtly different."

Did he think Zalman's approach to kabbalah as psychology too reductive, too concerned with the self?

"The four worlds are very much larger than the self and also mean something else. The cosmology has nothing to do with intellect or emotion. It has to do with irreducible energies, all of them deeply connected with how these energies vary in different manifestations of time. The *atzilut*"—what Zalman calls the world of intuition or spirit—"is reaching the place of the utterly timeless."

I was not entirely following Jonathan, but knew that I was on the edge of something I needed to understand. He must have seen the puzzlement on my face.

"Look," he said, repeating his idea, "the kabbalistic cosmology is a mystical exercise that has nothing to do with human psychology. It's seeing how different entities change when you move them through the different qualities of time." That was then like the Bereishit meditation.

"There are three dimensions in the Jewish cosmology, he went on, "*shanah*, *olam*, and *nefesh*.* Time, space, and life, and each of these different dimensions changes as one moves through the worlds. The key one is time.

"The full order of high energy comes in a flow." He paused. It's not surprising computer imagery came up: while Jonathan was teaching me, his office computer constantly buzzed, often with the distinctive crackling of a modem connection as e-mail uploaded. So he chose an image that owed something to the technology of communications software. "The flow is punctuated, or rather, the flows: *flow* makes no sense because it's punctuated in little breaks. It's like the bytes of information. You can't just get a single byte."

"There are packets of information."

"There are packets, but the space between the packet determines the nature of the packet."

In brief, the intervals of noncommunication, the intervals of absence of connection, define the shape of the energy received. As perhaps the silences in a conversation may be far more telling than the words spoken.

Here is a different angle on the question of absence and presence that had been haunting me ever since Zalman insisted on the reality of God. The absence of connection I felt to God—the beeper out of range—is itself an essential element of the communication.

"The space between the packets is what we call *gevurah*," Jonathan added. "Also *tzimtzum* [contraction]. The flow is punctuated. So the space between the packets turns it from incoherent

* Literally, "year," "world," and "soul."

light to coherent light. This is what happens when we look at the changing nature of time. The higher one goes up toward *atzilut*, the more things move from actuality to potentiality. In the highest world, everything exists in total potentiality. The first level after that is conceptualization—the world of *beriyah*. The world below that is the world of emotional movement. These are completely separate sets of forces. *Assiyah* is the world in which everything is packed into everything else."

*Gevurah* (or power) means here restraint: the endless flow of divine energy is restrained or constricted so that it can be received on our limited human scale. Otherwise it would blow our circuits, or, to use Torah language, burn us like fire. As Zalman would say, divine energy is a reality we can't observe on our human scale.

An infinite message cannot be read, but must be punctuated. In the same way, the flow of energy must be punctuated into smaller units, packets, for human comprehension.

"So in describing four worlds, we are not talking about psychological processes, but about creation, the processes of creation?"

"Yes."

"But can't I call it the psychology of creativity?" I felt that Jonathan was not being entirely fair to Reb Zalman.

"Yes. But . . ."

"But it's not personal, is that what you mean? It's an impersonal process."

"It's an absolutely impersonal process. For instance, when we talk about intellect we're talking about *seikhel elyon*—the highest intelligence. Which has nothing to do with normal understanding of intelligence. *Beriyah*, the level of conceptualization, is the level of essence just short of the divine. In the divine level"— what the kabbalists call *Ein Sof*—"there's total oneness and unity and no discrimination of any kind, but in *atzilut* the very beginning of crystallization begins. Then *beriyah, yetzirah, assiyah*. Ultimately the entire system is contemplative."

The cosmology in itself is an object of contemplation. I saw the mistake I'd made. I'd pinned baby photos to the carousel: I'd lingered in the personal.

"One contemplates on the entire system," Jonathan said. "One doesn't really try to understand it, or understand *with it*, but one contemplates it because we get into the other worlds only by flashes."

Jonathan saw a danger in the four-worlds formulation of Jewish renewal, or, in fact, in other contemporary studies of the esoteric—the scholarship of Gershom Scholem or the literary criticism of Harold Bloom. They tend to create systems that are far too rational and dogmatic. The tradition understood prophecy—insight into the whole cosmos—as a much more ephemeral experience.

"It's like you're going down the countryside in the middle of the night," he said, "and suddenly there's a flash of lightning. For one second you see the entire landscape, and then it disappears. That's the nature by which you can understand the four worlds, that's the way you can understand mystical knowledge altogether." The image, he told me, comes from the Rambam. "The flash goes through all four worlds, it cuts through everything."

I knew my strong desire to command and understand mystical knowledge, the same ferocity I felt in Paul Wolff. But was I trying to catch lightning in my hands? Jonathan was warning me not to overschematize, overintellectualize, and certainly not to think I understood the four-worlds cosmology.

OK, but I'd been chanting those four names ever since the JFK airport, and did it all mean nothing? The connection to divine realms seemed so elusive.

Maybe, I thought, that was right. The infinite light hides itself. And this hiding is absolutely essential because it makes space for us to be. Just as a pause in a conversation allows the other person to speak.

The secret is hidden in its giving forth: the elusiveness of God is on purpose. Our light is punctuated by darkness. The first immense act of creation—which is the very image of creativity—is not expansiveness, but restraint. In the kabbalah of Isaac Luria, this restraint or contraction is called *tzimtzum.*

Luria was describing a cosmos, but in hasidic teaching the same terms become profoundly psychological. That was the spirit of Zalman's teaching as well. At the human level, in the intimate conversation, we also *tzimtzum*, we also contract to make space for the other person; such restraint is a sign of my own confidence and strength. Again and again in my travels I would come to such moments of encounter based solely on the fact that I'd finally learned to keep my mouth shut!

But there is a similar process of dialogue in prayer. Hasidic masters paid a great deal of attention to what happens in prayer, especially in ecstatic states of mind. Dov Ber of Lubavitch (1773–1820), son of the founder of Chabad, wrote a tract, *On Ecstasy*, which indicates that ecstatic prayer too requires a *tzimtzum*, a contraction of self, to a state of nothingness.[2]

That is why in working on ourselves to prepare for prayer, silence is so important, why Marc Lerner had a point in suggesting that silence rests at the heart of Jewish spirituality. To prepare for prayer I empty all my words, busy thoughts, selfish whirling, to the place of no words, no thoughts, no self, no images. And only from that place of humility—of nothingness—can I begin to have enough room for God.

I am holy, you are loved, all is clear, it is perfect. It had been a very pleasant opening. But now I understood: "I" could not identify with the I in "I am holy." If I think I am in a state of ecstasy, then with that thought, I am not. Rabbi Steinsaltz puts it quite beautifully: "The beings of the lower worlds feel their independent existence with greater intensity than the beings of the higher; they are more aware of being separate individual selves. And this consciousness of their separate selfdom blocks the divine plenty"—the *shefa*—"and at the same time obscures the truly unchanging essence that lurks beneath the individual personality. In short, the lower the world, the more it is pervaded by a sense of the "I," and consequently the more it is subject to the obscuring of the divine essence."[3]

Zalman opened up the doors and let me in; Jonathan cautioned me not to think the doors were that easy to open. In a sense this tension plays throughout the history of the Jewish esoteric: there are always warning voices like Jonathan's and beckoning voices like Zalman's. But in general, regarding the esoteric, Jews certainly erred on the side of caution, Jonathan's side.

To Jonathan a danger of kabbalah's becoming a watereddown psychological system is that it leads pretty quickly to exploitation. I never saw that in Jewish renewal, but certainly predators lurk out there teaching kabbalah for profit, selling expensive translations of the Zohar, and promise cures for illness by merely passing your eyes over the text. The history of every Jewish mystical movement, as it becomes popularized, shows the same tendencies—whether the disastrous messianic movements of Shabbatai Zvi or Jacob Frank, or the decay of the hasidic movement into opulent courts and corrupt dynasties. This is what Reb Zalman insisted Jewish renewal could not become. When kabbalah becomes a head trip, the sense of mystery and awe disappears. Or it becomes sentimental and sloppy, a quest for fun that amounts to self-validation, self-gratification.

## Big Defeat for the Ego Brigade

Jonathan believes there is much confusion about meditation. We'd talked about it over coffee on Monday in his office, a couple of hours before I interviewed Rabbi Judith. "Sometimes the boundaries between the different psychic exercises are not at all clear. Some people prescribe lots of visualizations and guided meditations and they call that meditation. They leave out a major part of what meditation is about."

"Namely?"

"Exercising the minimal amount of directive control on the mind—and to do it with as little energy as possible. Like riding a horse or a chariot. One has reins but uses the reins as little as possible. If you have a very tight hold, that's not what it's about. Or—to use Plato's imagery of the two horses—the light and the dark, and one controls them as lightly as possible. Many of these visualization exercises are extremely controlling, very tight pressure. You know: 'blue sky with seagulls and a lagoon and you see footprints in the sand and you follow the footprints and they disappear' and you realize . . ."

". . . it's somebody's bad poem you have to run through," I said, finishing his thought.

This spoke to me. My control of the reins was too tight, my search was blocking my search.

But these ongoing lessons in meditation, this exposure to Jonathan's thinking, teaching, and being, chipped away at my sense of my mission, and redefined it. I had started with a simple proposition based on my own admiration of certain Buddhist practitioners: that developing equanimity is vital to a Jewish path. Several times in fact, I'd asked Jonathan to teach me a Jewish "equanimity" meditation, and many times he'd rebuffed me or redirected my search. He'd sent me to talk to Rabbi Judith, to Mark Borovitz, to Paul Wolff. Mark led me to Beit T'shuvah, and Beit T'shuvah back to Paul. The *Maggid* diverted me further, insisting I learn about the blessing path. His story touched on my own deepest grief. In all these encounters, I was growing. I was not at the stage where I could make the spiritual ascent of the meditative masters of Beit El, or endure the Abulafian intensity of chanting vowels of Elijah. But I was attuning, in my own way—a writer asking questions and hearing answers, working on my listening, refining it, becoming a better receiver.

There's no point in seeing Jewish meditation, or any meditation, as a panacea. That leaves the ego in charge, seeking levels of spiritual achievement as if they were mental BMWs.

Rather, the effort is to break set, break habits, work on purification, purification, purification—slowly refine oneself, break down old associations, and, as with the Shema meditation, move away from old mental grooves. This difficult venture requires patience, practice, purification.

I was struggling with myself. I felt within a contradiction between being culturally Jewish and the real teachings of Judaism. So many Jews believe, without examining it, that being born Jewish creates an automatic genetic channel to the wisdom of Judaism. Yes, Judaism is a family religion, a covenant given to families, and there is clearly a genetic component to Jewishness—as recent research on gene markers in Jewish *kohanim* (priests) confirms. But there's nothing automatic about the process. Buber, who moved outside of halakhah, sought to find some essence of Jewish disposition and in his early lectures spoke about Jewish "blood." Freud replicated Buber's mistake in *Moses and Monotheism* when he speculates on genetic transmission of guilt. But Judaism can be passed on only through culture and practice; the wisdom of the Torah is not something you pick up just because your parents happened to be Jewish. Yet many Jews cling to this confusion between Jewishness and Judaism. In the end, their presumed Jewishness blocks their coming to a deeper Judaism.

I knew it well. I'd written, "Nervous is my religion." Yet I'd found *hishtavut*, equanimity, a very important trait—*middah*—to develop. When I speak in public about developing equanimity as a Jewish practice, I am often met with disbelief. To some, Jewishness means either chutzpah or anxiety, either Alan Dershowitz or Woody Allen—but not calm. Jonathan felt it almost impossible to teach *middot* like equanimity and humility to the Jewish world at large.

"Anyway, I don't see equanimity and humility as connected." He pointed to his Metivta library shelves. "In all these books, humility is the first virtue to work on. But I get people working on generosity instead, because no one could buy it. It didn't mean anything in the context of our life to talk about humility."

"Why?"

"Because they think it antithetical to Jewish values."

"Which is chutzpah."

"And, 'I'm the junior partner with God.' Or maybe full partner."

"Yet every single Jewish sage recommends that you can't even experience God unless you have extreme humility."

"Yah. Of course one has to have humility. I work on humility much more by chipping away and putting out areas in ego that get in the way, by humor, than by positing humility per se. It's a major part of the work. It's also very elusive. You must know the story of Erev Yom Kippur? The rabbi comes into the synagogue by the open ark and says, 'O Lord, I am nothing.' Then the *gabbai* [synagogue official] comes in and says, 'O Lord, I am nothing.' Then the *shamash*—the doorman—comes in and says, 'O Lord, I am nothing.' and the *gabbai* turns to the rabbi and says, 'Look who thinks he's nothing.'"

"It's one of my favorite stories."

"It's a very difficult point, because there are rewards for everything one does. Any practitioner of humility can easily be deflated."

"So you're reporting that humility is so counter to today's Jewish culture that you can't even address it directly? What about equanimity?"

"They can't distinguish between equanimity and passivity. You know the lines from Yeats: 'The best lack all conviction, while the worst/Are full of a passionate intensity'"?

"Sure."

"Try to teach that poem to a group of Jewish leaders. They will fight against it. They will not get it. I mean, passionate intensity is the ultimate booster of the ego, and we Jews use it a great deal. Let's put it this way: some parts of the Jewish world are so threatened by that concept, so aligned to drumming up passion on an ongoing basis, that the passion is more important than the object of the passion. It infects large parts of the community, and others don't know how to stand against it." I assumed he meant the fund-raising campaigns certain Jewish organizations run based on threats to Israel, or anti-Semitic incidents. Yet also I understood that passion. I'd felt it strongly in the struggle against David Duke.

Jonathan paused. "Listening to myself talking to you in the last three days, apart from realizing that various things that have nothing to do with this are upsetting me and I'm slightly depressed and agitated, there is an awareness that I've really given up on trying to change the mainstream, which for a long time was a goal. Basically I'm just doing my work."

To do his work, he had to let go of his mission. "Well," I asked, feeling some chutzpah of my own, "do we have an exercise in equanimity, or is it just through prayer?"

"You're impatient."

"I'm not impatient."

"I told you I was going to give it to you. It requires a certain space to do it, and it will either be this morning, later this afternoon, or tomorrow morning, or sometime you'll get it."

I laughed at the way he drew it out. "I'm impatient for equanimity."

As I look back on it now, that moment was a turning point. By the time Jonathan taught me a specific visualization for equanimity a few days later, my question had changed. I learned that equanimity is not the goal of meditation but, as Jonathan said, "a by-product."

I'd been too goal directed, and this disposition was a barrier. I was stalking Elijah, pursuing non-chutzpah with chutzpah. You can't stalk Elijah; you can only encounter Elijah in the person before you.

O

But that afternoon, I stalked on and asked Jonathan what Jewish meditation is and what it is for.

"I answer that question in a number of different ways," he said. "I mean, it's a question I always avoid."

"Fair enough." After all, if the purpose of his teaching is to get people to ask deeper questions, he had to fend off the questions that lead nowhere.

"I talk much more what happens if one meditates. On a simple utilitarian level there is no answer. If the question comes from a utilitarian place I won't answer. If it comes from true curiosity I will say it's a way of transforming who one is. It's a way of making oneself a more perfect vessel, aligning one's will to the divine will, learning equanimity, discovering that sovereignty is only acquired by acknowledging every other sovereignty, especially the Boss's sovereignty—that one lives in a world of multiple sovereignties." Jonathan often referred to God as "the Boss" (a pretty exact translation of *Adonai*). The phrase, for all its humor, had implications about the relative value of the ego. As Reb

Zalman said to me once, memorably, "The ego is a great manager, but a lousy boss." Putting the two concepts together: the Boss is the boss, not the ego.

"One of the really important teachings," Jonathan said, "is that to be the sovereign human being you don't have to be the CEO."

"This is a path you referred to in Dharamsala as *keter malkhut*." The phrase means "crown of sovereignty."

"*Keter malkhut*." He whispered, "Yeah. One is open to the occasional profound intrusions of the divine into one's consciousness. One observes how the nervous system works so that we learn more about how to get out of one's own way. And that's a big one."

"It requires a certain humility to recognize that I am not fully in charge," I said, thinking how ironic it all was. I'd been pressing him with questions about an equanimity meditation, and he was telling me to get out of my own way.

"That's a battle that no one ever finishes," he said. "Yesterday, we were all going crazy because my son lost his homework." Another time he was reading a passage in my book that described him as a "gentle mystic"; a few minutes before, the "gentle mystic" had been roaring around the house chasing his teenage son and screaming, "I am going to kill you!"

"I found the trip to India to be the most wonderful teaching," Jonathan added.

"How so?"

"When we asked the tourist guide, Tsang Po, 'Can you get us to the airport on time?' and his answer was 'I hope.' It was the most reasonable answer in the world, but it drove certain members of our delegation absolutely crazy. We have this incredible belief that with enough information we'll be able to control the world, and it's just not true. I find that, especially with my limited mobility, I have to give things up and just not do them, or basically say, 'I'll see. I just don't know.' Of course, the Indians take it to ludicrous extremes, by accepting things that don't have to be accepted."

"Such as?"

"Well, the most obvious—that disability disqualifies one from an economic role in society. Or their acceptance of caste, of the punitive nature of poverty."

"They accept too much."

"They accept clearly too much. And we don't accept enough. I found it incredibly refreshing to find that balance, the balance between surrender and submission."

"What's the distinction?"

"Surrender is positive, willingly aligning oneself with a higher will. Submission means being broken by that higher will."

I told Jonathan my own sense of surrender comes from my morning prayer practice. After washing the hands, "*Reishit ḥokhmah yirat Adonai*"—the beginning of wisdom is fear of the Lord. The background noise of anxiety can be dispelled if I redirect it toward awe. If I have true fear of the Boss, I don't have to be scared of anything else.

Jonathan put it differently. "When one accepts that we are not the source of our wisdom—and that our wisdom is a tool and a gift and it isn't us, ultimately it's *yirah*—that awe becomes true humility. Whereas anxiety is an ego space. Anxiety is basically identifying with one's emotion of anxiety."

"A feedback loop?"

"I know when I'm in a state of anxiety it's totally about myself," he said. His words had more point for me because he'd just confessed his state of discomfort.

"So how do you balance it? How do you practice *keter malkhut*? Do you use images of kings in the Bible?"

"Oh no. You see, the human king is the wrong image. A few years ago I taught someone working as a hostess in Junior's Restaurant. Now, hostess is a long way down the pecking line, and she was becoming very anxious. I asked her, 'Who is the most sovereign person there?' Her immediate answer was 'The boss.' I said, 'Let's stop back. Who is the most sovereign person there?' Then she laughed because it was the janitor. He was outside the pecking order, and truly in a place of equanimity. He used to sit in the back room with his buckets, smoking whatever he was smoking. When called upon to do something, very often abruptly, he just smiled and did it. I mean, I believe one can achieve equanimity without marijuana, but in his case, that man was sovereign. The idea is to discover our royalty. We are not kings and queens, but we have sparks of royalty. That spark can inform us in our quest for sovereignty. How am I sovereign if I am God forbid in a prison cell with absolutely no discretion whatsoever in any aspects of my life?"

"That's the question you ask yourself."

"I mean, this prison cell is a really tough one."

I nodded. Did he mean the world around us in general? Or his own predicament?

"It's very important to look around us to see people who manifest different degrees of sovereignty. A sovereign is not someone who manifests power. It can be a person who has power but does not exercise it. The nonexercise of power is a sovereign act. The Dalai Lama is clearly a sovereign human being who has a great deal of power and knows exactly when to use it and knows ultimately it isn't his power."

"Was Hitler a sovereign human being?"

"No. Hitler was completely dominated by inner passions."

"So there has to be a distance from one's passions?"

"Yes. Sovereignty has to be a conscious act. When one is governed entirely by one's passions or unconscious urge, that's not sovereignty."

"Is sovereignty recognizing the sacred obligation to choose at every moment?"

"At a certain point the ultimate sovereignty is the choice whom to serve. It's the Passover story: in Egypt one serves Pharaoh, which ultimately is ego. In the land of Israel one serves the other, which is the divine."

By this time, we were sitting outdoors at a café restaurant across the street from his office. We were being served as well: grilled chicken sandwich for me; for Jonathan an egg, asparagus, and rosemary toast. An old character actor got into a beat-up Chevy with the help of a young woman. It was Monday, March 27, Academy Awards day, and of all things we were talking humility and sovereignty on Wilshire Boulevard.

I saw *keter malkhut* as a spiritual antidote to chutzpah. Sovereignty is a spiritual concept drawn from deep Judaism; chutzpah, I would argue, is a cultural conditioning of the Jewish character under the immense pressures of assimilation and persecution. Each is authentically rooted in Jewish experience, and yet the concepts are antithetical. But people who live within the boundary of ego cannot experience sovereignty—only chutzpah. As Jonathan had suggested, they cannot see humility or equanimity as anything but weakness and passivity, for that is how it looks through the ego glasses. It's not a simple dilemma, the struggle between humility and chutzpah, between equanimity and passion, between Jewish and Judaism.

To move from chutzpah to *keter malkhut* requires a practice, and a community. I saw Jonathan's Metivta classes as a community in formation. His students clearly formed a network; they popped up in different settings, such as Ohr Hatorah synagogue, Beit T'shuvah. I'd see them again that evening at a meditation class.

Before class, Jonathan and I ate together at Milk and Honey on Pico, a small kosher restaurant he favored just around the corner from his home. Over dessert he apologized again for the interruptions in our conversation—the times he'd had to lie down or just stop altogether. The punctuation in the flow. After the obvious hints Judith dropped in our interview earlier that afternoon, I knew the real problem. He confirmed that and went into details, which were immediately anguishing.

A conversation we'd had came back with new significance. I'd said, "It seems that so many people only come to recognize a spiritual dimension to their lives because of a moment of outrage. They've come up to a door of pain. Before they reach that door of pain God doesn't occur to them." I was thinking of the polio that changed his life.

"Except," Jonathan had said slowly then, "there's more than one door of pain. You think you've been through and there comes another one."

After dinner, Jonathan drove me to his meditation class at Kehillat Ma'Arav, a Conservative synagogue. A dozen students sat in folding chairs. We started with a chant based on the prayer *Adonai melekh, Adonai malakh, Adonai yimlokh le-olam va'ed.* God reigns, God reigned, God will reign through eternity.

"We do it with head movements," Jonathan explained. "*Adonai melekh*, you move your head to the left; *Adonai malakh*, your head to the right; *Adonai yimlokh*, head forward; and *le-olam va'ed*, move the head back. All four directions. After about seven minutes, when I detect a change in the energy I will ask you to fall into silence and then we will meditate for a few minutes —trying to find a place of emptiness. For many people who do the chanting, the mind completely empties and the being empties and they move into a different space."

The chanting sounded for several minutes. At Jonathan's signal we hushed, while still moving and saying the prayer mentally. Then we resumed, but from a quieter place, not so demonstrative. We had become more unified, one voice with many resonances instead of separate voices. The exercise ended in sighs and long exhalations.

"Before we go further," Jonathan asked, "would anyone like to comment on what just happened?"

"I got hooked up to a battery," one student said.

"Are you recharged?"

"Yes."

Another: "I felt very calm and at peace with myself."

Another: "I kept hearing that person with the automobile. I wanted to get up and punch him."

"Do you think," Jonathan asked, "the meditation made you want to punch or made you want to calm down?"

"I'm not sure."

"It's a pretty good exercise for excluding external noises," Jonathan said. "So if you hear them your level of irritability is probably—I'm not saying it pejoratively—your sensitivity must be pretty high. I've got my hearing aid on maximum volume and I didn't hear it."

A man spoke about hearing an underlying drone. Another spoke of embarrassment, then relaxation. A woman said the first time the exercise irritated her, but now "it moves me fastest to non-ordinary reality." An hour's doing it and she might do something "real weird," enter a "spiritual dimension," or leave her body.

Jonathan answered calmly. "If you note, this is very structured. We chant for a limited time. I keep my eyes opened. If anyone feels he is leaving his body," he joked, "make sure you leave the door opened."

"I wouldn't mind, actually," she said.

"Well, I would." Jonathan was subtle, but clearly did not want to encourage flights of fancy—especially out of the body.

Jonathan reassured the group that the meditations he gives are safe. "I would never suggest doing this for a long time by yourself. An extended chant should only be done with a group and a leader taking care of you. It's like going on a trip into the desert. There's nothing wrong with it, but you should tell someone you're going so if you don't come back he'll look for you. The same is true of a spiritual trip. One can explore anywhere, but you should have a friend who cares and will say, 'Kathryn?'—" He snapped his fingers twice. "That's what you need. Many years ago when I started on this, I tried some Abulafia meditation." Abraham Abulafia is a thirteenth-century Spanish mystic who practiced ecstatic meditations on the Hebrew alphabet, similar to the one on Elijah taught by Joseph Mark Cohen.

"Abulafia gives you a one-way ticket to outer space," Jonathan said and paused. "But we don't do anything like that. We're cementing horizontally as a community as well as developing vertically along the spiritual dimension."

Soon we stood in a healing circle. We held hands and Jonathan led us in a chant, the direct and simple prayer of Moses for the healing of Miriam. *El na refa na lah.* God, please heal her, please (Num. 12:13).

We repeated the Hebrew in a soft chant. "Anybody can put into the circle the name of someone for whom they wish healing," he said. "Then we chant loudly again. Then anybody who desires healing themselves will stand into the circle. When you step into the circle, the people on either side of you will close the circle so the energy will not leak out."

The chant began, slowly, mournfully; as the group chanted more softly, I heard: "Chaim," "Eva," "Sidney." It was a touching ceremony. Jonathan asked those needing healing for themselves to "please step into the circle." A woman came forward and we surrounded her with our chant. She withdrew and then, unexpectedly, Jonathan, on crutches, made his way inside the circle.

The students chanted very loudly. Even in exposing his vulnerability Jonathan manifested the dignity of his path of *keter malkhut*. We chanted for healing for our teacher as he stood with his head bowed in a cone of light.

Then a silence; we too broke up and went our separate ways.

○　◑　●　◐　◑　○　◑　●

On Friday, Jonathan gave me the blessing teaching. The night before I'd given a bookstore talk in Brentwood—and, with the O.J. prosecution going full blast, couldn't resist eating pasta with a friend at nearby Mezzaluna. Jonathan beeped me in the middle of my talk. He told me he had decided not to leave town for the Jewish renewal rabbis' meeting. Since he'd already canceled his class in preparation for his trip, he offered me that time for another study session. That's why we were sitting early Friday morning in his office at Metivta. I was running out of time.

"The *Maggid* thought the blessing path very important—so much so he accused you of sitting on it," I said.

Jonathan paused. "I am not sitting on it," he said quietly. "Except to the extent that, to the extent that I am . . ." The phone rang and I shifted in my chair. Jonathan leaned forward.

"As you are completely involved in all the gossip of this area, you have to hear the latest piece. Rico Cardinale is moving out today."

Rico Cardinale shared Metivta's Tudor-style office building. Cardinale was a hairdresser with an outstanding collection of junk vehicles. His late-sixties big-finned convertible with the top permanently down sat in the lot, rotting and peeling in the sun near the modest sign posted outside the building that read: Metivta, A School for Jewish Wisdom. I appreciated the humility of "*a* school."

"Where's Rico going?"

"He left a message yesterday: 'I am leaving tomorrow. They're going to cut off the electricity'—which we share."

"Amazing he could move that car."

"Oh, he leaves it with the wheel off in the middle of the lot. Anyway. Blessing." Jonathan made an abrupt transition as if we'd just left *assiyah* for higher worlds. "If you ask Jews to define themselves religiously, they'd probably call themselves the mitz-vah people—active, doing as opposed to being. But blessings are a very large part of our path. In traditional practice one says one hundred blessings a day. Not as many as it looks when you con-sider there are eighteen of the *Shemoneh Esrei*, which you do three times a day. Still, the idea of doing a hundred blessings[1] a day leads us to look at the question, What is blessing? What does it mean when we bless?"

I'd generally thought of a *berakhah* as a formula of muttered words, not a meaning. That changed at the '91 P'nai Or *kallah*. One exercise involved blessing a partner to his face. I had to search within and find a way to bless a person properly. It got in-tense. Once I broke loose, for a day or two I went around blessing people profligately. It certainly made me feel good. Sometimes, when the mood strikes me, I'll walk down the street blessing every face I meet, wishing that person good health or well-being.

Jonathan asked if I blessed my children on Friday night. "What do you think you're doing? What do you think happens when you do that?"

"Extending my protection. Making my daughters feel com-forted—that everything is OK."

Jonathan laughed. "It's not nice of you to screw up my theory. You say your blessing is entirely between you and the child. Most people feel they are channeling divine energy."

"Oh."

"But as a good reconstructionist—"

"I wouldn't say that." I finished his sentence, laughing. "I'd have trouble saying it. Too big a claim."

"OK," Jonathan said, acknowledging my stubborn core of re-serve, "but if people say 'I am directing it,' I answer, 'No, the blessing is there the whole time.' We don't get God to act, don't turn on the switch or open the faucet—but something arises in the interaction. This brings out the major point. Within blessing there's always three: the blesser, the blessed, and the source of all blessing."

Jonathan views blessing as a discipline. It forces you to give full attention—which is different from awareness. "One can be aware but involved in oneself. Blessing gives attention to something beyond oneself. Also, blessing isn't entirely spontaneous. One can't just be driving down the freeway—and oh!"—he snapped his finger—"God brings bread from the earth. Blessing has structure. It isn't impulsive."

That was a good corrective to my own spontaneous fits of benediction. And he added that although some say blessing is a moment of joy, one also blesses extremely sad moments. For instance, on hearing of a death, the *Barukh Dayan ha-emet*. Blessed is the true Judge.

"I always basically translate it as, 'Even though I don't believe it I'm saying the Boss knows best.'"

I knew that blessing all too well. "It seems the *berakhah* wants to take you out of that very lonely situation," I said. "It adds in another person."

"Yes," Jonathan said, "once again it triangulates. There's you, the dead one, and the Boss. Like everything in the spiritual life, it extends from immediate pain or joy to a context larger than ourselves."

The blessing path begins in the Torah with Melchizedek, whom Jonathan called "the first of all blessers. He blessed Avram on the mountain and said, 'Blessed is Avram in the most high, blessed is the most high in Avram' [Gen. 14:19].Ultimately this establishes a principle of triangulation. Melchizedek is extremely important in the Jewish esoteric tradition. Mainstream Jews have difficulty because Melchizedek is a goy, and how come a goy would go blessing Avraham? They really say that. Instead of seeing him as the prime initiator of Avraham."

The passage in Torah reads, "And Melchizedek king of Shalem brought forth bread and wine, and he was the priest of the most high God" (Gen. 14:18).

Rashi's commentary on this verse explains the bread and wine as "an intimation" of the meal offerings and libations Abraham's descendants would offer in Salem "which is Jeru-salem." Abraham learns from Melchizedek the basics of the Temple sacrifices.

At an early age I learned the words for blessings over wine and bread, over candles and reading the Torah. With my prayer practice I'd added the morning blessings and the blessings of the *Shemoneh Esrei*. I knew how to bless my children at Shabbas, a sweet ceremony. I had multiplied the number of blessings I could recite. But what did I know of their spiritual meaning?

Jonathan answered, "When we try to understand what happens when we take a piece of bread and bless it, we are led into deep kabbalah." He paused in thought for a long moment. "In addition to the *Ein Sof*, the divine beyond, sparks of the divine in exile hide in the world. A spark of the divine hides in a piece of bread. The divine beyond—the *Ein Sof*—can't be seen."

The *Ein Sof* is the God beyond all four worlds, the ultimate God with no descriptors. "The only way you can know the divine is through its reflection in yourself, and your reflection in the divine spark in the bread. When we make a blessing we become aware of the divine in the bread. We make—through an act of consciousness—a unification between the bread and the *Ein Sof*. We draw ourselves into the triangulation."

Jonathan added, very softly, "That is the essence of the teaching. The blessing isn't a high moment necessarily, but a very low-key event. Blessing is seeing the bread with one's eye, acknowledging it, closing one's eyes, making the *yihud*—the unification—and doing it a number of times a day. It's an extremely powerful teaching."

I saw how the blessing path speaks to the problem of connecting with an infinite reality.

Did I have questions before he moved on? I had plenty. What is an "act of consciousness"? Does that mean an act of imagination? Or an intention? Does wishing make a blessing real?

Also, how to imagine the divine energy? I assumed he did not mean the elementary particles or the vibrating molecules of the bread. "Not the physics of the bread?"

"No," Jonathan said, firmly, "but sometimes one knows it through sensual appreciation. Crushing a crumb between palate and tongue. It often means paying full attention to the bread."

He leaned forward in his chair. "Let me show you something." He touched a key on his computer and the printer whirred. "The exile in the bread—the exile of the spark in the world—can be of different depths. There is deep, deep exile where one can hardly perceive the spark. Like if you're going through McDonald's drive-through because you're on the freeway and you're hungry—and you say, 'Please scrape the cheese off the hamburger because I can do nonkosher meat but I can't do cheese too.' Then the blessing becomes almost inaccessible. That's a deep exile."

"So every blessing," I said, "is also a meditation on the depth of exile?"

He nodded. "It's an awareness," he said. "For instance, when you do your absolute best to bless someone whom you don't like." He handed me a sheet from the printer. "Please don't discard this page," he said, "because it contains the four-letter name of God, which is holy." He pointed to a drawing that looked like this:

Metivta
Advanced Seminar on Blessing
The Basic Unification

"This is the source," Jonathan said, pointing to the הי (*Yod Heh*), "and this," pointing to the וה (*Vov Heh*), "what is in exile. By the act of mind one puts them together. This is the most basic of all the unifications."

It looked like divine algebra to me: YH + VH = YHVH. "So הי is the source beyond and וה is the divine in exile. Do you visualize the letters as you do the blessing?"

"It depends if you are a visualizing kind of person. I'm giving you theoretical background, which sometimes comes to the foreground. Different people do different things. If you read the kabbalistic prayer books, they all start with the *leshem yiḥud*, which is basically the unification of the *Kadosh Barukh Hu* (the Holy One, blessed is He) and the Shekhinah (the indwelling presence)."

The two halves of God's four-letter name are divided into male and female. By bringing them together through our prayer, *Yod Heh* plus *Vov Heh*, the transcendent and the immanent become one. (The transcendent name YH is a name of God in itself, *Yah*; the addition of VH makes it possible for us to make a personal connection to that transcendent being through the complete name YHVH.)[2]

"So," I said, trying to sum up what I'd received so far, "blessing intimates holiness in our world: it unifies for a moment this world with the *Ein Sof*, the whole that is beyond."

"I'd put it this way," Jonathan answered. "When we bless, are we inviting holiness in the world? No, holiness is there the whole time. So—we remove the veil. For an instant—never more than an instant—there's no distinction between the place of holiness and our place. When we bless we remove the veil."

On cue, another erring student poked her head through—not the veil, but the doorway. Without missing a beat, he turned and wished her well. She smiled, realized her mistake, and left.

So when I pray, I asked Jonathan, am I reflecting a greater unification? Or do I passively allow it to be manifested through my blessing?

"Look," he said, "our knowledge of the divine is always passive. Now, this is missed by Reconstructionist, Reform, Conservative, modern Orthodox—all the way through until you reach that wonderful crazy place of ultra-Orthodoxy who ultimately know: our knowledge of God is passive."

So why had I been running all over the country? If our knowledge of God is passive, what does it mean to be a spiritual seeker?

"We do active things to reach the place of the passive knowledge of God," he answered. I took that to mean we work on opening ourselves in order to be able to perceive the divine. "But this incredibly important teaching is just not understood. People don't get it. It's never acknowledged. It's just such a basic teaching: We do not grasp God with our intellects."

"The knowledge only comes to us, we cannot come to it?"

"We prepare ourselves for it. If you like, we are the flower bed waiting for the seed. We have to prepare the flower bed, we have to work the soil, but ultimately we are passive. At the moment of blessing one removes the veils, so that for a second the name of God, the *Yod Heh* and the *Vov Heh*, become united through our active attention."

The ArtScroll Siddur, an Orthodox prayer book with kabbalistic teachings, explains the unification or *yiḥud* in detail. There are *kavvanot*, or specific intentions to be recited before saying a blessing; one might call them the warm-up for the blessing itself. For example, before putting on the tallis, for morning prayer, many recite the following declaration of intent: "For the sake of the unification of the Holy One Blessed is He and His Presence, in fear and love to unify the Name—*yud-kei* with *vav-kei*—in perfect unity, in the name of all Israel."[3]

The *Yod Heh* and the *Vov Heh* are united through our active attention, *leshem yiḥud* יהוך לשם, for the sake of the unification of the Name.

The four-letter name of God is divided into two parts; the first two letters refer to the divine beyond, the second two to the divine in exile. In kabbalistic teachings these are identified with masculine and feminine principles, but I think of them without gender markers—simply that our sense of living in a broken, imperfect world reflects itself in the division of God's name. And that at some level, through our blessings, we heal that division.

"We don't do it," Jonathan corrected me, "but certain actions facilitate its manifestation. From God's perspective there never is a division. There never is an exile. Only from our space is there an exile. At that point we abolish it."

"We do nothing," I said. "Then how does the unification process [*yihud*] differ from mindfulness in Buddhist thought?"

"Phenomenologically—very similar. Theologically different."

I reminded him of the training Buddhist teachers give, to simply look at bread, to be with the bread before eating it. Eating a piece of bread, one realizes the interconnectedness of being, or what the contemporary Vietnamese Buddhist teacher Thich Nhat Hanh calls "interbeing." You meditate on the truck driver who delivered the bread to the grocer, the baker who baked the bread, the miller who ground the flour, the farmer who grew the wheat, the wheat tips shining in the fields, the breeze and the sun and rain that nourished the plants. All partake of the moment of eating the bread, and all deserve thanks.

"Oh, it's the same training," Jonathan said. "Truly the same. When we compare Jewish meditation to Buddhist meditation, the techniques are the same but not the contexts. Just as, when it comes to the psychology, to the physics and the anatomy, Anna Karenina is the same as Madame Bovary. They're almost inter-changeable—but they are not."

"Right."

"It's the same between Buddhists and, uh . . ." He paused for a minute and then smiled ". . . and, it's just my mind is focusing on women who throw themselves away, but that's, uh . . ."

I laughed. Judith was leaving him. Which is why he'd can-celed his travel plans and we were sitting together. Jonathan laughed too. "Well, enough of that today."

I realized that all during our time together, Jonathan was wrestling with jealousy, anger, and a sense of loss and abandonment. Now I understood why he'd had trouble focusing, why sometimes he stopped our lessons to lie down and rest: it wasn't just the effect of Rob's funeral. In my presence, only small hints emerged to the surface. But lofty teachings and powerful emotions contended side by side within him.

Still, the healing circle he'd stepped into had begun its work. Perhaps just asking for that healing had done a great deal in itself.

In the selfish way of students the world over, I had anticipated that my perfect teacher would have a perfect life. I had simply assumed he would be an automatic watercooler of wisdom. Push the button and the truth flows out. But I learned more from him this way—as a whole person, with cracks and flaws.

"So," Jonathan said, "it's important to recognize the generic similarities between different spiritual traditions that really do illuminate the process—but," he added, "only in one dimension, phenomenology. In the dimension of context, they are very different." Jewish meditation helps Jews discover their spiritual context.

"That's what happens," he explained, "when people say, 'Well, it's all one really, all the same. Why do you need something different?' They're right on the phenomenological level, but on the context level that statement becomes meaningless."

Religious practices, then, are context sensitive. Of course many people would like to ditch context in the name of freedom; they want to mix and match spiritual languages, partly to escape the particular claims of any one tradition. A universal generic spirituality has always attracted a following, a soup of Native American wisdom, yoga, Buddhist meditation, Christianity, and other spices, including a dash of kabbalah.

But religious traditions are languages. Each language has its own rich history, its nuances, beauties, distinctions. As Wallace Stevens reminds us in "Thirteen Ways of Looking at a Blackbird," half of poetry is "the beauty of inflection." There's no poetry in Esperanto, no nuance in a universal spirituality.

Another student meandered into the room.

"There's no class today," Jonathan said, smiling.

"What," she said, "there's no class?"

"I'm only by chance in town," Jonathan explained. "I think I announced last week. I'm sorry."

She turned and left, still puzzled.

"Isn't that interesting?" I said, grinning.

"That's two so far. It's just as well I'm here, that I can say it in person."

"How do you interpret the grammar of *Barukh Atah Adonai*?" I asked. The Hebrew for the *petihah* or opening of most blessings translates as: You are blessed YHVH. "What does it mean for us to say that this awesome being, YHVH, is blessed by us? Shouldn't it be the other way around?"

"Look," Jonathan answered, "Various things happen there. The Hebrew moves from second person to third person. *Atah* is second person, *Adonai* is third person."

The grammar of blessing is peculiar in that way. Consider the simple blessing over wine. In the usual English translation we get: Blessed are you, *Adonai*, Our God, King of the universe, who creates the fruit of the vine. Recast in ordinary English syntax: You are Blessed, *Adonai*, Our God ... who creates the fruit ... [4]

It doesn't sound right. The prayer slips from second to third person in a subtle way that I'd never noticed, though I've been saying these words all my life.

To Jonathan this grammatical movement represents the essence of the triangulation. The prayer moves from the personal to the impersonal, from God addressed familiarly as You (*Atah* or *At*) to God accessed or acknowledged as YHVH.

I begin a blessing addressed to a You. And in the next word of the blessing I invoke the name YHVH. The move from one to the other leads, as Jonathan said, to deep kabbalah.

It's clear in reading the Spanish kabbalist Joseph Gikatilla that he saw the same "problem" in the Torah that scholars like

Wellhausen and others later seized on in formulating the documentary hypothesis. Gikatilla was a student of the Rambam's philosophy, and he saw many names of God in the Torah and that they are used in different ways. But Gikatilla wished to use this knowledge not to fragment the Torah, but instead to unify it. The key to such unity is the name YHVH, which to the kabbalist, ultimately, is the only word in the Torah; every other word is derived from YHVH.[5] To Gikatilla, "the great Name that is called YHVH, may He be Blessed, is the source and the trunk of the tree which extends above, below and to all sides. He dresses in the other Holy Names and the other Cognomens . . . and He does so in accordance with each activity that He enacts in His world." In Gikatilla's metaphor, the root name YHVH "dresses" in the garment of *Adonai* or *Elohim* depending on the action being described. "For He will be dressed in the garments of the Name that signifies His conduct."[6]

In his *Gates of Light* Gikatilla lists the familiar cognomens or names of God, among them those we translate as God, Lord, Lord of Hosts, Lord God, and explains the activity and power of each name. But he also describes more recondite names of God. One is *Atah*, or "You." The "You" in our blessings, "Blessed are You," is an acknowledgment that the God we are praying to can be reached.

Gikatilla explains, "Since the Name that is called YHVH is accessible to the created in His activities and His awesomeness, we call Him by the word AtaH, as if He were present and approachable through speech."[7]

The "You" implies accessibility, nearness; but the YHVH implies distance, and awe. In prayer, Jews do not even vocalize the word *YHVH*. That is a privilege reserved for the High Priest in the Holy of Holies on the holiest day of the year, Yom Kippur. In the tradition, awesome powers and terrible consequences attend that moment of pronunciation. One must be in an entirely pure state to even approach it.

In other words, when we read the four-letter name in a prayer, we are touching on a distant, awesome name of God. To reflect that, Jews in prayer pronounce YHVH as *Adonai* (the Lord), a substitute name that derives from the Hebrew *adon* (lord, master).[8]

But there's another way of looking at the etymology of *Adonai*. Jonathan reminded me of a teaching from Gikatilla. He found *Adonai* rooted in *eden* אֶדֶן—"doorsill."[9]

"The *Adonai* which is the doorsill opens to a much larger place," Jonathan said. I thought of the door of pain, our experiences of fear and turmoil. Jonathan stricken with polio. Judith alone with two children in Mexico. Mark Borovitz turning the street corner. Paul Wolff crying out for his daughter. For many, pain is the doorsill to a larger awareness. But blessing is another door.

"In blessing, you can only strip away the veil for a very short period—an ephemeral event. Like the curtains in the poem we discussed." In a Metivta poetry class on Tuesday morning, we read Rilke's description of a caged panther:

> As he paces in cramped circles, over and over,
> the movement of his powerful soft strides
> is like a ritual dance around a center
> in which a mighty will stands paralyzed.
> Only at times, the curtain of the pupils
> lifts, quietly—. An image enters in,
> rushes down through the tensed, arrested muscles,
> plunges into the heart and is gone.[10]

"Rilke knows that that curtain opens just for a second and no more."

"The image sinks down deep."

"Way down deep—and then disappears probably."

He sat for a while in silence. Jonathan often emphasized for me the evanescence of attainment, the slipperiness of awareness, the impossibility of holding on to higher knowledge. Which explains why such knowledge is passive. All we can do is be prepared to bump into Elijah.

Jonathan had given me several images for the Jewish path. A veil that lifts for a moment of blessing. A curtain within the eye of the caged panther, an iris that unfans in the dark, and then closes down to focus at the rush of sudden light. The image of a glimpse—and the glimpse of an image, for in poetry, image is glimpse, a momentary blessing where two unrelated worlds emerge as one.

Catching lightning in my hands . . .

Now I understood why we say Blessed are You, YHVH. Because the blessing is always here, already here. It's just that I don't know it, don't feel it. The blessing is hidden, in exile, in the wine, or the bread, or the face of a child at Shabbat. Through my acknowledgment of its ultimate source, YHVH—I liberate the blessing. And in that moment YHVH is blessed. The veil lifts and the remote and the near are one—*Yod Heh* unites with *Vov Heh*—in unification, *yiḥud*. When YHVH is acknowledged as the ultimate source of the blessings we see around us, God is blessed.

"Why do you think this teaching is important to Paul?"

"Paul came from the Gurdjieff world in which being present is the absolute first thing one does. In Judaism very few exercises involve being present. Blessing is a way of being present."

"But there's so little time and so many blessings. Most of us don't know the Hebrew for the more unusual situations."

"No need," Jonathan said. "You just do one bread a day."

"One bread a day."

"For starters."

"I'd like to do more. Yesterday I was doing blessings. It was really quite nice. I can get into it like Ginsberg or Whitman: hail to the holy palm leaf! Hail to the setting sun! Praise God for the wind ruffling the feathers of the jay! Do you think it gets too ecstatic?"

"According to the Talmud," Jonathan said, "one cannot make up one's own blessings. But at a certain point about fifteen years ago I was at Fellowship Farm on my way to visit Zalman, a crisp ten degrees under, cold night on the prairie, and I realized it was absolutely absurd to say you can't make up your own blessings. If you don't you're nuts. There's something else. Sometimes our making up our own blessings is our flow of praise. Did you see the air last night round about six, between six and seven, before the sun set?"

"That's when I was doing my blessing." I'd been standing outside a school, waiting for Heidi Singh to pick up her son—she's the Buddhist chaplain at UCLA—and the rose light of the setting sun had hit an adobe wall perfectly. A bright green palm leaf flowered there. I uttered spontaneous words of praise, trying to connect that experience of beauty with something beyond it. I made up a prayer: "Blessed are you Lord our God who creates such beauty in our lives."

"The sky was wonderful," Jonathan agreed. He'd seen the same serene light, filtering past the honking horns of Los Angeles traffic, like a blessing in disguise. "I don't know whether what you said was blessing or just an expression of thanksgiving or praise."

"So the discipline, as you are defining it, is the conscious intention to open, to lift the veil, to unify your moment with something bigger than you. What's in back of my mind is something Paul said, which is that Judaism has a huge transcendent deity, which is vast and somewhat impersonal . . ."

"And zaps Egyptians," Jonathan finished dryly. Pesach was much on his mind.

"Well," I said, recalling my conversation with the *Maggid*, "I have a very hard time with a personal God. Intellectually I find it pompous. It seems to me absurd that a force that could create galaxies, with such a vast amount of space and time to deal with—how could there be any concern with the local ups and downs of one individual? I find that very hard to appreciate."

"The difficulty you're facing is also the greatness of Judaism. If you go to a Hindu temple they will separate the *bhakti*—the devotional—from *jnana*, the wisdom path. You come with a bowl of rice to the god and say, 'Please help my brother-in-law get insurance for his motorcycle,' and that's the devotional level. Then you go through a certain number of chambers and relate to Atman—the utterly impersonal. But Judaism says, 'Hey, you don't have two different temples. They are one. They're one.'"

"I guess the *Shema* also says that."

I'd been practicing Jonathan's *Shema* meditation, taking the familiar prayer out of its old grooves. Hear O Israel, the Lord our God, the Lord is One. It's clearly also an algebraic equation, one of several found at various points in the Torah.[11]

The *Shema* sets up an equivalency. I read it this way: wake up Israel, this *Adonai* we think of as our personal God, *Eloheinu*, is in reality YHVH, vast and beyond all limitation. They are one and the same.

"Absolutely the *Shema* says that. Spiritual practice will take you from *Adonai* through to *Yod Heh Vov Heh*."

"I want to believe it," I said, "but I find it very hard to believe. [The physicist] Richard Feynmann once said that given the vastness of the universe, the idea of a God who cares about a nation or individuals seemed too local."

"If one accepts," Jonathan said, "different levels of consciousness and one moves through them . . . You know my exercise of crying out to God?" He'd mentioned it several times. "It always takes me to the place of the impersonal," he said. "I absolutely agree with you that God has no features, no face, no personality, but saying, 'Help me please, I'm stuck' can open things up. The practice becomes the *Adonai*, the door.

"One of the problems of Richard Feynmann and many bright people is that they would never in a million years accept such a level of nonsophistication of questioning in their own fields. It's like Richard Feynmann saying, 'I just don't believe that matter is divided between negative and positive, it must be one at base.' What would you say to him? That's the level at which he's really approaching the discussion. It comes from a kind of assumption that expertise is permissible at every single level of human endeavor except the knowledge of God.

"Rodger, as a Western intellectual you expect your theology to be consistent, but these books"—he gestured to the loaded shelf behind him—"like the Tanya know that although God has no personality, you can't be a complete human being unless sometimes you call out in a personal way."

He was touching on my place of most resistance. My reservation. Chanting, all right. Meditating quietly, all right. But calling out, calling out in a personal way? I drew back, as I'd drawn back from the *Maggid* when his preaching seemed too insistent.

I'd told Paul I was uncomfortable with the notion of a personal God. I found it much easier to accept an impersonal one. And he'd said, "Spirituality is highly irrational, which is why people don't like it. It's irrational but it's completely sane."

Jonathan was saying I couldn't be complete without the personal calling out. It went back to his important distinction, between personal prayer and liturgical prayer.

Jonathan understands the movement from the personal to the universal in two different ways. "I used to think I was a Sufi-type Jew," he said. "Now I am a Buddhist-type Jew. I don't know whether it's age, I don't know." I heard brakes squealing in the background. He shrugged. "I used to joke that I'm an inhibited ecstatic—and I am. But really I'm much more a contemplative who moves out of the personal realm altogether. That the יהוה [*Yod Heh Vov Heh*] is the true level at which everything exists."

Throughout our conversations Jonathan alternated between northern and southern Hasidism, between Chabad and Nachman of Bratzlav. Nachman of Bratzlav proposes that the world is broken, and that by experiencing the brokenness, the shattering of the vessels, we can grasp a more profound joy. This is the union from below.

But Chabad says we are already in the universal light and the shattering is an illusion. Jonathan confided to me that he'd made a great discovery and wanted to send it out on e-mail to all who would understand: the vessels were never shattered, never really broken.

O

I wondered what he meant by that: for him personally, for his current difficulties, as well as the permanent difficulty of his life. Was he dreaming an escape from the broken world he lived in, the problems and particulars of his own suffering and of others around him? Or did he truly find in every moment, no matter how painful, this larger universal joy? Hadn't he also said that we lift the veil only for a moment?

I'd spoken on the phone to Marc Lerner, who does spiritual counseling work with cancer patients. He told me, "People aren't going to go through the door unless they're forced to. Only with immense pain." I asked Jonathan if he agreed.

"I don't believe in the apotheosis of pain. I leave room for the experience through joy. There are different traditions. Rabbi Nachman would say you have to go through the shattering. The *ḥasidim* knew that you have to force yourself to get to the place of joy. And clearly joy and fun differ."

"I don't know what it would mean to have a path of joy," I said. "You described this to the Dalai Lama. How can you always find a place of joy wherever you are, whatever the situation? That seems very difficult."

"But that's what this exercise I've been teaching you is all about," he said, "this unification. Even the *Barukh Dayan ha-emet* [the prayer at death] can be a place of joy if one reaches it with the totality of one's being. Any moment of true mindfulness that involves a unification is a moment of joy. Not necessarily a moment of happiness.

"Making a blessing establishes a level of intimacy by creating attention. So just as one by-product—but not the goal—of meditation is peace of mind, so one by-product of blessing is enhancement of blessing. Another word I use is *freshness*. Blessing refreshes one's connection to a person or a thing. Does this help? Do you pick up what made Paul so enthusiastic?"

"Yes. You're suggesting that it becomes a practice . . . because occasions for blessing rise up throughout the day—every time you eat, for instance. It raises consciousness."

"Yes. For me blessing—and meditation—define my most basic practice."

"That's what carries you from moment to moment?"

"And from day to day. It has a cumulative effect."

He suggested I take the *yihud* sheet and practice. "This is a very low-key exercise. The practice needs to be steady. There's an enormous difference between davening once a week and davening daily. Davening once a week, you expect something exciting. Davening daily, you can't." Compared to the initial lightning of the revelation at Sinai, "the *mishkan* is a forty-watt lamp. Keep the forty-watt lamp on. This practice draws you." He suggested that in time I could look at other blessings, then added, "A spiritual exercise, even a nonliturgical one, is blessing other people."

"How do you bless other people?" I looked into Jonathan's kind face and felt an answer already.

"An act of consciousness. You look at them, you see the divine spark within, you connect it with the source."

"Is there a prayer for that?"

"Not necessarily. When you see the other person in a completely noninstrumental way, just as another unpredictable manifestation of the divine in the world, with the spark of the divine which you see just for a moment . . ." I looked closely to Jonathan—my own unpredictable spark—and silently said good-bye. I didn't know when I'd learn from him again.

"I wonder," I said, "if you can see a person in terms of how she is uniquely expressing the divine purpose . . ."

"That's too much in the head, Rodger," Jonathan said with quiet insistence. Then my teacher, who'd already given me a bushel of blessing, added one more. "Just say, 'Wow.'"

## Calling Out
JOSHUA TREE
APRIL 2, 1995; 2 NISAN 5755

I saw Jonathan one last time, at a Shabbat dinner with one of his students. Before we said good night for the evening, we embraced. This meant a lot, because Jonathan is not given to such gestures and neither am I. But we had moved through so much territory together—emotional, intellectual, spiritual; our relationship had changed. He said he felt we had become friends. I could think of nothing finer. And at that moment of farewell, I wished I could stay, to study with him and benefit from keeping better company. But I had my family and my life to go back to. I felt again the pull of wandering off, of *lekh lekha*—and also the difficulty of having the wisdom to change your life from where you are.

I watched Jonathan for a long time as he made his way up the walk to his house, as he opened the door, and as it closed behind him. I stared at the door to his house, where we'd studied Torah together over a kitchen table, then turned away.

Our work was done for now. I'd come thinking I knew what I wanted: meditation techniques. But I saw now that what was wanted of me was different. Yes, after my persistent urgings, Jonathan taught me an equanimity exercise in his office that involved visualizing an internal ball of light and sending it through the body. But by then, I knew: what I thought I wanted was not the point.

Jonathan said the essence of religious practice is keeping better company. In Los Angeles, I'd kept company with many whose lives had been transformed, and who in turn opened themselves to me: Mark Borovitz and the men at Beit T'shuvah, the *Maggid* of

Hollywood, Eliahu Pinchas, Rabbi Judith Halevy. And other Elijahs who'd surprised me on the way, like Marc Lerner. Through them I drew closer and closer to my own door of pain. Was that also, as Jonathan insisted, the doorsill, the place of *Adonai*?

"What happens when you pray?" Jonathan had asked me once. "Does anything happen? Does anything happen objectively in the world? Do you change anything in the world?"

"I don't know," I'd answered. "I've been doing it for months now, but I'm not sure of the answer. My wife says I'm less grumpy in the morning when . . ."

Jonathan chuckled, then challenged me again.

I told him that I thought of prayer as a dialogue. Buber defined it that way. "With the Boss?" Jonathan asked. "Gikatilla talks about this. We say *Adonai* when we're on the dialogic level, the level of *malkhut*, of sovereignty, of causality in the world. But *Adonai* is in fact just a lower level of *Yod Heh Vov Heh*. With *Yod Heh Vov Heh* there is no dialogue—it is timeless, spaceless, the eternal. The meditative exists on the level of *Yod Heh Vov Heh*. According to the kabbalah, according to all of Jewish practice, and this is what I most of the time believe, the only way to get to *Yod Heh Vov Heh* is through the *Adonai*. It's wonderful that it's written *Yod Heh Vov Heh* and you say *Adonai*. You have to go through the devotional, the pietistic, in order to reach the mystical level."

The devotional, the pietistic—I understood from our earliest conversation—meant not just liturgical prayer but personal prayer, prayer from the heart. But to make such prayer? All my pride said no.

When Jonathan first described the crying-out exercise, I doubted I could do it. My skepticism abhorred it. My sense of humor found it horribly sincere. I wasn't alone in my resistance. Jonathan told me, half joking, that "only two groups of people have enormous difficulty doing this exercise: rabbis and lawyers.

Both have complete control over their voices; they don't want to move out of control."

I'd read about *hitbodedut* (literally, "self-isolation") in various books, including Herbert Weiner's classic *9 ½ Mystics*, where he describes the Bratzlavers of Jerusalem who went at night to the outskirts of the city to shout and scream.

"That was before '67 when he wrote that book," Jonathan said. "That area is now a housing development. They have to go further afield."

"Do people do it still?" I asked.

"I get all my students to do it. Third week of the introductory class you go out and scream."

"Here in Los Angeles?"

"Yep."

"Can you tell me how that's done?" I had the sense that what I'd been thinking of as an entirely theoretical discussion was much nearer at hand.

"By the ocean. Parked car by the ocean. Last week three people described how they did it in their showers. Which is strange. Some people drive up into the mountains. Everybody here has cars. Ultimately doing this exercise reveals one's vulnerability to God."

"When doing this, is there something you need to know?"

Jonathan paused. "Yes," he said, gently. "That no one ever goes mad doing it. And it never happened yet that someone could stop the crying, stop the tears. One thing that reassures people with this meditation is that anytime you want to"—he clapped his hand—"you just stop. That's one reassurance. Another is you're not going to become ultra-Orthodox if you say, 'Please God help me.' Some people feel if you open the door a bit the whole thing comes in. Overcoming the fear of inauthenticity. These feelings of inauthenticity have no more significance than flatulence."

"You must shout?"

"Yes, it must be above normal voice volume. It shouldn't be controlled."

Then Jonathan told me a hasidic story. "A king had a favorite son. He said, 'My son, I want you to perform a task for me. At the bottom of the yard is a very narrow tower. Beside it is a boulder. Raise the boulder to the top of the tower.' The son tried to lift this huge rugged boulder, but he couldn't do it. He rolled it to the entrance, but it would not fit into the staircase. After a week he said, 'Father, I tried and I failed.' The father gave him a hammer. 'Break it to pieces.'" Jonathan paused. "That boulder is your heart."

○

The Bratzlavers find calling out in the Passover story. When the Hebrew slaves call out to God in their anguish, they evoke a response.

Indeed, the Bratzlav *ḥasidim* read Adam's silence when banished from the Garden of Eden as a failure of faith. Had Adam protested loudly enough, had he called out, God could have reversed the decision. They do not read the Torah, by the way, as a storybook. Adam, as Jonathan remarked dryly, is not some citizen of Mesopotamia. Instead, Adam is each of us, and the story speaks to the stony despair we freeze into when our hearts are shattered, in that critical movement in our lives from innocence to experience.

Calling out originates from a deep place of protest. It stems from the intuition that regardless of reason or reasons, a dimension of experience lies beyond reason—that the unreasonable cry for God's presence can cancel out the reasonable punishment of our guilt, the accumulated weight of our past. "When God says NOW," the Breslov Haggadah teaches, "He means, forget the past."

○

I was not sure I could call out. I rather liked my big boulder, in spite of the cracks in it.

"That's where people realize this isn't a game," Jonathan said. "It's an acknowledgment that most people past the age of twenty have broken hearts. There's no way you can't—if you are a whole person in the world. Whether of people very important to us dying, going mad, abandoning us or just—I don't like the life I'm living, I'm disappointed, my life seems meaningless . . . Nobody denies having a broken heart."

Jonathan told me he did not advise particularly fragile individuals to do this. But as far as he knew, no one had ever "freaked out."

"I guess if you don't cry out, something inside you cries out and it's demonic," I said. I was thinking of my own inner voices in Dharamsala years before.

Jonathan whispered, "Yeah."

"I have experienced that."

He paused. "It's the punitive voice used when one argues with one's loved ones. That punitive voice can get you."

"Yeah."

"As sure as eggs is eggs, that punitive voice is gonna get you."

"And it knows all your faults." I laughed. "It's pretty knowing."

"It feeds off them."

"It's pretty damn smart. It's almost a reversal of crying out."

"Yes. I get people to see if they're whining."

"You want people to listen to what they are saying?"

"Yes. This exercise leads to a very important distinction between essential or conscious pain and voluntary suffering."

Mark Borovitz first mentioned this.

"Voluntary suffering is the social way we protect ourselves against the exquisite nature of unbearable pain. Statements like: 'Poor me' or 'I can't stand it.' These statements or behaviors often have an audience. Now, voluntary suffering is an essential part of the way the organism works. We can't live with the exquisite pain for much of the time. It's like a cast we put on our arm. But by listening to their voices calling out, people discover their true pain, the true essential pain of their condition. When you touch that, it neutralizes the energy and the pain becomes easier to live with."

Robert Frost wrote that "the subject of poetry is grief, not grievances." "Voluntary suffering is grievances," I said. "Essential pain is grief."

"Griefs, not grievances," Jonathan said. "Exactly."

○

So what would I do? Jonathan said, "*Adonai* is the doorway to the *Yod Heh Vov Heh*." He'd added as a challenge, "If you want to stand in that revolving door the whole time, fine, but you can go out the other side."

That was on my mind my last day alone in Los Angeles as I drove down Wilshire to gas up the car. Jonathan had suggested a drive to Joshua Tree National Park. I stopped at the shopping center at Crescent Heights and Beverly, and ordered a tuna sandwich at Subway. I rolled down the window, peeled down the wrapper and, remembering Jonathan's image of the McDonald's drive-through blessing, tore a hunk out of the roll. I held it in my hand, stared at it, the brown outer covering, the spongy mass—soft tissue, white-webbed openings, labyrinth of wheat . . . I whispered, *Barukh Atah Adonai Eloheinu Melekh ha-olam*—saying it to myself, to my bread, fixing my mind on whatever is out there that is wide, generous, strange, and beyond. Then I looked down: *ha-motzi lehem min ha-aretz*, pinning down that large wide blessing onto the bread itself—hoping to connect the divine beyond to the divine spark in the bread, the particles, the crumby crumbs. I took the first bite slowly, chewing, tasting the gluey wheat mass, swallowing. The actual event was very simple. As Jonathan said, the forty-watt bulb. The *mishkan*, not Sinai. For a moment, I felt very high and connected and then—tuna again.

The curtain opens. The eye of the panther shuts. Tuna again, green peppers, jalapeños, nice sandwich eaten in the shopping-center parking lot on Wilshire outside Beverly Hills. I took a swig of cola, ate half my sandwich, saved the other half for later. I was on the blessing path: Definitely I'd go to Joshua Tree.

I headed east on the San Bernardino Freeway. Lots of early-afternoon traffic, brilliant sun shining, but a thick gray scrim obscured the hills. It soon got very hot and dry, traffic slowed down about an hour out of town, and then we were all just sitting on a giant hot parking lot. I thought, "Gee, this is the equivalent of going out in the woods and shouting, so maybe it's time to do it." I began to shout, over and over, "Please, God, tell me what you want, God," pushing myself to say it louder and louder until I was red in the face and rocking in the front seat, and just as Jonathan had suggested, tears came to my eyes—I heard the anger in my voice and frustration and a welling up of years—and then, I didn't know how, a plea shouted through me: "Open my heart! Please, God, open my heart! I've got to open my heart, please open my heart," again and again, howling, deeply anguished. My plea: to open my heart—to my wife, to my kids, to my friends, to strangers, everyone around me; make me generous, make me open, open my heart. I understood my failures of seeing, my blindness to the man in the airport, my blindness to others, my own preoccupation with myself and my ideas, my stiffness, my relying too much on the head, and being too quick to judge others as a failure of heart. Traffic moved, and I pulled over to the shoulder. Shouting at the windshield while other folks drove by. I felt the strength of doing this, that calling out hard enough, I penetrated below the level of grievances—hot day, frustration in the traffic—to the level of grief.

And from there, I heard a response. The beeper was in range. I picked up a new thought, a message that needed to be heard.

Open my heart.

○

I knew why I'd resisted the exercise. It came to me, later, that after all, once before I had done this calling out. "Everyone prays in the trenches," Paul Wolff had said.

When my son lay in the neonatal-intensive care unit, neither awake nor dead, I saw him hovering—the promise, the hope of an infant, hovering outside his body. In the evening, after spending all day beside him hoping he would open his eyes, I hurried home before returning at night. I walked my dog in an empty field across the street from where I lived. I called out in an empty field, cried out, not to heaven, but to the grass, the trampled flowers, dirt, discarded beams rusting against a metal shed, the August weeds dried and spindly, mounting towers of seed. I chanted his name in an abandoned field because I joined all hurt and damage there, crying to a boy who never raised a cry.

I remember searching the eyes of that dog. I caressed the dog, who stank in the hot August light. I prayed quite simply, "Come back to this world." Nothing answered, and nothing added up. I called a name against nothing. The dog barked and barked and broke free from my arms.

I called out my son's name. Come back to this world. I said it as a personal prayer. I didn't know from *Yod Heh* or *Vov Heh* or *Adonai* or doorsill. I was calling out the name of a boy lying a few miles away in a hospital, but I was calling out as well to—what? To the compassionate place in the universe. Address unknown.

I had called out then. But incompletely, in a broken language, in a field of weeds. I had felt completely alone. No triangulation, just me and my anguish. Paul Wolff understood in the hospital that all the parents were praying for the same thing, that in our suffering we are not alone. Now I understood. I called out, I shouted, I screamed, I scraped the bottom of my heart. And then a quiet place emerged, and from it I heard a quiet voice ask for one thing: open my heart.

O

When I got to Joshua Tree I felt very refreshed. I stopped off at a shop in one of the small towns for a soda. The storekeeper said, "There won't be much light left," then gave me directions: "You can go through the gates, the gates are open." In my state of mind, every phrase sounded like spiritual advice, every direction was for the heart as well.

The Joshua trees are delicate candelabra with bent arms holding sprays of green in their fists; they dot the landscape of the park, among large hollowed rocks like pelvic bones or chunks of ankle, broken femur, white and bare, smooth, with lots of reds and the preliminary green of sunset. It was cool after I entered the park, and I pulled over at a roadside marker. I wanted my feet on the ground. I hiked out in the sand, past clumps of plants here and there, large rocks ahead, like piles of rubble, stone on stone, some old disaster, and all the life bare and clinging: small purple flowers amid sprays of dark green plants like weeds in clumps and wisps of witch's hair and the Joshua trees everywhere like sentinels and sounds of birds calling back and forth, as in Judith's exercise.

I climbed. Some prayer is just praise, Jonathan said, and so since I knew no *berakhah* for the beauty of the landscape I sang "*Ma tovu . . .*" in the melody from Friday night at Beit T'shuvah; how moving to be in that tent in the middle of the city, "*ohalekha Ya'akov . . .*"—the tent of Jacob. The chandelier hanging in the middle there rimed with the Joshua Trees, so everything was displaced, but as the early *ḥasidim* understood so well, everywhere is a dwelling place of holiness. I could hang mezuzahs on the rocks like bones and on the Joshua trees' prickly arms, with the birds calling, the sun casting the shadow of the rocks behind me slowly on the hills. I stared long enough to see the shadow move. I thought of Shefa's psalm setting, "*Mah gadlu ma'asekha Yah*"—How great are your works, *Yah*, how deep are your designs (Ps. 92:6). I chanted it to myself, blessing, praising this moment, this place on earth, a temporary dwelling place of the spirit—a *mishkan*. Then I sat quietly, took it all in, a chill in the air—stood up and slowly walked back toward the car.

I heard a bird calling and stopped. On top of the highest arm of a Joshua tree, calling out. A small bird with an orange crest, orange going to salmon. I called back and he answered. We called back and forth. I stood very still.

A group of these birds ran past, upright—quail. They moved just out of sight behind scraggly weed hair, a spray of green to hide them. I edged slightly a few feet and saw them again. They detected me and ran on just out of sight.

Then I played the calling game with another one in a tree. Calling out. Calling out. The heart of the world and the spring of the world. I felt delighted to have such contact, such calling out again. My heart was open but with no human creature in sight, heart open to them and the land around me.

Judith's exercise, her favorite tale, the tale of Rabbi Nachman's crooked beggar, reset in the great American West. Two birds called one to the other, the cherubim on the ark cover who turned their backs after the great destruction calling back in longing, the universal longing we all feel. To hear and to be heard. Nachman's story taught me that the crying out we do in our anxiety and fear echoes the great longing of the heart of the world. Which is the pain that, if we only look, we can see all around us.

I left Los Angeles the next day. For a connecting flight out of Houston, we boarded a small bus. I noticed a woman traveling with her grandmother. The old woman had difficulty getting up the stairs, and her granddaughter carrying her bags could not aid her. Dozens of us watched and did nothing, thinking the usual—Not my problem. Then I heard my heart. We rode the bus to the airplane, waiting on the tarmac. I eyed them the whole time: this old lady and her tiny granddaughter. I stood at the bottom of steps of the bus and waited. When she came, I climbed up and took this old woman in my arms. "My leg does-n't work," she said. I lifted her. She was so light to lift off this earth and to hold and to help her down step by step as I backed down. It felt good somehow. Like I was supposed to be there.

○

A month later, I heard from Jonathan by phone. He told me that Judith's leaving him felt like he'd gotten off an ocean liner and found himself in a rowboat. But it was a good place to be, he said, a big ocean. At the close of our conversation I said I hoped he moved soon from the rowboat to a sailboat. He said he had to stay in the rowboat for a while.

I told him about calling out on the freeway. And a second time. I'd been driving this time between Baton Rouge and New Orleans. I was under pressure, because I was about to leave town again for Boston, where I would meet with Rabbi Arthur Green.

Meanwhile, my life was in chaos. After years of talking about it, Moira and I had decided to move from Baton Rouge to New Orleans. It all seemed overwhelming. Buying a new house, rent-ing our old one, finding decent schools for our kids. I had gotten ill from a bad meal, had no sleep, was exhausted from driving back and forth, my life divided between the two cities. I was full of anxiety, and not having anywhere to go with it. I called out. "God I'm angry, I'm so upset, I'm tired of being tired . . ." I was screaming, and when someone passed me and saw my lips mov-ing they sped out of my way: here I was going eighty-five with the radar detector on and shouting at God.

I prayed for balance. Then when the shouting was over, these words came up: "A thousand years are but a moment in thy sight, a thousand years are but a moment in your sight."

I repeated them over and over, loud and then softer, and I re-laxed. I'd combined primal-scream therapy, very dangerous dri-ving, and true calling out. And heard exactly the correct verse.

I took it to mean: you may be going through a very intense, anxious time right now, but from another perspective, it's a brief moment.

It's a slightly garbled verse from Psalm 90. "For a thousand years in your sight are but like yesterday when it is past, and like a watch in the night." And later I realized with a certain sense of coming full circle that it was from the same psalm Zalman quoted to me years before in Dharamsala. "So teach us to number our days that we may get a heart of wisdom."

When I told Jonathan, I could almost hear him smiling over the phone. He told me the universe was saying, "Lighten up, Kamenetz."

*Rabbi Arthur Green: Dancing on the Shores of the Sea*
Newton, Massachusetts
April 8, 1995; 8 Nisan 5755, one week before Pesach

●　　◐　　○　　◑　　●　　◑　　○

I came to Newton to see Arthur Green, rabbi and Lown Professor of Jewish Thought at Brandeis University. For many years, as a teacher, writer, leader, he has charted the heterodox Jewish spiritual path. I hoped he could help bring together my experience, help me understand the divisions I felt in Jewish life—between the mystical and nonmystical, the heterodox and the Orthodox, the female and male.

When I heard Arthur Green in 1993 at the Jewish Buddhist conference in Barre, Massachusetts, I learned that his connection to Buddhism is partly theological, but also personal. Raised in a secular household, he'd become devoted to Judaism, and his sister Paula was active with the Buddhist Peace Fellowship. Though very clear about his own views, he seems to understand, from the heart, the attraction of Buddhist teaching.

A few years before, he'd published a "contemporary theology", *Seek My Face, Speak My Name.* He told us at the conference he'd been accused of being a closet Buddhist, probably because his conception of divinity is closer to the *Ein Sof* of the kabbalists—the no-name, no-attribute God—than to the Lord who, with a strong arm and mighty hand, intervenes in history.

The blessing practice Jonathan taught me connects *Adonai* to YHVH, the lower and upper worlds, the broken bread crumbs of experience with the inconceivable light of the One. But in going through the doorsill from the personal to the impersonal, what about the historical?

The problem is already implicit in the Rambam. How can the God his philosophy describes, a God about whom nothing positive can be ascribed, be active in history or be the source of halakhah? This paradox led some pious Jews to burn the Rambam's writings and declare him a heretic.

I felt it personally: how can I connect this being, who escapes language, with the very concrete stories of the Jewish people? It was harnessing a locomotive to a whisper, tying rope around a soap bubble and hoping to rise to heaven. I found that Art Green, as a theologian, was asking the same questions.

At the Barre conference, he had told us gently, but with quiet emotion, "I've been on a journey of return to God through Jewish language for as long as I can remember."

But he added, "The journey has not been an even one. I've had moments of fullness and moments of emptiness and longing, lots of longing." In Rabbi Nachman of Bratzlav he found "a great master of longing—knowing emptiness is also fullness. When you say that to Buddhists it means something else," he added, smiling at Joseph Goldstein, the Jewish-born founder of the Insight Meditation Society.

But Green's personal journey has also been communal. After graduating from Brandeis in 1961, he studied at the Jewish Theological Seminary five years and was ordained as a Conservative rabbi. He returned to Boston to begin a doctorate at Brandeis. With a group of graduate students, he started Havurat Shalom (the peace havurah) in 1967. It became the most influential havurah group of its era.

Starting Havurat Shalom meant creating a community, he told me, "that wanted a different approach to Judaism—which we hadn't articulated yet. We knew it wasn't the coldness and the nonspirituality of the American synagogue and it wasn't the ultra-Orthodoxy of the hasidic world. We knew elements of warmth and intensity were going to be there. Many of us had read Buber on the hasidic community. Several of us were [Rabbi Abraham Joshua] Heschel's students. But we never felt the American synagogue had much room for the spirit of either

Buber or Heschel. So the community would incorporate some of the rebelliousness and freedom of Buber, some of the spiritual intensity of Heschel, be traditionalist in form and open to experimentation."

In short, the havurah was a vehicle through which non-Orthodox Jews could experience some of the fervor of hasidic prayer, and the beauty of hasidic teaching. The havurah model quickly spread to New York, Berkeley, Washington, Chicago, then, through *The First Jewish Catalog*, whose editors were members of Havurat Shalom and its offshoot, the New York Havurah. Under Art's leadership, and Reb Zalman's influence during the formative stages, the initial bent of Havurat Shalom was strongly mystical, modeled in part on the mystical Beit El group in Jerusalem, Ahavat Shalom. (Havurat Shalom, the peace havurah, began also as a yeshivah where Vietnam-era students could receive draft deferments.)

By American measures, the sixties is ancient history. But the continuing impact of the havurah model became clear in August 1994, when I taught at an annual meeting of the movement, the Havurah Institute. Rabbi Leonard Gordon, a Conservative rabbi from Philadelphia who studies the theology of havurah, told me, "The move from an architecture in which the rabbi is up on a bimah and the congregation below, to one in which the Torah is at the center of a circle, implies a whole new theology. In the old model, the rabbi is a professional holy man, living an exemplary Jewish life on our behalf. In the havurah model, there's a bit of God in each of us, and the Torah is at the center."

Rabbi Arthur Waskow, of Aleph, found his own Jewish bearings in the Fabrengen, a Washington, D.C., havurah. "Davening in circles was from the get-go not even planned, just the way you did it. A conscious theology grew out of it. If you spend five years davening looking at your comrade in the face, it becomes very clear that God is right there in the middle, not somewhere off very far away, not up there."

Judith Plaskow considers herself a "havurah Jew." She described the early havurahs as male-centered groups, but added that "many women, myself included, had our first experiences of egalitarianism in the context of havurot. I grew up in a Reform congregation that supposedly was totally egalitarian, but the religious role for women was to light candles on Friday night. I remember very clearly my first *aliyah*\* on Rosh Hashanah in the New York Havurah. I must have been about twenty-four. That *aliyah* was an incredibly moving experience for me."

As Plaskow indicates, the havurah experience underlies feminist Judaism and the Jewish renewal movement. Also, Reconstructionism, the fastest-growing formal denomination in the United States, experimented early with havurot and is closely allied with the movement. Art Green's pivotal role was confirmed by his appointment in 1986 as president of the Reconstructionist Rabbinical College in Philadelphia. He'd left that post for Brandeis in fall 1994. Now I visited him for an informal Shabbat *shi'ur* or study group, held with members of the local Newton Center minyan, some of whom are "alumni" of Havurat Shalom.

○

Art and his wife, Kathy, have a big and generous house with tall ceilings and large archways, and a staircase leading up to second and third floors. I arrived early, and as I waited on a green velvet couch, I noticed the coffee table loaded with new books, including essays on Gershom Scholem edited by Paul Mendes-Flohr and Herbert Levine's book on Psalms. Soon the room filled up. Art seemed surprised by the turnout—close to fifty at its peak, with some folks sitting at his feet. Thirty years since the movement started, our generation of Jews is still sitting around talking Judaism in a living room—though with greyer hair. When

---

\* *Aliyah*, in this context, means the honor of being called up to read from the Torah.

Kathy, Art's wife, saw the unexpected size of the crowd, she quickly retrieved some folding chairs.

Art grabbed a wool tallis and tossed it to Moshe Waldoks, who in one motion wrapped himself, rose, and began singing "Ashrei," the antiphonal hymn that opens afternoon prayer.* Later, at the standing prayer or *Amidah*, Moshe and others shukeled, lots of rapid bowing back and forth. I read the *Amidah* slowly. The traditional prayer book used exclusively masculine names for God.

We sat back in our seats for Art's *shi'ur*. As an early bird I had a prime perch on the velvet green couch. Art read from an old leather-bound volume phrase by phrase in Hebrew, translating on the spot, then commenting. Doing Judaism in English is a necessity with some advantages: translation stimulates contemplation, wrestling with meanings. In the interstices between the two languages interpretation seeps in like pure water finding its level.

The volume he held was *SHLAH* [*Sh*enei *l*uḥot *h*a-brit]: *The Two Tablets of the Covenant*, by Rabbi Isaiah Horowitz (1564–1630).[1] Horowitz is also known as the Shlah, after his book.

The Shlah had been the chief rabbi of Prague, but yearned for the Holy Land. In 1621, after his wife's death, he journeyed to Tzefat and Jerusalem, where he was received as a kabbalistic master. Through his extensive writings, meant as a legacy to the grown children he left behind, the Shlah transmitted the Lurianic kabbalah of Tzefat back to Eastern Europe, where it influenced the hasidic movement.

As Jonathan had done with the Breslov Haggadah, so Art selected mystical passages commenting on Passover. To the Shlah, matzah represents the *sefirah* of *binah*, the divine potency of understanding. Matzah is also the pure light of the first day of

---

* The hymn is a combination of Psalm 84:5, Psalm 144:15, and Psalm 145, and is also recited twice during morning prayer.

creation, spiritual light. Just as matzah has no leaven, so this pure light has no darkness, no shadow.

So the kabbalist sets out a poetic equation: matzah = pure light = *binah* = compassion.

The light of compassion, as reflected light, can be seen in the light of the moon. Art describes the Jewish people as *am levanah*, people of the moon, explaining that hidden beneath the cycle of religious holidays are full-moon festivals. Pesach comes with the first full moon of spring and Sukkot with the first full moon of autumn. For the settled agricultural society of ancient Israel, the three major pilgrimage festivals—Pesach, Shavuot, and Sukkot—represent the beating of the unsettled nomadic heart. The bright light of the moon over the desert is a nomad's beacon. The matzah is nomad's bread, cooked hastily over an open campfire.

Jewish lore conceals a deep poetry of experience. The trick is to find the gold behind the stove, to relive powerful moments of revelation, of discovery, when the world is seen anew.

These are the eternal moments in Torah. One is the gathering at the foot of Sinai. But Art points in his writing to another eternal moment of revelation in Torah of equal importance.

It is the moment Judith Halevy also recalled with a scrap of paper on her dining-room table: "A maidservant at the (Reed) Sea saw that which prophets did not see."[2] In the rush of exultant freedom comes a direct encounter with God. The dancing women and men have God at their fingertips. Pointing, they cry, "*Zeh eli*"—This is my God.

To Art, the Reed Sea and Sinai "are spiritual moments. As [German Jewish philosopher Franz] Rosenzweig says, of his three moments—Creation, Revelation, and Redemption—they are eternal. Not moments you experience only on Passover. They are modes of being or modes of relationship. So the liberation [at the Reed Sea] is a moment that can always be with you, that can always recur, that you always have to recall. That's one way of living, living in one's liberation, living in 'I am free of'. . . or 'I am free to.'"

The Reed Sea is our rebellious side, and Miriam's dancing a very different revelation from Sinai. "The 'Sea' is radical liberation," Art said, "seeing your enemies drown, knowing you're not going back there, you're going to be free."

Though, now in his full professorial authority, it is hard to see him this way; even Art's adolescent impulse toward Judaism was a rebellion against his atheistic father. Then in a new phase at Brandeis there came a second rebellion. He fell under the influence of some intellectual friends, and of Kafka and Nietzsche, those penetrating, uprooting questioners. He'd left "commitment"—celebrating with a gustatory rite of passage. "I went to a diner in Waltham and ate two treif hamburgers, and that was it. I gave up on observance." As he told the writer Bill Novak, "I soon came to feel that my Judaism was little more than a neurotic wall I had built to protect myself from the pain of dealing with my mother's death."

Paradoxically, even rebellion against religion can be holy. "When I stopped being observant, I felt terribly free and exhilarated. I look back on that time as one of great liberation, a kind of emotional *yetzi'at mitzrayim* [Exodus from Egypt.]"[3]

So how to accommodate rebellion within a religious structure, how to bring the energy of liberation back to the constancy, the *keva,* of commitment? Art Green's personal rebellion found an echo in the larger youth rebellion of the sixties. The havurah provided a constructive answer. It was a new holy space, a new *mishkan,* a shul for rebel Jews.

Art's theology takes up the same theme. "That Sinai is preceded by liberation from Egypt," he writes, "forces us to recognize that, for others as well as ourselves, liberation takes precedence to commitment. The struggle to be free in all of its many forms (including freedom from religion itself when it becomes a source of bondage), is a sacred struggle."[4]

After the *shi'ur* broke up, I rode home with Moshe Waldoks. Moshe has a Ph.D. in Jewish studies, but he's a natural nomad himself. Several years ago he left academia to freelance as a traveling entrepreneur of Jewish renewal. Now he was studying with Reb Zalman, Art Green, and Rabbi Everett Gendler for private rabbinic ordination (which he later received in the fall of 1996). Moshe's outdoor davening in Dharamsala was spectacular, and I was delighted the next morning when he asked me to daven with him.

We sat at his dining-room table, with racks and shelves from the oven spread out on newspapers for Pesach cleaning. As the last days ticked away toward seder, I missed being home. After my return from Los Angeles, I'd reviewed the four questions with my younger daughter—and she was doing well. But I felt guilty not being home so close to Passover.

Moshe and I recited the morning blessings and psalms. He taught me a *Shema* he'd learned from Reb Zalman. We used one long breath for each word. *Shema* on one breath and then prolonging the vowel sound *aaaaa* until it resonates with a metallic tinge. These sounds were not just being said, but made through and between us, a community of sound in and out of our bodies, echoing against the walls, windows, the metal racks on the table before me: one big *aaaaa*. Then came a long *ayl* in *Yisrael*. Then *ai* in *Adonai* and *uuu* in *Eloheinu*. That reminded me of the chanting I'd done with Joseph Mark Cohen, of the vowels of Eliahu.

After the *Shema Yisrael*, we chanted the *Ve-Ahavata*, very slowly, syllable by syllable. You shall love the Lord with all your heart, it commands—a strange and extraordinary command. How can you command love? The Hebrew reads, literally, "with all your hearts." A midrash explains: love the Lord with your divided heart, with your divided states of soul and mind. Love the Lord even with your doubts and conflicts.

We chanted together intensely as the sounds echoed into eternity's temporary home address: Lombard Street, Newton, Massachusetts. We then davened the *Amidah* together silently, Moshe finishing very quickly, while I much more slowly read word by word. I said, "Let's sing the *Sim Shalom* together," and he gave me a melody.

Afterward, over coffee, he confessed he's on the right wing of Jewish renewal because he prefers the old melodies over the new ones composed by Shefa Gold, Hannah Tiferet Siegel, and others. I said the old *nusah* (liturgical music) was entirely male and that women brought a new range to our davening, both melodically and in other ways. Yet I enjoyed my prayer with Moshe, the fellowship of two fellows, and felt how very male my world of Judaism often is.

I wanted to ask Art Green about that, and had an extraordinary opportunity about four days before Passover. We spoke also of his search for a Jewish language, why he prayed in the old one, what the Buddhist questions about Judaism meant to him as a theologian. Our conversation moved, along the path of dialogue, to a true encounter.

I'd spent the day being interviewed by Laurel Chiten, who was making a film inspired by my book *The Jew in the Lotus*. There were technical interruptions, time spent fussing with purple gel paper, to make the light right. Then the camera came on, and that lens sees everything. Toward the end she told me that she'd been discussing the project with a well-known Buddhist teacher, an author born a Jew. Laurel revered him. He'd informed Laurel that Judaism is a lowly religion. What did I think of that? she asked.

Not much. I'd heard that sort of thing from some Buddhist teachers with Jewish backgrounds—who ought to know better. It only demonstrated the work they had to do on themselves. I said, "Imagine him standing before his ancestors and telling them that the tradition that they preserved, often at the cost of their lives, is a lowly religion. That's what it looks like to me, Laurel."

She got it. Yet I wasn't entirely happy with my answer. It felt a point too self-righteous and defensive. And it begged the question. What if some religions *are* higher than others?

Laurel drove me over to Art's house after the taping. Art came to the door with a little dog trailing behind him, ferociously barking, but no sound coming from his mouth. He apologized for not feeding us, but explained that as Pesach was approaching and with the kitchen in tumult, this was no time for dinner guests.

I heard faint rattling of a teakettle and Art invited both of us to sit. He posted himself in a comfortable stuffed chair, with arms hanging down, his mute sheltie beside him, licking his palm extravagantly. Laurel could stay for only a few minutes, so, still rankled by her question, I decided to ask Art.

"We were talking about a statement by a Buddhist with a Jewish background who decided Judaism is a lowly religion."

"Nn-hunh," Art said, mildly and absently scratching his dog's ear. Art is a very large man—I would guess over 250 pounds.

"Wondered what you think of a statement like that," I said, laughing, and he laughed too. His laugh was rich chestnut brown—warm, generous bassoon notes.

"Well, God is in all the lowly places," he began. "Why shouldn't religion be lowly? God is lowly. God is lowly and uply, high and low and everywhere, so I don't see why religion shouldn't be lowly. On the contrary, the whole hasidic teaching is that you have to go down in the lowest places to find God, not just preserve your pristine holiness in the high places. So. Lowly isn't a very dirty word for me. You have to get dirtier than that to get me upset."

I thought Art had it right on the money.

"I spoke in Phoenix, Arizona, last fall," he went on, "and a guy came up to me and said, 'Yeah, but Judaism is really that angry god who makes Abraham kill his son and who wants child sacrifice and who makes people suffer and who kills people. And how could you have such a religion with such an angry . . . ?' This guy was so angry! Who's angry here?" Art laughed low and bubbly.

To me the whole lure of Buddhism is its strong take on anger. Buddhist practice directly addresses anger as a poison, and many

Jews, by virtue of our history, are contaminated by it. Becoming a Buddhist doesn't always clean out the corners of anger; the place you feel you have left behind is likely to be the darkest.

I was glad anyway that Laurel heard Art's answer. It hadn't occurred to me to answer so neatly that lowly is a good place to be. But, of course, where else is the door of pain? I wanted to test that notion with Art.

"How do people come to a deeper commitment to Judaism as a spiritual path?" I asked after Laurel left, feeling too formal and pompous, alone now in Arthur Green's formidable presence.

"I want to stop your sentence."

(Please, I thought.)

"How do people come to a deeper commitment to Judaism," Art repeated. "How do people come to a *deeper*—? Stop right there. How do people gain depth? So pain is probably the easiest, most obvious way. We don't like to recommend suffering as a recipe, but it sure helps. It's probably a more obvious way to depth than other ways. But I have to believe there are other ways. Not because of personal experience, mind you . . . but . . ." He paused, listened and listened, closed his eyes and held his head to the side. I wondered what he touched on in his memory. The sheltie panted and Kathy slid drawers open in the kitchen. "I just do," he finally said, opening his eyes. Then he added, as if it were a lucky thought, "The Baal Shem Tov is a very different path. An opening to perception, to joy. There is a way of wholeness that finds its way to depth. A path of compassion for other people not necessarily born of one's own suffering but which goes to a very deep open place."

Art added that when he asked people "about the moments when they met God, what their Sinais were," he often heard stories about birth. A "pain story" for the woman, he admitted, but "mostly a joy story—finding God in exultation."

The question reminded Art of a midrash. "To what may Abraham our father be compared? To a man walking through the wilderness who sees a *birah doleket*—this seems to mean 'a burning tower.' He says, 'Could there be no master of this tower?' Then the master of the tower looks at him and says, 'I am the master of the tower.'

"So Abraham saw the world was a *birah doleket*. God looked out of it and said, 'I am the master of the world.' Most people translate that as 'a burning tower.' Heschel translated it as 'a castle full of light.' Because *dolek* can mean 'burning on fire' or 'glowing with light.' So I take that as two paths. You can find God by seeing the world is on fire—an existential crisis—or by seeing that it's so glowing with light . . ."

I understood. I understood better thanks to Jonathan and my time on the San Bernardino Freeway, yelling my head off to an unknown address, and then arriving at Joshua Tree and suddenly being open to the beauty there. At times the burning and the light are one, the pain and the joy are one. These are individual moments, glimpses. But how do they connect to Torah?

I recalled again my conversation with Rabbi Nehemia Polen. Rabbi Polen stressed that Judaism is primarily communal, which is why his favorite book is Leviticus. I replied that mine was Genesis, the favorite of Jewish mystics. I read there paradigms for individual spiritual encounters: dream visions, night visions, the personal prayer, the calling out to God of women and men, Hagar and Eliezer, the anguish of Sarah, the growth and transformation of Abram to Abraham, and Sarai to Sarah, of Joseph the dreamer to Joseph the dream interpreter, of Jacob to Israel. These stories speak to the individual search for a Jewish inner life.

Such moments need affirmation, especially now in Jewish life, where they are so often suppressed or ignored. A Jew who seeks a spiritual experience is told to join a synagogue, pay dues, send kids to Sunday school, and contribute to the UJA. What in this program speaks to the individual moment of revelation?

There are such moments, of calling out and hearing a response. Yet I could not stay in those moments. Every ecstasy leaves a trail of questions, some from the idiot questioner, some from deeper places. As Franz Rosenzweig writes of his own spiritual experiences, "The reasoning process comes afterwards. Afterwards, however, it must come."[5]

There are such moments, and they need to be understood in a Jewish language.

More, they need a Jewish meditative practice so they can be cultivated and understood in a Jewish context. Or as Jonathan put it, Jewish meditation creates a Jewish context.

I told Art about a friend, a former Catholic monk who meditated by visualizing biblical passages, the ecstatic moment when David dances before the Ark of the Lord. Were there, perhaps, similar Jewish meditation practices to bring us back to the Reed Sea?

Art paused a long time in reflection. "The answer," he said, finally, "is those practices are not much developed in the tradition. They're there and nobody has developed them. Or they're there and they've lain fallow for a long time. And they are waiting to come out again."

I felt my friend Eliahu Pinchas beside me, with all his urgency for a Judaism lived from moment to moment. Where's the beef? he would say.

"Why was it decided," Art mused, "in the seventh or eighth century that we'd recite the Song of the Sea [in the morning prayer] every day? What does it mean to do that? How much is the liturgy meant to be visualized and not just mumbled? We are so conditioned by people who treat it in a pedestrian way that it's hard to get back to the moment when the people who first did that really had it as a living tradition. In general that's the problem with Judaism."

What of Jonathan Omer-Man's emphasis on *keva*, the regularity of spiritual practice, and how such regularity could be boring? "It's impossible to expect that every morning you will have a revelatory experience."

Art agreed. "You can't always reach there, but you want to be open to it. You keep the watch wound so that sometimes, something exciting and important will happen." Then he added that his own prayer practice was sporadic. That surprised me, because when I first heard him in Barre, prayer seemed central to his religious practice. Now, he said, "it has ups and downs, regular periods and irregular periods. Of course I still have hopes of such [revelatory] moments or I wouldn't pray." He paused. "Maybe that's too strong a formulation."

"You'd pray anyway?"

"Yes."

Art went back to my question about the Reed Sea meditation. He suggested places to look: the commentaries on the siddur, midrash, Zohar. Then he put his finger on the question behind my question, my own need to tie every move I made to a Jewish text.

"We worry too much about what's in the texts," he said, "and I don't think that's the criterion for everything. The religious form—the act—I believe, preceded the text."

I was taken aback again. He had deftly uprooted my question. I knew Art's deep devotion to Jewish text; his whole life is spent immersed in it. I'd witnessed the day before the loving way he'd midwifed new life from the old bound volume of Shlah.

"For us Jews," he said, "the beginning is always the text." He paused. "No," he announced, "the beginning is not always the text. There's another Torah behind the written Torah."

To me this sounded like the experience of the divine that Shefa Gold spoke of, that comes before the words we use to describe God.

He told me a story. "The Vilna Gaon is the great opponent of hasidism, the master of the law who opposed the new teachings of the hasidic masters. So somebody asks him a very difficult legal question, the most difficult of his life. He studies and comes back with an answer, permitting a certain action to save somebody's life. The man says, 'I want you to know, I asked the same question of the *Maggid* of Mezritch two weeks ago and I wrote down his answer. Here it is.' The Vilna Gaon reads and it's the same.

"He says, 'This is impossible. I gave my answer only on the basis of the Jerusalem Talmud, which nobody studies but me, and on the basis of a *gersa*, a manuscript version of the Jerusalem Talmud, which nobody else has. So this is impossible.'

"The man says, 'Here it is: I have it written down for you.'

"And the Gaon says, 'You go back to Mezritch and ask this *maggid* where he got such an answer.' Of course the man goes back to Mezritch. The *Maggid* says, 'Tell the Vilna Gaon I got the answer the same place the Jerusalem Talmud got it from.'"

"What place is that?" I asked.

"I talked the other night of going back to the primitive memory of the tribes that became Israel when they ate the nomad's bread by the spring full moon. That came before Pesach was an historical festival, before it was the story of the Exodus from Egypt." He paused and breathed in deeply, as if to succor his speculation. Sometimes he'd enter a college-lecture mode in our conversation, holding his head to one side, not looking my way. "But maybe, even, there's a before-the-before-the-before-the-text, and the text came to explain things people were doing already. I'm saying there's a level of—not only historical antiquity, but also of depth of spiritual antiquity. There's an antiquity of the self, antiquity of the soul. In Hebrew *'atik* עתיק means both "ancient" and "deeply known,"—deeply well known. So it comes before the text." He paused and looked into the distance again. I thought, Come on, look my way, and finally he turned and his face opened. "You asked me if there were visualizations for the Song of the Sea. The Song is there, and you sing it and become the text. You dance it and you become the text." He pointed at me, hopelessly sunk in his green velvet couch.

"The same with the seder?" I asked, smiling.

"Yes, reliving. The Exodus happens to you. It happens now. I want to push a step further. We're judging so much. Maybe I have our friend with the 'lowly religion' still in mind. We get into a mind-set: 'If the texts are good enough, we'll like this religion, we'll take this religion. If there's nothing real great in the texts, then it's not good enough for us.' We want something great in the texts. Maybe great isn't in the texts. Maybe great is in you." He gave me a long, searching look.

I understood: he was giving a kind of permission, a blessing. If I want to make a Reed Sea meditation, the way is open. The time for creating new language is now. He was also answering the Bentley question. Judaism is a great vehicle, and you do have to fix it yourself. That's the beauty of it.

Art thought Buber missed something when he described the traditional forms of Jewish practice as merely inertial. "The ancient forms have an accrued holiness because all these generations have lived them—and then there's you doing this form."

Did only holiness accrue? Did Buber have a point?

"I'm in dialogue with Buber all the time," Art said. "At one time I said, 'I'm a Buberian,' but I'm a traditionalist. I love the forms. I understand Buber very well when he says how dangerous the forms can be and how much they can block one's spiritual life. But Buber didn't create anything. You can't live his religion."

"In other words, what's the practice?"

"There's no practice. And without a practice I don't think you can do it. Buber would say the practice is whatever you are doing. The practice is right now. The practice is this conversation."

"It's our encounter."

"Right. You don't interrupt this practice to go daven. You daven right now while we're doing this conversation. That's the davening. That's the practice. That's very intense, very demanding, very hard to live with, and very hard to communicate and build community around." Yet Buber seems to be articulating the Judaism of the moment that Paul Wolff and Mark Borovitz speak of.

Buber rejected any division between religious experience and everyday life. This was for him the essence of hasidic thought, what he derived from the hasid's insistence that there is nothing else but God. Buber did not even want to distinguish between meditation and everyday life. He told the story of a young man who came to see him after Buber had emerged from an "ecstatic" meditation. Buber felt he failed to be fully present for the encounter. When the young man committed suicide shortly thereafter, Buber felt some responsibility. He decided the truly holy practice is always to be present for the other person.

Buber confronted in this incident a dilemma many meditators feel, between the sublime and blissful states achieved in private meditation and the demands of living in the world. Buber vowed from that time on never to leave the world solely to cultivate states of mind.

Traditional Judaism also struggles with the tension between this-worldly concerns and spiritual aspiration. The rabbis ask, 'Which mitzvot, laws, are most important?' Or, 'When is it right to interrupt the mitzvot of study, or prayer, to do another mitzvah?' 'What about to save a life?'

But Buber felt mitzvot and halakhot, the commandments and the laws, were in themselves spiritual slavery. I don't agree, but at times I share Buber's impatience. "Do we keep *everything* in Judaism because we don't know what to get rid of?" I asked Art.

He said the question softly to himself. "We're so afraid. The traditionalists are so afraid to let go of anything. It's the legacy of persecution, of being a minority group for so long."

"I'll tell you why I asked that," I said. "When we were in Dharamsala, Zalman's question for the Tibetans in exile was, 'Which practices do you keep and which do you jettison?' But we unorthodox Jews are also in that position. We are trying to find a path of spirituality while choosing and selecting which practices to keep. Yet we have no criteria for picking and choosing. If I decide not to keep Shabbat in the traditional way because it's inconvenient for me, then my criterion doesn't travel any higher than the ego. How can you have a spirituality in which personal convenience is the highest authority?"

Art paused. "Let's talk about that." Then he rested, with his brow furrowed, just thinking. "Until now," he said, "the great challenge to my Judaism, the sister faith from which I've learned most, was always Roman Catholicism. I've always been attracted to the way the Catholic Church preserved its spiritual life. Monastic communities were the great bastions of spirituality in the West. I could listen to Gregorian chant for hours. I feel a kinship to a deep classical Western spirituality that the Church has preserved. I also feel tremendously challenged by the legacy of Vatican II. *Aggiornamento*—the Church could really do it. It jettisoned a whole lot of stuff that for many people was essential to being Catholic. Fish on Friday for God's sakes! Saint Christopher and lots of saints in between . . . The Church said, 'No more. We don't need it anymore.'"

"Mass in Latin," I suggested.

"Mass in Latin. I thought they were wrong on that one, because we tried it in Reform Judaism and it doesn't work, we're going back to Hebrew. But they managed to do it. Though the Church has suffered tremendously in thirty years and lost a lot of people, it has come out spiritually more healthy for having let certain things go. It shed the heavy baroque accrual of tradition. Because the Church was able to say, 'The real question is not fish on Friday, the real question is Christ.' For a long time, the Catholic Church had lost that question to Protestantism and was able to recover that in very powerful, wonderful ways.

"So now I'm beginning to feel the challenge of this dialogue with Buddhism. One way is on this question of letting go. Buddhist practice seems so much to be detachment and shedding things. Judaism is not about that. It's about making commitment and joining, carrying it all with you. Jews went out in the wilderness with *milchik* pots and *fleishik* pots,* and sets of books, big multivolumed commentaries, on their backs. It's very hard to do a Jewish spiritual life and travel light. Yet the traveling-light image does attract me, I must say."

"There's that nomad in the moonlight again."

"That nomad again—and this guy has been carrying too much around for a very long time." He looked down at his stomach and then back at me. "Right, that's true too."

I laughed nervously.

"No," he said with emphasis, "I'm serious about that. It's an issue that touches my spiritual life as well, that's related to my spiritual life." I nodded. The more we talked, the more deeply personal our conversation became, as if we were traveling down Buber's path of holy encounter.

"So," Art said, "it's hard to do Judaism and travel light. Judaism is not mostly about letting go, but mostly about attachment to God, through attachment to tradition, attachment to forms. You meet God in the halakhah, the practice, the Book. The Baal Shem Tov is unusual in just meeting God without all those accruals."

"But, does God have admission requirements? Is there an entry-level test?"

He paused a long time. "I think yes. I think I say yes." I was anxious to hear if I could pass. "That is, recognizing God's image in other human beings. If you can't be a mensch in the way you treat others, then God doesn't want you messing up the courtyards. But that's the only entrance requirement I know.

"In terms of a knowledge requirement or observance requirement," Art added, "no. The entrance requirement is that you walk in. You have to walk in the gates and not just stand there

---

* Kosher cuisine necessitates separating *milchik* (dairy) and *fleishik* (meat) cooking utensils.

like the character in Kafka's 'Before the Law' and make yourself an outsider and feel alienated your whole life and scratch your behind and say, 'I'm alienated.' You have to walk in."

Kafka, I said, should be added to the Jewish canon, our own Ecclesiastes. Art replied that Gershom Scholem and Walter Benjamin also proposed adding him to the canon. But he didn't share that enthusiasm. Having "wandered in Kafka land" himself, he said that the writer offers no way out.

"Kafka was the best describer of the pain of our situation," Art said. "Nachman went to those same deep mythic places—but did so with faith."

Art had found in Nachman answers to the questions that prompted his rebellion against observance. For many readers, Green's penetrating psychological biography of Nachman, *Tormented Master*, offers a paradigm of the hasidic master as a spiritual seeker. He makes of Nachman our own rebbe of doubt.

After my time with Jonathan, I understood well Nachman's appeal in our time even to liberal Jews, an appeal Art Green had done much to foster. Nachman spoke of "the philosopher in the heart"—the inner voice of doubt and skepticism. I'd heard that voice often. Sometimes even in the midst of dancing at the Reed Sea—at a Jewish renewal Shabbat—I'd pinch myself and rub my eyes. Is this real or a delusion? I thought about how difficult it had been for me to try the calling-out exercise, Nachman's *hitbodedut*, which his *hasidim* describe even today as "the door to heaven." I loved the moment when I let go of my questions—and settled for ecstasy—but it sometimes took a lot of work on myself to get there.

For Nachman, who felt the winds of Enlightenment change coming to the shtetl, even the moment of doubt is sacred. In fact, especially sacred. The moment of supreme doubt is a main gate, another door to God.

But, as Nachman predicted in despair toward the end of his life, for most of us the crisis has gone beyond doubt. Today, there's an absence of questions. We don't know that we don't know, we don't care that we don't care. I wondered how Art would define this moment in Jewish history.

"I would say the Jewish people is shrinking, we will be a smaller and more spiritually interesting body a generation from now. That includes both claimants for the mantle of authentic Judaism, the Orthodox and the heterodox. There will be two of them; the divisions are growing.

"However you slice it, this is a new age in the history of the Jewish people. Even if you go to the broadest divisions"—biblical and Diaspora Judaism—"the biggest piece, this long Diaspora period, began to end two hundred years ago, first in Germany." He defined it as the period when the Jewish people defined itself in terms of loyalty to halakhah. "That's gone now for about eighty-five percent of the Jewish people. We left the later Middle Ages and went through a crisis of modernization and transformation. Now we are in a postmodern period, which is to say a good number of us are trying to come back to a spiritual life through Judaism on the other side of a great divide. We have lost our naive faith. The great divide is that we have lost our naive faith. We no longer believe in God as the personal figure who rewards and punishes and rules history and conducts the universe. We are no longer believers in the redemptive quality of history, largely because of the Holocaust, though for many of us that would have happened before, or without the Holocaust. And we're no longer literal believers in knowing divine will—in knowing what God's will is. If God's will is the Torah—it no longer is to us. So we've lost our naive faith in all the major questions: God, creation, revelation, and redemption. And yet we want to rebuild."

Art explained that was why he felt comfortable heading the Reconstructionist Rabbinical College for seven years. Not that he is a Reconstructionist by dogma, but that the founder of Reconstructionism, Mordecai Kaplan, affirmed that "people had the right to say yes, we're trying to re-create a Judaism for people who can no longer pretend to have naive faith. To me, that's the real place that should be dividing us from Orthodoxy. It shouldn't only be the question of halakhah. We want a Judaism that responds to the far side of the crisis of faith."

I asked him to explain further.

"By naive faith, the sense that there's still a beneficent, personal God who rules history, who rules the external world, providentially guiding the fate of individuals and nations."

"Don't you think when we talk of uniting the transcendental and the immanent, then we have to believe that's the case? If only for a moment?" I was thinking of the blessing path Jonathan had taught, my Subway sandwich to heaven: prayer to unite this world, down to its bread crumbs, with a world beyond. The divine algebra of YH plus VH. I'd had such moments, many times, and lost them many times. "Maybe we lack the nobility of the past, but can we live without faith?"

"We don't eliminate faith," Art corrected me, quickly. "Of course we can't eliminate faith, but we have to not pretend. We have to not pretend. But that's too . . . " He hesitated. "I don't like what I'm saying. That's too judgmental." He paused. "Sometimes it's nice to pretend." He let that hang and went silent for a very long time. He was clearly unsatisfied with that statement as well. We were entering together another intimate moment. I remembered the mezuzah meditation, how in a conversation like this, one sees a door, and a mezuzah, because such a passage is guarded by the Holy One. It was ironic given the crushing frankness of what he was about to say. "I guess honesty is very important to me, Rodger," he said, speaking personally, very tenderly. "I want a faith about which I can be honest. And not have to hide from reality, not have to lie about how reality is. Too much of religion is a lie." He breathed out slowly. "Too much religion is lying about the way reality is." He spoke these words very softly and wistfully, like a sigh given to words, then quoted from the morning prayer, where God is praised for miraculous powers. "*Someikh noflim ve-rofei ḥolim* [who lifts the fallen and heals the sick], you know?" he said softly, regretfully. "And the stumbler remains fallen and the sick die."

"The dead aren't raised."

"The dead aren't raised. And here we are. We want to say those things and we reinterpret them like crazy, and reinterpreting is OK—but there comes a time to remind ourselves that no, that's not what we believe. We are not literalists, we are not naive about any of those things."

"What about *matir asurim* [freer of the captive]?"

"Yeah, there are moments when God does that. Moments when God does all of them."

"That's true."

"There are moments when God does *meḥayei ha-meitim* [gives life to the dead]. I know that's happened to me many times, but . . ."

"You don't mean your death, you mean what?"

"I mean deadly."

"Being deadly?"

"I mean dead to my own spiritual life. Dead to the presence of God in the world. Dead to that deeper reality. Then God comes and kicks me in the butt and wakes me up again through an interview with Rodger Kamenetz, or a death, or things like that."

"Dialogue with something outside yourself."

"Sometimes. You never know how God's going to do it. It's full of surprises. The old fellow is full of surprises."

I was touched, deeply, that he felt our conversation, our encounter, had such qualities of depth. When he gets into his professorial mode, Art projects a certain austerity—but in the course of several hours of conversation, we had passed through that narrow place, had moved to a feeling of intimacy. "Is it hard for you to remain open," I asked him, "when you are constantly asked to be the expert, the solemn authority?"

"I'm not constantly asked to," he said slowly, "but it's hard for anyone to remain open. But open is how we are supposed to remain. So yes, it's hard. I close up and as I say, I have great fortune, great good fortune that I keep getting kicked open again and again. The door into my heart has been pounded on so many times it seems to open pretty easily. So I then become open again. I feel like an old warhorse a little bit, you know. And my war is to remain open. There are people who demand more of it and people who demand less. My problem is that I'm usually among people who demand too little of it. So then it's easy to close up again."

"What do they ask?"

"Sometimes footnotes. Sometimes pats on the head." He laughed with a deep, ratcheting sound. The sheltie licked the chair leg. It was time for a confession of my own.

"Jonathan Omer-Man suggested I try the Bratzlav technique of crying out." I paused. "Where do you cry out in today's world?"

"In the car," Art said.

"On the freeway in the car. When I started calling out, at first it was like playacting, then got more and more serious. The prayer was three words. Over and over. 'Open my heart.' I thought I'd tell you that."

"You didn't have to," Art whispered. "I know it well," he said, a little louder. "That's what I pray for. That's how my prayers always begin."

"Really?"

"There's not much else to pray for," he said, very quietly. "To remain open. To remain vulnerable. To be willing to live enough on the edge so it stays right there. To feel the fullness and feel the presence—you have to have an open heart to do that. Open heart to be able to give it to others, because others know when it comes from the heart."

I know. I knew.

●　　　◐　　　○　　　◑　　　●　　　◐　　　○

Art and Kathy were putting dishes away for Passover. After we broke from the interview for hard pretzels and coffee, we spent an hour or so carefully moving chametz food from the kitchen cabinets to the basement—pretzels, flour, anything not kosher for Passover. We stuffed non-Passover silverware into paper bags and stored other items in high cabinets. Art stood on a stepladder and sealed the doors with masking tape. Art and Kathy consulted back and forth about different items. We loaded forks, spoons, knives, nut picks onto metal trays and carried them into the dining room, along with stacks of dishes. Must a corkscrew be banished or could it remain? Is putting up silverware a spiritual practice? Is it a meditation—the "endless tea ceremony," as Paul Wolff put it? All this fine consideration and careful thought seemed more complex because Art and Kathy did not consult books of halakhah.

What were they consulting? Art explained that his sense of the rules derives from his memories of his childhood, "all of the cousins going to my grandparents' house the Sunday before Pesach, and carrying the *pesadike*\* dishes down from the attic. It was a big deal, who was a big enough grandson to carry a big platter. That was a real ritual event of early childhood."

"So it's not in relation to law?" I asked him.

"No no no no no. I'm not a law person. I'm very Buberian. When it's law, it's frozen. I'm not a law person," he repeated.

"Well?"

---

\* Kosher for Passover.

"It is a living form that somehow has been passed down from one generation to the next as an expression of love. Does it come from God? The answer is yes and no, but the love passed down from generation to generation has a divine presence in it. God is there in the love with which these forms are passed down. That love somehow shines forth from the form, is discoverable in the form. Radiates from it. I don't believe with Buber that the form is necessarily a trap. The form is brimming with light and love put there by the generations. We can discover that love and find it in the forms. That's where I disagree with Buber. The idea that all forms are never real bearers of the divine presence seems mistaken. But once it's law and it's codified . . . I never look things up. I never go to a law code to find out can you do this or can you do that. I'm really not a by-the-book Jew in that sense."

"So what are you thinking," I said, "as you decide what to do with that corkscrew?" It lay on a tray in front of us. Art hefted it for a moment, thinking out loud.

"It's what I know," he said. "It's what I remember, from the way we did it last year and the year before." He turned the screw absently, then tossed it into the reject pile—banished from the realm of *pesadik*. "A corkscrew has movable parts—they're attached different ways; no, it can't be kashered. I know it by instinct—the instinct of my kitchen."

He cited the sociologist Haym Soloveitchik's article in *Tradition*.[1] Soloveitchik is the son of the late Rav Joseph Soleivichik, the great teacher of modern Orthodoxy. "He talks about the decline of the mimetic tradition in contemporary Orthodoxy. In Eastern Europe people learned to keep kashrut by watching their grandmothers or watching their mothers, and people kept Shabbas the way their parents kept it. Today in Orthodoxy everything is by the book. You look it up and find out what the proper rules are because many of the people"—the *ba'alei teshuvah*—"weren't raised Orthodox and even if they were they're trying to be more Orthodox than their parents were. I am in that sense a traditionalist rather than a legalist. I don't care about doing precisely right in the legalistic terms. I really care about doing it the way traditional Jews do it. If I have a question, I don't look it up in a book, I ask an Orthodox rabbi friend."

Yet, like Jonathan, Art is not a strictly halakhic Jew, and though this had its own complexities, I could see that for some Orthodox his path might be seen as the easy way out. He told me how one Orthodox critic approached him after a lecture and asked him to stop calling what he was doing Judaism. "'You're creating a different religion. We know what Judaism is, Judaism is the halakhah. This is not Judaism, call it something else. Truth in advertising,' he said."

Because of our difference in backgrounds, Art and I viewed halakhah from different angles. I'd felt undernourished, he overstuffed. The Reform Judaism I grew up with—in many quarters it's changed—stripped the halakhic menu from a rich banquet to fast food. But the Conservative Judaism Art knew had spent too much time niggling over details. He described his time at the Jewish Theological Seminary in scathing terms. "They had great thinkers in their midst—Heschel, Kaplan—calling for two very different but very powerful spiritual remakings of Judaism. They rejected both of them and worried about whether you can drive to shul on Shabbas and whether cheese is kosher and whether you can eat fish out in restaurants—little things. The energies of the Conservative movement went into the Law Committee for all those years, and that's not what the people needed. Nobody cared about those decisions except the rabbis. Meanwhile the movement could not talk about 'Why should we keep this thing going?' 'Why should we observe at all?' 'What's the spiritual meaning?' We didn't begin to have a language for that. So I have been overfed halakhah and want to step back from it somewhat. That's my own personal story as a former Conservative rabbi."

"Are you on a halakhic diet?" I asked him, letting my stack of dishes down on the dining-room table.

He laughed. "[The Hebrew poet] Bialik has this wonderful essay, 'Halakhah and Aggadah,'[2] and he talks about the interrelationship between the two and how one is the crystallization of the other. A new halakhah will only come out of a new aggadah. Finding a theological language, finding an aggadah, is important."

In other words, the poetry of Judaism—not the law—is the first step of the path. I did not think Orthodox Jews would agree with that formulation. But Jonathan, in a different way, had also stressed that the Torah in all its dimensions is a poem of poems before it is a law book.

Art told me we are in a crisis in both areas: a crisis in faith and religious language, and a crisis in praxis. Aggadah and halakhah. "We need to develop new faith and religious language. Practice will come out of that, rather than concentrating too immediately on it."

I went back to the kitchen for some more plates, wondering what he meant by *praxis*. When I came back and set my dishes I told Art I didn't think of halakhah that way. "It's a system of laws, some with deep spiritual wisdom and power, and others, not. I'm not sure which are which."

"I'm not sure either. I don't have an answer for you. It's a very serious problem. Halakhah began to run away with itself very early in Jewish history. The New Testament authors who made fun of halakhah already knew what they were talking about. You know, plucking ears of corn on the Sabbath, healing the sick on the Sabbath. Paul came along and said, 'It's the law that condemns you, the law always makes you feel guilty and therefore condemns you.' He and the gospel understood the problems of halakhah very early."

I followed him for more dishes as he talked, thinking about halakhah running away with itself as I ran back and forth from dining room to kitchen. Why were we doing this, then? What were we enacting? Was it a wistful home movie of Art and Kathy Green's childhood? Or the preservation of a living spiritual tradition? What was appropriate when dealing with the law—rebellion or submission? The Reed Sea or Sinai?

Art spoke of these issues as a "tension," and I could see the tension within myself as we prepared for Passover. The traditional Jewish claim, and one I take very seriously, is that each mitzvah holds a kernel of spiritual wisdom, which can be known only in the doing. But still the philosopher in the heart is not as pious and ridicules me. Does God want me to move a dish into Art Green's living room? For moments in my life I am willing to say wholeheartedly yes. But only to those commandments I feel as a strong calling. Given my background that is where I begin—with what speaks to me.

In my morning prayers, I recite a list of *mitzvot she-ein lahem shi'ur*—mitzvot without measure, boundless mitzvot. They can be done as often as we like. They are beautiful practices I try to integrate into my life, guidelines for being a decent person, and for the possibility of holy relations with others. *Gemilut ḥasadim:* deeds of loving-kindness. *Ha-pe'ah*—literally, leaving a corner of the harvest for the poor, but now, direct acts of charity. *Talmud Torah:* study. A second list of mitzvot has rewards both temporal and eternal: among them, honoring mother and father, welcoming guests, visiting the sick, honoring the dead, rejoicing with bride and bridegroom, enabling friendships. Many we do naturally, Jew or non-Jew alike, but to think of them as mitzvot adds to their power for me. Then the doing becomes more than doing, it becomes possibly holy.

Yet that is a long way from what is called "Torah Judaism," the faith that commits itself to doing all the mitzvot, both from the Torah and from those derived (in the formation of rabbinic Judaism) through the halakhic method. It is an all-or-nothing faith that says that either all the Torah *and* rabbinic mitzvot are grounded in divine will or none of them are. Here I find myself on the far side of faith, naive or not. (I am not willing to say such faith is purely naive.) But I do not believe literally in the assertion that opens the Pirkei Avot, that an oral teaching was passed down from God to Moses at Sinai, to Joshua, to the men of the Great Assembly and on to the rabbis. There the skeptic in me shouts out loud, as Jonathan would say.

As we went down to the basement with some boxes, Art told me of his own halakhic wrestling. "I am a great believer in Shabbat," he said, "—one of the great institutions the Jewish people has created. As Kathy said one Friday night, 'Whoever invented Shabbas really did a mitzvah.' So whether it's from God or Torah or the soul, the basic form of Shabbat seems to work. I like keeping Shabbat in a pretty traditional way. But when you look at the details of laws of Shabbat—how to celebrate Shabbat in all the thirty-nine categories of work and all that derive from them, and the thousands and thousands of things you have to be careful not to do because you might be violating Shabbat in some ways—it's just crazy, it's overwhelming. Spiritually choking. Living in that environment is not at all attractive to me. So how do I draw the line? Do I draw the line at the things my family said were silly? Not necessarily. I feel more strict about some things than the halakhah. To me it's outrageous that people have the TV going with a Shabbas clock. Say if there's a big game on, and the teenage son wants to watch it. I'm more traditionalist than that. Yet I am very selective. The problem is I'm a non-Orthodox Jew, and halakhah ultimately doesn't matter to me."

I might not have put it that strongly, but Art has clearly thought these things through with some rigor. He continued, "There aren't absolutes. There are no more absolutes for me— except probably something like the seven Noahide commandments and treating other people like the image of God. Those are probably my only moral absolutes. Maybe they're enough absolutes."

What, I thought, not even the Ten Commandments?

"I'm a traditionalist," he said. "I really like keeping Shabbas— staying home on Shabbas and walking to shul on Shabbas and doing nothing else. But I had six Shabbatot in a row, working this spring. I should never have taken them. One was in suburban Boston. I decided I'd rather travel back and forth in the car to that synagogue and be home with Kathy and be in my own home with my wife than staying in some strangers' house who themselves aren't *shomer Shabbas* [Sabbath observant] and would have to play some silly games to try to make me comfortable there. It didn't make sense. All right, so it's not halakhic, it's not absolute anymore, not riding on Shabbas; it's relative. It's just something I don't like to do."

Now I understood why he talked about the Noahide laws, since honoring the Sabbath is one of the Ten Commandments. I set down my box and asked how he weighed the decision. "Were you testing it against your feelings, the value of not driving on Shabbas versus the value of being home with your wife?"

"It's one among competing values. It's my spiritual life, and I make the decisions."

That is the crux of the matter. Yet Art confessed he wasn't comfortable with his choice. "Once I get in the car, it just doesn't feel like Shabbas. Once I get in the car it feels like I'm kidding myself. You get in the car, you've got to have your wallet with you. You've got to have your license. Take the money out of your wallet? Well, that seems a little silly. Should I turn the car radio on or not? Awf, drive without the radio because I'm driving on Shabbas? But I'm driving already . . .

"Hmm," I said, "a slippery slope." His argument with himself resembled those frenetically reasoned passages in Kafka, where guilt and reflection bounce along at a madly neurotic pace.

"It just doesn't work," he said. "It just doesn't work for me to drive on Shabbas. I can play the game. I got there. I did my lecture, I got paid. But that's work, that's not Shabbas."

"Isn't that interesting, in general?" I said. "All over America we have rabbis working on Shabbas. After a time they don't know what Shabbas is."

"Right, because nobody in the congregations keeps Shabbas anyway. It's funny. One reason liberal Jews have rabbis is to get the few liberal Jews committed to Judaism to work on Shabbas also and be like them." He laughed, wiping his hand absently over the top of a cereal box. "It's pretty strange."

I wondered if I disobeyed halakhah for a serious reason, or out of weakness. Given the rebelliousness of my generation, how could I know?

Art thought the right question was, What relationship do we want to have to the new emerging halakhah? Is it for all the time, or for when we feel like it? Is it for every week or every day?

"We need a vastly, vastly simplified halakhah," he said. "There can't be a Judaism without some halakhah. One reason the Conservative, Reform, Reconstructionist movements have not yet succeeded in creating a serious religious alternative to Orthodoxy is that we have not been able to articulate a halakhah and say, 'Yes, we will live this. We will raise our children with this and promulgate it. This contains the real presence of God.' We're not serious enough to be able to do it. It's very painful to admit. That we're ultimately not serious. Because then we are saying only the Orthodox are really serious. That can't be. We can't leave seriousness only to them. So we just have to do this thing." He spoke quietly, with some sense of resolution. "So I've begun to know for myself what the form of that halakhah will be."

Shabbat is basic to it, and he mentioned an article he'd written giving ten rules for Shabbat.[3] (The ten rules include five do's and five don'ts. Do: stay at home, celebrate with others, study, be alone, mark the beginning and end of this sacred time. Don't: do anything you have to do for your work life, spend money, do buisiness, travel, use commercial or canned video entertainment.) He said *kashrut* would take the form of vegetarianism. He mentioned the religious calendar and the life-cycle events, "living the stages of one's life as a Jew and living the cycle of the year as a Jew. These are the vital rhythms of Jewish life." Judith

Halevy had expressed this well, speaking of the festivals as windows opening on moments of joy, of revelation.

Other things he wanted to change.

"I still like davening," he said, "but I can't teach it. I can't tell people, 'That's the way you should be praying.' For me it's vestigial, a leftover from my grandparents' shul and the hasidic *shtibl* where I davened. If people who don't know anything ask me how to pray, I recommend silence more than learning to mumble a lot of psalms very fast. Though that's what I do, it's hard for me to teach that anymore or advocate it. So I'm very much for reintroducing of silence and silent inwardness back into our tradition. That's one thing I really want to learn from the East."

Art Green had found much of that silence and silent inwardness in the hasidic tradition. Like Reb Zalman, or Jonathan Omer-Man, many of his models of Jewish practice derive from Hasidism. With Barry Holtz he'd translated and edited a collection of hasidic prayers, *Your Word Is Fire*. But is this neo-Hasidism authentic?

"I remember a guy," Art said, "on the circuit teaching Hasidism, who said to me, 'What are you talking about Hasidism for? You're not even Orthodox!' He couldn't fathom that somebody not Orthodox might also have a spiritual life, might also be interested in the insights of Hasidism. So Orthodox comes first and then hasidic. I said, 'No, hasidic comes first. You don't need to be Orthodox to learn from the hasidic masters. Did the Baal Shem Tov come only for the Orthodox or for all the Jews?'"

"Of course the Baal Shem Tov came for everybody. The last thing he was worried about is who's Orthodox."

"But," I said, "isn't one element of the lack of conviction in non-Orthodox Judaism the rebellion? At some level people aren't willing to submit. That element of rebellion is also a lack of seriousness. It's a refusal to submit to anything at some level."

"What you say is in some ways true, but not necessarily bad. Sometimes there's good reason not to submit, sometimes too much submission is also not good. One has to maintain tension between freedom and submission. It's never easy. Yes, we have too much willfulness; we don't submit to God, and submission to God is essential to religious life." He paused. "But is submission to halakhah the same as submission to God? Is that what submission to God should be for us?" He shook his head. "I don't know."

I went back in thought to Reb Zalman's *shi'ur* (class) at the '91 *kallah*, when he spoke of the need now for Judaism to accommodate both natural science and the natural: the extreme asceticism of the Chabad yeshivah that Zalman rebelled against because the asceticism meant a hatred and fear of the body and sex that no longer spoke to him as holy.

I'd felt the conflict, not as directly. The teachings of Rebbe Nachman had opened me up; the *hitbodedut* Jonathan conveyed to me from those teachings is profound. Perhaps I also could have learned them directly from a Bratzlav teacher—such as Rabbi David El-Hara in the Los Angeles area, whom Paul Wolff, for one, raved about. I have learned from Chabad teachers and could learn from Bratzlavers, but I could not honestly enter into a Bratzlav or a Chabad community. I cannot accept all of Nachman's teachings as true. They are rooted in a worldview too out of touch with the truth as I know it. I mentioned to Art a book put out by the Breslov Institute, *Rabbi Nachman's Tikkun*, an incredible text, with very deep teachings about language.[4]

"There's also much to filter out," I said. "There's a big discussion about masturbation as a major sin."

"Yes there is. A very basic reason I'm not a Bratzlaver *ḥasid* is the load of sexual guilt in that stuff. It doesn't interest me. I'm not interested in going on that trip with them."

After we moved all the dishes, I asked Art to show me his collection of fine antique glass, lovingly displayed on a wall of shelves from floor to ceiling. On the back roads of Pennsylvania and New England he's known as "Art Green the glass man."

Some of the glass dates from the early nineteenth century. I saw a very beautiful blue pitcher and many whale-oil lamps. He pulled down a rabbit-ear lamp, so called because the wicks are set wide apart. Then he put an old whale-oil lamp in my hands. It was small, with a wick from 1830. Art said glass collecting is his escape from his life as an academic—and even his life of the spirit. I asked him why. He likes the concrete quality of the glass. He showed me a lamp with a spiral pattern of intersecting lines. It was blown into a mold with vertical ridges and then slowly twisted.

I wondered if the glass is entirely an escape from the life of the spirit. In his work, he also collects what carries the light. Yet the light itself can not be gathered, only what holds it.

And what mainly holds it, for us, is, somehow, language.

In *Seek My Face, Speak My Name*, he writes of two truths embodied in the words of the *Shema* and its traditional response, "*Barukh shem kevod malkhuto le-olam va'ed*." Blessed is the name of God's glorious kingdom for ever and ever! The *Shema* expresses the truth of a transcendent God, where "nothing but the One exists." "*Barukh shem kevod*" expresses an immanent God, where "we encounter God's oneness in and through the world, not despite it." After seeing Art's glass collection, I was struck by the metaphor he used to write about these two truths. "They represent the same finely wrought transparent vessel, here seen in emptiness, here in fullness."[5]

He loves old glass, but wants to encourage a new Jewish theological language. Reb Zalman speaks of a psycho-halakhic process, a method of extracting the intention of law from its old context to a new one. In a similar way, I think, Arthur Green sees himself responding to both contemporary philosophy and competing religions—especially now, Buddhism.

"We started talking," he said, "about the particular time in which we stand. We are at the beginning of a new age in the history of the Jewish people. And for that new age a new Judaism is going to emerge. Not the Judaism of the eighteenth century, the Judaism of the shtetl. And so the attempt of Orthodoxy to idealize and romanticize Eastern Europe and say that's the Judaism we have to have more of and reassert and reinstitute over the lives of Jews makes no sense at all. The Jewish people, after all, fled that Judaism."

I knew that in my own family history. The town of Kamenetz was once visited by Rebbe Nachman. Yet my grandfather, an immigrant tailor, had little enthusiasm for the *hasidim*. He used to chase away the men in long beards and black coats who came by with pushkes, asking for religious donations. "Get a job," he advised them. He told my father once, "They'll steal your last chicken." He meant that literally. He'd lived in the corrupt milieu in the southern Ukraine on the downslopes of hasidic inspiration. When as a young man from a poor family he'd wanted to leave for America, he needed the local rebbe's blessing. But the rebbe exacted a price, a poor family's last chicken. I'm sure my grandfather would have found it highly ironic that his grandson was poring over the texts of Rebbe Nachman.

"When the gates of the modern world opened," Art said, "Jews enthusiastically were willing to leave the shtetl and its spiritual life behind in order to enter modernity. That was not only because modernity was so attractive, but because the religion of the shtetl had really outlived its time in some ways, and become repressive. Once modernity began its challenge, the rabbinate and the forces of religion became reactionary. Opposing any new thought, opposing any change, opposing anything they didn't consider authentically Jewish enough.

"In the Middle Ages, the greatest Jewish thinkers freely borrowed from Plato and Aristotle, and the Islamic philosophers and commentators. Maimonides and others are proud of their knowledge of these people and treat them with the greatest respect. Only in a hasidic text of the nineteenth century do you see someone referring to 'that uncircumcised Philistine, Aristotle, may his name be blotted out.' That's hasidic, that's reactionary, and much more pervasive in the nineteenth century than in the twelfth or thirteenth.

"Modern Judaism in Germany could take from Kant and Hegel in the same way. But if the twelfth century can do it with Aristotle and the twentieth with Kant and Hegel, the twenty-first century will have to do it with the philosophy we're going to learn from the East—particularly Buddhism. The other religious language will challenge us. The language of absolute oneness and nothingness. The refinement of that language, including a refinement of descriptions of psychological states that we learn from the East, which is—and now I will agree with the person with whom we began—much more highly developed in Buddhism than in Judaism. That's OK and it doesn't mean we have to abandon our Judaism. It means we're going to learn some of that language and Judaize it the same way we've done with other thinkers. We can do that partly because we have no negative legacy with those people. This is not like taking Catholic thought, which would be very hard with Jews. It would obviously have to be done abstractly, detached from the particular devotional symbolisms of Buddhism so as to be integrated into Judaism. But there's room for that to happen. It's probably the next important philosophical, theological step Judaism will take. That's why I think this encounter with Buddhism—which you and I have fallen into in different ways—is going to be important." He added as a caution, "You and I are not the ones to do it, because we don't know nearly enough on the other side to be able to know what would be useful." That was certainly true.

"When I talk about the move from monotheism to monism and trying to redo Judaism in a nondualistic framework,* I'm preparing the way for that kind of dialogue and am already open to that sort of influence." Monotheism would be the belief in one

---

* In *Seek My Face, Speak My Name.*

God as asserted in the *Shema*; monism states that everything is one, as in the *Barukh shem kevod*. "Judaism can live with that philosophical change while still retaining its essential symbolic language, maybe even retaining its prayer language, though the prayer language is Judaism at its most dualistic."

In *Seek My Face, Speak My Name*, Green writes about this One in terms of the *yiḥud*, the unification, which I'd encountered through Jonathan's teachings about blessing. The two truths, represented by the same transparent glass vessel, are really the same truth. Jonathan had asserted when he taught me the divine algebra of the blessing path that you cannot approach the impersonal God except through the personal. In the same way Arthur Green writes, "We cannot reach the inner gate of understanding the eternal and unchanging One unless we go through the outer gate of discovering and embracing the divine presence as it fills this world. The way to God is *through* the world, not around it." At the end of his book, Green concludes, "We are on a journey, a journey of *yiḥud ha-Shem* ("unifying the Name"), one that proceeds from *proclaiming* God is one, to *making* God one."[6]

I told Art how I'd already felt the challenge of Buddhism, which had led me on my search for a Jewish meditation on equanimity. One phrase from Shabbat davening had stuck in my mind. *Ve-taheir libeinu le-ovdekhah be'emet.* Purify our hearts that we may serve You in truth. Could we not use meditation practices to purify our hearts? To read Torah right, to pray right, first one must purify the heart. Violent and angry people read out a violent, even homicidal, Torah, even though they are Orthodox practitioners. I was thinking of Baruch Goldstein—and the shocking support he'd had from the heads of several Israeli yeshivot.

"What does it mean," Art asked himself as much as me, "to purify the heart?"

I spoke of *vipassana* meditation. "It allows everything in the heart to rise up and be acknowledged, and pass away, and loosens the attachment to the particles. It's like loosening the dirt particles so your clothes can get cleaned. Then the purified heart can open up to new dimensions."

He took that in, pausing to reflect, then treated me to an instant midrash. "I try to understand what in its native context the phrase means: *Ve-taheir libeinu le-ovdekha be'emet*. What did the *ba'al ha-siddur* [the author of the siddur] who wrote that have in mind? Well," Art said, quoting a line in Hebrew, "*Leiv tahor bera-li Elohim ve-ruaḥ nakhon ḥadesih be-kirvi*.[7] Create for me a pure heart O God and renew in me a bright spirit. A psalm is in the background of that phrase, *ve-taheir libeinu*. It's a *mikveh* of the soul. You're getting in to a place which is the *mikveh* of the heart, cleaning out the heart." Art smiled. "I think you are right, meditation can be that kind of cleaning out of the heart. One thing *ve-taheir libeinu* has to mean has to do with ego, with competition with others, with improper motivations for prayer, praying for the wrong things, praying for the wrong reasons, praying in the wrong way. All that is preparation for prayer, seeing everything pass by and accepting it as is. I think you're right, that's a good way of making the heart ready for prayer. The Talmud says the early *ḥasidim* would be still an hour before prayer[8] and for an hour after prayer, and so prayer comes between meditations. We can't take whole hours for all of these things, but we can take a time of preparation." Art was referring to the first *ḥasidim*, the pious ones of old of the Talmud, whose practice of *shohin*, stillness before prayer, I'd connected to Jonathan's meditative practice of emptying.

Though some scholars—Leo Strauss, for instance—warn against interpreting the Rambam as a mystic, his texts read like prescriptions for just such meditative experiences. In *The Guide of the Perplexed*, the Rambam suggests that one could in fact "come near" to God, not spatially but in knowledge. How? By systematically examining in our hearts what we wish to say of God. And then systematically and thoroughly understanding why such attribution is nonsense, why such language is inadequate.

It is a meditation of emptying, as Jonathan suggested, emptying of categories. And emptying of desires. Even if we wish to call God kind, wise, gentle, understanding, beautiful, great . . . even this praise is dispraise. The Rambam shows us why: ultimately God is incomparable.

Such meditation is coming to a place of stillness, an emptying out of projections. Not to project onto God my anger, my pride, and my arrogance; not project on God my weakness, and passions, and indifference. Not project on God the face of my father or grandfather, mother or grandmother, or Father or Mother, or King, or Queen . . . To empty and empty until I am as nothing, and in that nothing to come as close as I can to the presence. The more I am, the less room for God; the less I am, the more room for God. And that is what I would do in the *shohin*, in the silence before prayer.

Art has a proposal for making space for that silence.

"Every major Jewish community now should have a meditation service somehow once a week, in addition to its wordy prayer services. Maybe a Kabbalat Shabbat at sunset, or early in the week, but it should be a time when the synagogue is open. It could begin with chanting a *niggun*,\* and then have a long period of meditation, then just end with a *Shema Yisrael*." He wanted to welcome people with meditative experience, regardless of where acquired. "Let them bring that silence home."

"After I came back from India, we came to the moment in the Reform service of silent meditation. I said to my rabbi, 'Can you make that a little bit longer?'"

Art laughed.

---

\* A hasidic melody inducing contemplation.

By purifying the heart, by working on our own equanimity, we can also read the Torah in a new way. "My interpretation of the prayer for Oral Torah—*Ve-ha'areiv na Adonai Eloheinu et divrei Toratekha*—sweeten for us, God, the words of your Torah—implies to me that there must be some process by which we can read the story more sweetly, and it needs to be read more sweetly. We're called upon to do that."

Art paused and corrected my bad Hebrew. "*Ha'areiv na* doesn't really mean 'sweeten.' It means 'make pleasant.' *Ha'areiv na*, make pleasant for us words of wisdom in our mouths and in the mouths of our children."

"It is something we must do."

"We must make Torah more pleasant," he said. "More pleasant for us and for our children and for our children's children, and each one of these is different. We can't do it for them. We can make it pleasant for our generation. Each for each generation. The words of Torah keep changing. The *hasidim* understood that so well in the beginning. They've lost that message, but they understood it so well. With each generation, new words of Torah come out of them, the words mean something new because of the need of that generation. That's why, when the Gemara has a difficult passage, it says Elijah will come and answer that question. Levi Yitzhak asks, "Why Elijah and not Moses?" Elijah, after all, is not a Torah figure, Moses is a Torah figure. The answer is, Elijah was a miracle worker because *Eliahu ha-navi* never died. *Moshe rabbeinu* died.* You can't learn Torah from a dead man. Because he can't teach you the Torah of this generation. But Elijah is alive in every generation, so he can keep doing it. It's still alive for him."

And with that latest summoning of Elijah, our conversation came to a close. I said good night to Art and Kathy. Before retir-

---

* *Eliahu ha-navi* is Elijah the Prophet. *Moshe rabbeinu* is Moses, our rabbi—the traditional rabbinic honorific for Moses.

ing, I called home to make sure my younger daughter, Kezia, was ready for the seder. This part of the tradition was, as Art would say, brimming with love.

When she got on the phone I didn't even say hello. I just chanted, "*Mah nishtanah ha-lailah ha-zeh . . .*" My dear one answered without missing a beat, "*Mi-kol ha-leilot.*" *

---

* I chanted in Hebrew, "Why is this night different . . ." and she completed the first question: ". . . from all other nights?"

## A Seder in Dharamsala
APRIL 14, 1995; 14 NISAN 5755, EREV PESACH

## Dharamsala
MARCH 20 1996; 29 ADAR 5756, FOURTEEN DAYS BEFORE PASSOVER 5756

Passover 5755 was a real homecoming. Perhaps our family seder was not yet the existential seder of Art Green or the mystical seder of Jonathan Omer-Man. But the brimming-with-love part was vital that night, especially after weeks away from my family. I had the joy of hearing my younger daughter sing the four questions. Later she carefully investigated the cup of Elijah, to see if the prophet had made the trip to Louisiana to take a sip. But if Elijah had whispered in my ear how the next two years of seders in my life would go, I wouldn't have believed him.

For instance, a year later I did a seder in Dharamsala. All that I'd learned since my last visit would be tested: a final exam where I'd stood with Reb Zalman six years before.

Laurel Chiten's film project brought me back. First I met with the Dalai Lama. I wanted him to know concretely how his dialogue with us had brought many Jews to a deeper appreciation of our own tradition, so I presented him with a copy of *The Jew in the Lotus*. I was a little afraid he might be offended by the title, which plays on "the jewel in the lotus"—*om mani padme hum*—the Tibetan national mantra. Often Jews didn't get the pun, and some Western Buddhists were too pious to laugh. But the Dalai Lama seemed to think it was a riot. He touched the book to his forehead in the Indian gesture of acceptance, and I felt maybe I'd finally made up for that stupid moment five years ago when I'd hastily handed over my autobiography.

But with all the joy of being in his presence, I did not forget that the Dalai Lama leads a martyred nation. For nearly fifty years, the Tibetans have endured a ruthless Chinese occupation. Sadly, since our visit to Dharamsala in 1990, the situation has worsened. The ancient capital of Lhasa now has a non-Tibetan majority. Old monks and young nuns, and all those who dare speak for Tibetan freedom, languish in Drapchi prison, many enduring cruel torture. The Dalai Lama has stated that time is running out for the culture and religion of Tibet.

With this in mind, I told him before we parted, "We are going to celebrate soon—at the next full moon—Passover. It's a celebration of freedom, when the Jews left Egypt, where they were slaves. We have a tradition that every nation is included and ultimately will be freed, and we certainly pray each year that Tibet will be free."

The Dalai Lama thanked me warmly.

I added, "At the end we say, 'Next Year in Jerusalem.' I believe some Tibetans once hung a banner in Dharamsala that said, 'Next Year in Lhasa.'"

"After we came to India we learned," the Dalai Lama replied, "how the Jewish community, the Jewish people, carried the struggle in different parts of the world and under difficult circumstances through such a long period; then we were very much affected. In the early sixties we often used to mention how we have to learn some of the Jewish secrets to preserve your identity and your culture and to develop it—in some cases, in hostile surroundings—over the centuries. So now we also use 'Next year in Lhasa'; I think that also we learned. We are copying your practice." He smiled broadly.

O

Filmmaker Laurel Chiten brought Marc Lieberman and me back to Dharamsala to bring the Jewish Buddhist dialogue up to date.

Over a period of a week, we met with His Holiness, and Marc and I revived our debates about Torah and dharma, God and nothing, over ginger tea at Kashmir Cottage and walking the streets and footpaths of McLeod Ganj.

I had my own personal mission. Back in 1990, Reb Zalman had proposed the seder as a model to teach Tibetan families living in exile. He felt that those emigrants living in India or the United States would lose their culture unless new family ceremonies were created for the exile situation. He saw the seder not as an old Bentley, but as a survival vehicle—one Tibetan families could customize. In 1990, Zalman's proposal had been met with strong objections from his colleagues. But I saw the wisdom in it, given the reality that Tibetan exile might last longer than we hoped. Now was a time to share with our friends this specific secret of Jewish survival in Diaspora.

Not that a Dharamsala seder would be easy. Laurel Chiten brought boxes of matzah from Boston, and at 7 A.M. the day we left for India, I rounded up the last of my supplies: a jar of horseradish from a New Orleans grocery. I was shlepping in my suitcase a Jewish catalog of Diaspora goodies: my personal silver wine cup, candles, candlesticks, a challah cover/matzah cover.

As for Haggadot, I'd called the Afikomen Bookstore in Berkeley and ordered twenty copies of *The Telling: A Loving Haggadah for Passover,* a sweet egalitarian seder I'd used the year before at home. Edited by Dr. Dov Ben Khayyim, it's a pure product of Berkeley Jewish renewal with feminist, mystical, Sephardic, Aquarian minyan, and Freedom Seder strains.

Our model seder would be close to traditional while addressing the concerns and questions of Tibetan Buddhists living in exile. We would also be joined by two notable Jewish Buddhists: Alex Berzin, a translator and worldwide teacher of Tibetan Buddhism, and Thubten Chodron, a Buddhist nun who teaches in the Seattle area, agreed to come. But even though Dharamsala in that Tibetan New Year season was crowded with monks, finding some to join us proved a challenge. That's why my wife, Moira, and I hit the streets early the morning of the seder.

Since my last visit, business had picked up in downtown McLeod Ganj, the Tibetan enclave. Now there were two main shopping streets, not one. Restaurants had improved. Shops were more sophisticated. Gone from shelves were thighbone trumpets and human-skull bowls—replaced by beautiful silk *thangkas* and rugs made by Tibetan exiles, displayed near Visa and American Express signs. With the continuing influx of travelers and curiosity seekers, the town had experienced growing pains. From time to time, tensions had erupted between lower Dharamsala, mostly a Hindu town, and the Tibetan enclave, McLeod Ganj.

Other cultures clashed: in the main streets of Dharamsala (they seemed innocent of names) the Middle Ages meet the Information Age. Slops and dishwater are tossed from second-story windows onto the muddy cobblestones. Four-wheel-drive sports utility vehicles flatten Westerners against buildings, though Tibetan monks and nuns walk millimeters from death and never flinch. Oxen plod by as old Tibetan peasant women in colorful striped aprons hurry around them. Ancient monks with lined foreheads and average Tibetan pilgrims whirl small prayer wheels of silver and wood. Western tourists from France, Germany, Australia, and the United States crowd the shops with identical backpacks on sunburned shoulders—pilgrims from L. L. Bean to eternity. A temple surrounded by large brightly painted mani wheels offers a pass-through from one block to the other. The mani wheels are like giant spinning mezuzahs stuffed with Buddhist prayers, so you can spin them, davening as you stroll. Nearby a shaggy saddhu with grey Adamic beard begs in a metal cage—half dumpster, half apartment. Information pilgrims stream steadily toward a universal destination, a tiny shop with a red-letter sign: FAX.

Moira and I visited FAX twice a day. The shop is always crammed, so it's customary to poke your head in the door and riffle through a pile of faxes on the counter, looking for replies to your own messages amid mysterious communications in English, Hindi, French, Hebrew, German, Tibetan. The proprietor watches Indian movies on fuzzy Indian TV—where actors scream in operatic tones and then dance like all get-out, like a Busby Berkeley routine on fast-forward. The screen bulges with messages: a line of text races across the bottom; cartoon ducks and dragons burst in the middle, balloons expand out of their heads stuffed with Hindi script. No one screen could hold all the information, pleading, selling, singing, dancing, and lovemaking going on in India at any given moment.

A row of patient petitioners waits on a bench to send a fax: an Israeli girl fresh out of high school, taking her last fling before entering the army; a wizened Tibetan monk clutching dark beads; a high-spirited tall blond Australian man with a backpack full of paperback dharma; and Moira and I, sending a message exactly halfway around the world to our children in New Orleans. Reb Zalman's vision of global telepathy through the media lives in the Dharamsala fax shop. Through such communication we live in several worlds simultaneously, as the kabbalah's reality map teaches.

One day while Moira was eyeing a chain-stitch Kashmiri rug, a distinctively American voice called out to her, "Don't buy that—I can tell you where it's cheaper."

"You're from North Carolina," she said, and wheeled around to see a smiling sixty-year-old American man wearing the maroon robe of a Tibetan Buddhist monk.

"Asheville," he said.

That's how Moira met Gerry, also known in Tibetan as "he who practices the perfection of giving." A retired tool and die maker, he'd earned his Tibetan name by contributing his monthly check, and eventually himself, to the Drepung Loseling

Monastery. His money supports six monks, full time—a stretch of the Social Security net Newt Gingrich probably never dreamed of. Gerry may be India's only resident redneck Tibetan Buddhist monk.

As we set out on our search for monks, we wound down the footpath from Kashmir Cottage to the cabstand. At the road we had a magnificent view of the Kangra Valley. A Tibetan woman in chuba sat on her haunches, and when I took her picture, she smiled. Mist gently filled the valley, and we saw, arced like a huge suspension bridge, a major rainbow.

We ran back up the cottage path to yell for Peter Wiehl, the cameraman for the film shoot, who soon came running, with his Arriflex, as though it didn't weight a hundred pounds, his assistant, Emelia, trailing behind him carrying light meters. Naturally, by the time they arrived and set up the shot, the rainbow shyly slipped off, but Moira and I had seen it: good luck in any language.

Dharamsala challenges boundaries and can evoke spiritual crises in her Western visitors. The crises come with the special air, the mountains, the exotic nature of this meeting ground of East and West. Pilgrims constantly perambulate a circular path cut at the top of a hill. They paint rocks bright blue, and red, and inscribe them with the Tibetan national mantra, *om mani padme hum*, in elaborate script, setting their offerings on the side of the hill. I almost had a crisis of my own when I saw painted on a large boulder in the middle of the path the symbolic key to the whole Jewish-Buddhist story: a Jewish star at the center, ringed by four swastikas in the cardinal directions.

But once I stopped reading it as weird Nazi propaganda, I remembered that the swastika is actually an ancient Hindu symbol. But what about the Jewish star? I asked a Tibetan pilgrim in sign language—pointing at the rock, shrugging my shoulders. She pointed at the Jewish star and then to the top of the mountain, toward the Dalai Lama's residence, where I had been two days before. The six-pointed star represented His Holiness. The boulder was a map of his world: a fairy-tale kingdom with the Dalai Lama as the chief wizard, and the Tibetan pilgrims and legions of monks circling him around the mountain, and all sorts of energies circulating with them. It was high season, right after the Tibetan New Year, Losar, when monks from all over India flock to Dharamsala to receive teachings and blessings from His Holiness. Many of the pilgrims carried a long sheaf of grain, which reminded me of the *lulav* or palm branch of Sukkot.

We headed for town and Gerry's monk lodgings, the Drepung Loseling guest house. He wasn't in, and no one knew where he was. (We learned later he was having his teeth pulled; we met him smiling and toothless a few days later.)

We were back on the street, standing in front of a shop. I was feeling tired and disoriented, Moira even more so: in the wild clear air of Dharamsala, she'd had trouble sleeping, and we spent the night in Kashmir Cottage discussing the competing claims of Jewish and Buddhist spirituality. Which spoke directly to the heart? What about survival? A thin, short man in his early fifties walked out of the shop and addressed me as rabbi.

He had an extraordinary face. He wore a wool watch cap, and his dark eyes slanted down in the corners, with deep crinkles; he could have been Elie Wiesel's brother. His accent told me he was Israeli.

I explained I was no rabbi and asked him what he did in Dharamsala. He pointed at the mountain peaks above us. He came quite frequently to meditate at Tushita Monastery. He pulled out a worn wallet and showed me a photo of a robust, smiling guru with a white beard. "Sikh?" I asked, judging from his turban. Yes. He'd encountered this master in Germany and had made his work teaching Sikhism in Israel.

I asked him if he'd studied kabbalah.

He smiled, squinting up at the light. It was an overcast day, but the clouds were breaking apart and the sky was bright in patches.

Yes, he'd studied in Jerusalem.

"Where?" I said.

"You can't seek them out," he said, as if anticipating my question. "They have to come to you." As he had come to me.

"How do they know?"

"They see the lines in your face."

I'd read about that. Some teachers choose their students by reading Hebrew letters in the wrinkles around the eyes and forehead. His own face looked like interesting reading.

He'd also studied Tibetan Buddhism for many years.

"The kabbalists have it," he said. "They speak of the *sha'ar ha-rahamim* [the gate of mercy]—" and he pointed to his chest— "the *sha'ar yerushalayim* [the gate of Jerusalem] in the heart, and you open that." I knew he was talking about the *sefirah* of *tiferet*, the heart *sefirah*, which is identified with *rahamim* or mercy. With those words, I smiled broadly—and looked at Moira. She knew what I was thinking, because we'd talked about it all night—what Buddhism said, what Judaism said, and how one could possibly reconcile their competing visions of reality. It was the old Ping-Pong match I'd played in Dharamsala before—God one, Nothing, nothing—only this time, mixed doubles. How could Judaism with its ancient dualism be an adequate spiritual vehicle in a pluralistic age? Tibetan Buddhism seemed to offer powerful spiritual answers for today. But could it really survive as a tradition? How could Tibetan Buddhism, which had been nurtured in geographic isolation, endure the rigors of exile, or the violent pragmatism of international realpolitik?

Yet here on the street of Dharamsala a mysterious stranger seemed to point to an answer when he pointed to his heart. Here at least, the two traditions meet. The same message with different words: open your heart, open your heart . . .

I never learned his name, but I call him the Elijah of Dharam-sala, summoned as mysteriously as chanting the vowels of *Eliahu* with Joseph Mark Cohen years before.

The debate that kept Moira and me awake at night is under-stood in kabbalah as the battle between *gevurah* and *ḥesed*, be-tween severe intellectual judgment and overflowing compassion. In the kabbalistic scheme, *gevurah* is on the left side and *ḥesed* represents the right side of the body. *Tiferet*, the *sefirah* of beauty, sits in the middle, reconciling the claims of love and restraint. *Tiferet* is identified with *raḥamim* (mercy), seen as the powerful impulse to respond immediately, compassionately, to the pain of others. It's when I know another is standing at a door of pain, and I respond with all my heart.

The Elijah of Dharamsala told us that the basic mystical teaching is all in kabbalah. But, he added, it's more hidden, be-cause Judaism works by constantly running and returning, mov-ing up and down the ladder between the two levels of dualism and monism.

This recalled Jonathan's teaching from Gikatilla, that the *Adonai* is a doorsill, a doorway from the level of earthly duality to the level of YHVH, where all is one. You have to work hard on yourself to climb up from the everyday level to this higher level. It's the spiritual work from moment to moment, the path of blessing, and the path of our compassionate encounters with others, our awareness of their pain. But to be there for others, you have to work on yourself, and the work is tricky.

I remember once at a lecture a woman told me, "I prefer Bud-dhism to Judaism because it's nondualistic." "Oh," I said, "I see: you're nondualistic—and I'm not!" She laughed.

"The kabbalists have it," the Elijah of Dharamsala said, "but the Tibetans do it plain and direct," and that's why he spent sev-eral months a year meditating at Tushita Monastery.

He certainly had a point. I could not deny that within the precincts of the monastery, the Tibetan teachers could get you to the gate of Jerusalem in a hurry and open the heart like nobody's business. And yet survival also has a point: the very question the Dalai Lama was asking us, about the "Jewish secret" of spiritual survival in exile, found its answer in the Jewish drama of distinctions. The Passover seder we would do with the Tibetans would make that clear. And so the inner debate continued: monism, dualism, inner vision, survival . . .

But I remembered something marvelous Jonathan had said. "I don't want to have debating societies in my head." So I called the debate to a halt. Rather than roiling up internal arguments, I just wanted to marvel at the eerie synchronicity of Dharamsala, as if the first person who approaches you on the street would quite naturally speak to your deepest spiritual yearnings and discontents. The only other place I'd ever been to that resembled it in this way was Tzefat, in northern Israel, once the home of the mystical Rabbi Isaac Luria and these days full of Bratzlavers, Chabadniks, artists, and mystics. And Jerusalem.

According to what "Elijah" had told us, the old kabbalists of Jerusalem would sit outside a certain gate of the city and watch passersby. They studied each face to see who should receive the hidden teaching.

As we made our way back to Kashmir Cottage, I thought we'd failed to find a monk but had found a prophet instead. I was trying to understand why the Israeli stranger had pointed to his heart and called it the "*sha'ar ha-raḥamim*" and also the "*sha'ar yerushalayim.*" Then I remembered that the "*sha'ar ha-raḥamim*" *is* a "*sha'ar yerushalayim,*" a gate of Jerusalem, specifically, the Golden Gate, the oldest of the seven gates. That is why the old kabbalists sat there: because before the 1967 war reclaimed the Western Wall, the Golden Gate was the holiest site in the city, the closest to the old Temple.

A year before I'd foolishly told Eve Ilsen in Boulder that the "gates" mentioned in the *Shema* were not relevant because we don't have gates to our cities anymore.

Yet I'd seen the *Sha'ar ha-Raḥamim,* the actual Gate of Mercy, myself. In the Middle Ages, the Muslims believed along with the Jews that the Messiah would enter through that gate, and so they blocked the passage with stones. Even today the gate is permanently shut.

Set in front of that gate is a cemetery, also built by the Muslims. It was believed that the forerunner of the Messiah would not walk through a cemetery because he is a *kohein*, a priest. That forerunner is Elijah.

We made our way back to Kashmir Cottage. I learned then that Marc Lieberman had also failed in his effort to invite a local lama of his acquaintance. Then Lakhdor, our translator from the original dialogue, who works closely with the Dalai Lama's office, called in with his regrets. So I would try to find Ruth Sonam and her remarkable teacher, Geshe Sonam Rinchen.

O

I'd first met Ruth Sonam in 1990 at a Friday-night Shabbas dinner at Kashmir Cottage. She'd come as translator for Geshe Sonam. I'd been struck by their close relationship, the clear love between longtime teacher and student. But she'd also come as a curious Jew. Raised in Ireland, the daughter of German Jews who'd fled the Nazis, she has been living in Dharamsala for many years, working as a translator at the Tibetan Library of Works and Archives. She had long ago left Judaism for Tibetan Buddhism, but in our conversations I could tell she still felt certain ties to her Jewish background. Laurel had invited her to the seder, but Ruth sounded doubtful. So I thought I would ask her myself.

Moira and I walked over to the Tibetan Library of Works and Archives, a museum, a shrine, and a school where Geshe Sonam teaches Buddhist philosophy to Westerners. After a few minutes, his class "Compassion, Bodhicitta, and Profound View" let out. A dozen students trudged downstairs, all carrying their shoes—some quite young, world travelers with lots of metal in their ears and noses, and one old Mr. Natural in a white beard and a yarn cap.

I climbed up the stairs. In the corridor on the second floor were a few classrooms. A sign, posted by the Tibetan librarians who worked in the office nearby, testified to the level of equanimity at the Tibetan-Western interface. "Students of meditation class will please not leave their STINKING shoes in the corridor as they are disgusting."

I peeked into a classroom at the end of the hall and saw Ruth talking intently to a student. I caught her eye and she disengaged briefly and said we should speak in the library.

I entered the small library/museum, full of *thangkas* and golden Buddhist statuary. Over the past years, this room had loomed much larger in my imagination.

I found Geshe Sonam Rinchen seated behind a desk. He's in his sixties, an exile from Tibet; his title, "Geshe," indicates twenty-five years of advanced Buddhist practice and study. I admired his very large shaved head seated magnificently atop his maroon robes, the otherworldly ears sticking out, and I looked directly into his eyes, which were very friendly and kind. I was delighted that he still remembered our conversation six years before. We had discussed everything from the meaning of Shabbas to group karma and the Holocaust—with Ruth translating. Geshe Sonam speaks English but prefers to speak through Ruth.

Now our conversation evolved into a very sweet diplomatic ballet. I knew I had to overcome some resistance in both Ruth and the teacher she called affectionately Gen-la.*

In any case, a diplomat must bear gifts, so I gave him a copy of *The Jew in the Lotus*. He remarked that he could not read English and handed it to Ruth.

"That's why we are making a movie," I said.

"And we want both of you to be in it," I added.

---

* *Gen* means "teacher" and *-la* is an endearment.

Ruth said she hadn't been feeling well. And Geshe Sonam had a visitor, a student leaving the very next morning for a monastery in South India, to begin studies to become a Geshe. They needed time to say farewell.

I said, "Geshe Sonam's friend would also be very welcome." I paused to let Ruth translate, and those pauses became part of our rhythm, like line breaks in poetry. Each time I spoke, I looked directly into his extraordinary eyes. Each time, he reflected back to me a certain wry calm. I felt that by paying attention to what was behind his eyes, I could somehow pick up on where he was coming from—the state of mind that he cultivated with such conscientiousness.

The first shift came after I invited the young monk. Gen-la asked through Ruth if it would be all right to visit briefly, not stay for the whole time. I said they would be very welcome to come for just a few minutes. Geshe Sonam asked, "What is the ceremony about?"

I said, "It is a celebration of freedom.

"And I am sure you know a great deal about freedom or liberation."

He said, "What would I have to prepare?"

I said, "In the seder we give answers and we ask questions. So you could either give answers or ask questions."

He said, "I would not know what to ask."

I said, "In the seder we tell the story of four types of children, who are four kinds of awareness.

"There is the wise, the wayward, the simple, and the one who does not know how to ask."

I added, "All are honored.

"But the one who does not know how to ask is the deepest. Because for his sake, we tell the whole story."

When he heard that, something changed. The next thing I knew, they said they'd come. Not only that, but they would stay for the meal.

○

That evening, after Moira and I set the table, a hailstorm flogged the mountainside and trampled the flowers. The first to arrive, carrying umbrellas and flashlights, were Geshe Sonam in his robe; Ruth, very dressed up in earrings and shawl and black dress; and a young monk, Champa, off the next day to Sera for twenty-five years of studies. We seated them in one of the nicely appointed living rooms, the one that we jokingly called the Green Room.

When we'd settled down, Geshe Sonam remarked that I had gotten bigger. (Maybe that explained why everything in Dharamsala seemed smaller!) He said, "You are not the same person you were five years ago."

I said, "I have benefited from my contact with teachers like you."

He said, playfully "And am I the same Geshe I was five years ago?"

I laughed and hurriedly explained to him the symbols of the seder that I'd learned from Jonathan Omer-Man and Art Green. That leavened bread, in its puffiness, represents pride and also the endless distracting chatter of the mind. Matzah, on the other hand, is pure awareness. Egypt is *mitzrayim*, the narrow place, the place of constriction in our lives; the Pharaoh is the ego; and the Exodus, our personal journey out of constriction and toward freedom. He picked up on all of this immediately—and just in time, as Thubten Chodron and Alex Berzin arrived.

Born and raised Jewish in New Jersey, Alex first encountered Tibetan Buddhism on a Fulbright visit to Dharamsala in 1968. He never left and has become an unofficial roving ambassador for Tibetan Buddhism and the Dalai Lama. He'd just been around the world, including a visit to Israel. While in Jerusalem he'd met with a kabbalist and later wrote an extraordinary summary of kabbalah from the Tibetan Buddhist point of view. I suspected his curiosity grew out of his 1990 encounter with Reb Zalman. That night he was in a jovial mood.

But as host I was nervous. In our conversation before the event, Marc Lieberman had stressed the need to discover points of contact between the Jewish and Tibetan historical experience. The task of explaining the seder, and indeed the whole history of the Jewish people, to Tibetans was daunting.

When we assembled, I started with the basics. The seder means a set meal, a ritual meal, modeled on the Greek banquet, or symposium. (When I thought of it later, this seemed another argument in Zalman's favor: we Jews had borrowed the seder from the Greeks; why not pass it on to the Tibetans?) It's another example of the cross-cultural borrowing that Judaism is full of—*contra* the narrow views of some particularists.

The parallels between Jewish and Tibetan history were striking: the rabbinic seder as we practice it today originated out of the shattering of the Jewish people, when all hope to stay in the homeland was lost and we were facing dispersion and exile, as the Tibetans are facing it today. In that circumstance, the rabbinic sages invented the seder meal to fulfill the mitzvah in Torah of remembering the Exodus.

In his living room, I'd asked Arthur Green how to meditate on the Song of the Sea—and he had told me to look within. But that night I would feel strongly how the whole seder is just such a meditation, a focusing on an eternal moment of liberation that is simultaneously past, present, and future. A meditation to change the nature of time.

Now I understood, through doing the seder in Dharamsala, that the search for a Jewish meditation doesn't have to involve complex techniques. It can be as simple as the mezuzah meditation Mark Borovitz taught me—or saying one blessing a day over bread, Jonathan's "forty-watt bulb." Judaism is full of such meditative treasures, which is why when people tell me they want to "add spirituality" to their Judaism, I smile. The meditative technology of an inner Judaism is as plain as matzah. Take it in hand, take it to lips, take it to heart; in the presence of a Tibetan master, we would.

As the seder began, I explained that Pesach is a festival to remember the deliverance of Hebrew slaves from Egypt and the hope of a promised land. I added a tradition I learned from Rabbi Arthur Waskow, who originated the Freedom Seder in April 1968 as a gesture of healing toward the black community in the troubled days after the assassination of Dr. Martin Luther King.

"It's said in the Talmud that in the days of *Moshiaḥ*, when the world is more perfect, we will remember not just the liberation from Egypt, but the liberation of all people from oppression. So to make things more perfect, to bring that day forward, we remember tonight the hope of the liberation of Tibet."

In Reb Zalman's original proposal for a Tibetan seder, each cup of wine would be dedicated to a different stage of enlightenment. But Marc and I decided instead that each cup would be dedicated as a toast—the first to Zalman himself. After we said the *berakhah*, I lifted the glass and explained that Rabbi Zalman Schachter "had a great dream that there would be a seder like this in Dharamsala. So. We'll think of Reb Zalman right now."

The richness of the seder as practiced cannot be captured in a book; as Art Green put it, Jewish traditions are brimming with love, passed down through generations. Marc Lieberman now mentioned his family's custom for the ritual hand washing. "A person washes her hands and has the person next to her dry them."

This was a very sweet ceremony. Added sweetness came from Thubten Chodron's reaction. Because of the rules governing the behavior of nuns and monks, she would not hold out her hands to be dried by Geshe Sonam. Finally Ruth took over and directed Chodron: "You wash, and have Gen-la dry your hands."

"I'm embarrassed," Chodron said, and we all laughed. But she held out her fingers, and Gen-la very sweetly and carefully dried them with a towel.

I was determined to give as much participation as possible to all, while struggling to bring out the meaning of the ceremony. I soon ran into the same problem any seder leader might encounter as I held up the ceremonial plate and asked Alex Berzin, seated on my right, the meaning of the parsley.

"Saint Patrick's Day?" he said with perfect timing.

I remembered all the seders where I'd played the wise guy and realized that Alex's joke was my karma. I saw the same difficulty Jonathan expressed: the inner seder is hard to create. But I found an ally in an unexpected corner—Geshe Sonam.

We passed the greens and salt water around while Geshe Sonam spoke with some animation to Ruth.

"He asks, 'What is the salt water for?'"

"What is the salt water for, do you think?" I said to Ruth.

"Well, I seem to remember from the past, the tears." I saw on her face a beauty of recollection; she was going back to her own childhood.

"The tears, yes," I said.

Ruth translated for Gen-la.

"The tears of slavery. And the tears of the Tibetan people too," I said. "Many of these ceremonies are mixtures of something tempering; the green is good, and the tears . . . a mixture."

Gen-la nodded affirmatively. To Reb Zalman, as he related to me when I told him the story, the use of "memorable" food is a crucial technique of the seder, a vehicle he hoped the Tibetan families in exile could learn to adopt.

I said the *berakhah* for the matzah, took the middle piece, and broke it in half. I hid some for the *afikoman*, and as far as I know it is still hidden where I put it. Marc explained, "Before you finish the meal, the children have to find it. It becomes a game for them."

I added, "And an inner meaning is, we cannot finish the seder until we discover what is hidden."

I rose for the showing of the matzah. "This is the bread of affliction which our ancestors ate in the land of *mitzrayim*, the land of Egypt," I recited. "Now we are here; next year may we be in the land of Israel." I turned to Gen-la and his friend, the monk Champa, and added, "Now we are here; next year may we be in the land of Tibet. Now we are slaves; next year may we be free people."

I said Chodron would be the perfect person to ask the four questions because in our many conversations she'd asked me so many penetrating questions about Judaism. That provoked laughter from Alex, and Gen-la said, "I know that."

After she recited the four questions in English, I thought she might want to add more of her own. But she smiled and demurred. Marc thoughtfully explained the human dimension of the ceremony, that the whole seder is designed to keep the interest of children. "Traditionally, as the youngest child, our turn came to say these questions. We were so nervous, but the adults were always so supportive. It was our first effort at public speaking."

As Ruth translated, I thought to ask everyone to join in. We spontaneously broke into the traditional Ashkenazi chant. As I looked around the table, at Chodron in her maroon robes and shaved head, and owlish Alex with his thick glasses and deep Buddhist scholarship, and even Marc in his brocade Hindu yarmulke, I felt how deeply the memory lived. I was seeing what Arthur Green had spoken of as "an antiquity of the self, antiquity of the soul"—the ancient depth of memory, and the depth of ancientness each Jew carries. Despite every transformation and change, somewhere in their Jewish Buddhist hearts lived these words and the plaintive Ashkenazic melody that went with them. The same words my young daughter and I recited back and forth over the phone at Art Green's house: "*Mah nishtanah ha-lailah ha-zeh mi-kol ha-leilot . . .*"

I told the familiar story of the seder, with Ruth Sonam translating into Tibetan. Once again, the pauses were very helpful in deepening our sense of the message, giving us time to absorb each moment. At one point, I heard Ruth pronounce distinctly *Pesach*.

"Oy," I said, "this is the first Tibetan Haggadah."

"Once in Canada someone translated a Tibetan ritual into Yiddish," Alex said. "It was equally lovely."

As I looked at Champa and Gen-la, and began, "Our ancestors were Abraham and Sarah," I saw from their expressions that they had no idea who Abraham and Sarah were. I thought, "Boy this is going to be a long night." Telling the ancient story to this unique audience, I reflected how much we Jews in the West take for granted the knowledge and understanding of our history. "They came to the land of Canaan. They had a son Isaac who with his beloved Rebecca gave birth to Jacob . . ." Marc said, "Rodger, can you roll it?"

"I can roll it." I did fast editing. "Israel and his children went to Egypt and they became slaves under Pharaoh.

"And Pharaoh wanted to kill the firstborn children of the Hebrews.

"So the people cried out to God.

"And God heard their voice.

"And took us out of Egypt with a mighty hand, an outstretched arm, with great visions, signs, and wonders." I swung out my hand and my outstretched arm, and Geshe Sonam imitated me, his bare arm thrusting out from his maroon robe. He was getting into the story.

We came to the moment of the Reed Sea. "They say the first one to enter was very brave.

"Then the Egyptians came behind.

"And when all of them were there . . .

". . . the sea collapsed over them."

Geshe Sonam laughed heartily along with the rest of the group.

"You may remember the movie," Marc added.

"All of this was promised to Abraham," I said. "So we lift our cup to remember the promise. The promise made to our ancestors holds true for us. For in every generation are those who seek to annihilate us, but the Holy One, *Barukh ha-Shem*, stays their hand."

Ruth Sonam translated.

"And it is said, and this will comfort Ruth, that when the angels celebrated the drowning of the Egyptians, the Holy One silenced them, saying, 'The work of My hands is drowning in the sea and you want to sing?'"

Ruth paused from her translating, her face full of emotion. She said, "I never heard that before." For many Buddhist practitioners, the notes of nationalistic triumph in the Passover story are distressing. Perhaps it touched her to learn that within the Jewish tradition there are authoritative voices—the rabbis of the midrash—who see the danger of celebrating violence.

Later, we sang a rousing *Dayeinu*, with Marc improvising original Jewish Buddhist lyrics. Somehow he got Mount Meru in there along with Mount Sinai, and dharma along with Torah.

Then Ruth said, "Gen-la wants to know, when the Almighty bestowed these hardships on the Egyptians, what profit was gained by that?"

All eyes turned to me. How I wished Reb Zalman had been there at that moment.

"This is a hard question," I said, hemming and hawing. "Of course I knew you wouldn't ask an easy one." A great round of laughter. Here was the place where survival and spiritual values met. In a situation where people face physical slavery, was physical violence a spiritual answer? "Um, I'm trying to remember. No one knew about the Almighty One except the Children of Israel. This way everyone would know."

Ruth translated, and Geshe went *uumm*. I was struggling to keep my diction simple. The Exodus in effect is the worldwide announcement of God's presence, a universal demonstration of God's power. It proceeds with maximal visibility, with signs and wonders, so that once and for all the full reality of YHVH would be universally announced.

"So each time when Moses asked Pharaoh to let the Hebrews go, they say that God hardened Pharaoh's heart. That made it harder for Pharaoh to say yes. But that way, in the end, the whole world would know.

"So," I went on, "Pharaoh would represent the refusal to be aware. This one time, God wanted to demonstrate to all that God existed. So that's why the Holy One did these hard things." I paused and looked at Champa, the young monk in exile, off the next day to South India to study for twenty-five years, preserving his people's tradition. I looked at Geshe Sonam, born in Tibet, who had spent his mature years in India and might never return to his homeland.

"So all the people of the world would know that slavery does not last forever," I said to each of them. "So that people who have no hope, and no friends, and no help, know that they can find hope, and friends, and help."

Now I understood the connection that had troubled me between the God of the Torah and the One beyond all naming and gender. Our God, at the dualistic level where we live and suffer, is the God who brings freedom to the oppressed. Therefore, if we are looking for God, let us not only look within, let us also look wherever we see masses of people struggling to be free. For we will see God working there, the God of Exodus, the God who is *matir asurim*, the freer of captives. That is why Arthur Waskow's Freedom Seder of 1968 made such a powerful connection between Passover and the civil rights struggle. It is also why he and others insist that Jewish renewal must have a political component—that to struggle for racial justice in America, or the environment, or freedom for Tibet, is holy work.

I had been struggling to answer the Tibetan question about the use of violence. And help came now from Geshe Sonam himself. He spoke a long while in Tibetan to Ruth, who translated: "I feel that these plagues were sent to the Pharaoh so that he would recognize what suffering really is. To really remind him that suffering has a cause. If you inflict suffering on other people then something happens to you as well."

"That's beautiful," I said. Marc Lieberman added, "Geshe-la, there's some idea of what you are talking about: the law of causation or karma. The first thing that the Pharaoh wanted to do was kill all the firstborn sons of the Hebrews. And the last plague, that broke the Pharaoh's hard heart, was the death of all the first-born Egyptians."

As Marc finished speaking, the lights went out all over town.

"Aw, the plagues," I said. "Darkness. *Hoshekh*. We already had hail." We all laughed. The power supply in Dharamsala was somewhat uncertain. The film crew brought in candles and I said, "I don't know why the Holy One has brought plagues of hail and darkness tonight."

Gen-la answered quickly, "This is to make us remember better." We laughed.

Marc had a good point. A similar idea appears in a teaching of Rabbi Aaron Samuel Tamaret of Miletchitz. The Holy One directly executes the judgment of death on the Egyptians. Why? So as "not to sanction the use of their fists for self-defense even at that time; for ... by such means the way of the fist spreads through the world and in the end defenders become aggressors." God tells the Hebrews, "Your abstention from any participation in the vengeance upon Egypt will prevent the plague of vengeance from stirring the power of the destroyer, which is in you yourselves."

Pesach too is a search for the destroyers within. "Before Passover begins," I said, "we must search the house with a candle and a feather and look for any crumbs of bread. And the bread is *hametz*, which means 'fermented,' bread that rises with yeast. But *hametz* also means 'pride.' 'Puffed up.' So we have no *hametz* in the house and no pride in the heart. At another level, *hametz* represents the busy mind, always going everywhere. Matzah is pure awareness."

Marc laughed: "I certainly never learned this." He wanted to give the plain, the *peshat*, explanation. "This holiday begins with seven days when we cannot eat bread; we can only eat matzah for seven days."

"Finally, this is the *maror*," I said, "bitter herb. The bitterness of slavery. So tonight we will taste the bitterness of slavery—or horseradish sauce from New Orleans."

"You could have used Tibetan medicine," Alex said and we laughed.

I made another substitution: I brought in Psalm 126, which usually comes after the meal. It spoke to me of the hope of redemption for the Tibetan people.

"In every generation you ought to regard yourself as though you had personally come out of Egypt," I read from the Haggadah. "You shall tell your children, 'This is what the Holy One did for me when I went out of Egypt.'" Then I added an explanation: "So at the Pesach seder, you yourself are being freed, not just people in the past. And because this promise will extend to all people, of freedom, we choose a psalm of freedom from captivity. We are reading it for the people of Tibet.

"When the Holy One will return the captivity of Zion/Tibet, we will be like dreamers. Then our mouths will be filled with laughter. The Holy One has done great things. Those who sow in tears will reap in joy."

I saw a tear in Geshe Sonam's eye as he heard the words translated, though he smiled all the while.

We came to the second cup of mango juice. "Rodger," Marc said, "since you introduced that nice idea of a toast, maybe Geshe Sonam would like to raise a glass of mango juice in honor of someone . . ."

The answer came through Ruth: "Rinpoche says, 'I would like to dedicate the glass to all suffering sentient beings.'"

"When we taste what is in our glasses, we experience pleasure," Geshe Sonam said. "May all living beings who are experiencing suffering at present experience happiness and well-being."

Geshe took a very small piece of matzah. Ruth explained for him, "If this symbolizes lack of pride, I thought it inappropriate to take a big piece."

I said the blessing and explained the custom of the Hillel sandwich. "We are about to eat the bitter herb—our suffering. The rabbis had compassion on the Jews. They said you could mix it with something sweet and they made a sandwich. This compassionate meal was invented by Rabbi Hillel."

I heard Ruth speaking Tibetan, and, mingled with it—distinctly—the words *Rabbi Hillel*.

"Rabbi Hillel was a great Jewish lama," I said.* "Once a mocker, a scornful person, said to him, 'Teach me the Torah while standing on one foot.' So he said, 'What is hateful to yourself, do not do to others. That is the whole Torah; the rest is commentary. Now go and study.'"

"Gen Rinpoche says that summary of the Torah is very important and wonderful. Gen Rinpoche feels it is important to mix the sweet and the bitter because if you taste only what is bitter, then you don't know of sweetness, but if you know both sweetness and bitterness then you will try to emerge from your suffering, from your bitterness, you will try to get away from your bitterness to the sweetness." This also I recalled as Rabbi Nachman's view of suffering, as the *Maggid* of Hollywood taught. The purpose of the darkness is to move us toward the joy.

As we began eating, Marc added more about Rabbi Hillel.

"The rabbi Rodger just told us a story from, Rabbi Hillel, was one of two great rabbis. [The other is Shammai.] They had two schools in complete disagreement with each other. Rabbi Hillel was the school of great compassion for the people, and the other rabbi [Shammai] was from the school of being very strict with the rules. And Rabbi Hillel has become the rabbi that the other rabbis in later generations followed."

---

* "Lama" is a fairly accurate translation of the Hebrew term *ḥakham*—sage—applied to Hillel.

Gen-la had a position on the ancient controversy between Hillel and Shammai. "Gen-la feels that both are very important. Rabbi Hillel's approach and the other approach. But ideally the two approaches would be combined in one person. Because one should observe and discipline very carefully oneself, and in addition one should be kindhearted and compassionate. Then you have the two things together—fine noble ethical discipline and compassion, the kindheartedness. Gen Rinpoche says, 'That's how I feel about it.'"

"Thank you, rabbi," Marc said.

"We already made the Dalai Lama a rabbi," I said, "so you have the yarmulke." Gen-la was wearing a sateen yarmulke I'd given him.

"But I do not have a beard," Gen-la protested.

"It's OK," I said. "We're from the Hillel school."

Our meal arrived, and the monks took great delight in eating the glistening mutton momos. According to their custom, they took three at a time.

O

After the final words of the seder, I thanked our guests for coming and asked if there were any more questions. Gen-la spoke to Ruth. "Gen Rinpoche says, 'I don't have a specific question, but today getting together for this meal and this ritual has been really wonderful. We can see there are many human beings suffering in great difficulty and other living beings experiencing great hardship. So what can we do? My question is, What can we do for all of them when we are here together?

"'Tonight we thought about freedom and human beings emerging from servitude and great suffering. But if we can resolve to give up all harmful actions toward living beings in general, if we can concentrate love and compassion, then our coming together will bear even greater fruit.

"'When we think in this way and of trying to cultivate nonviolence toward living beings, that means we need to protect our environment, in which all living beings dwell. Because when we protect it, we protect all of them from harm. If those who keep a religious tradition alive can think in this way, then it will be truly of benefit.'"

"Good Torah," I said, "good dharma." The Tibetans in general and the Dalai Lama in particular have been strong champions of the environment. Just as Reb Zalman stressed that Judaism has to go natural, and Arthur Waskow had made environmental work a key issue for Jewish renewal, the Tibetans likewise see the environmental cause as a spiritual issue.

I asked him, having seen the seder, "What most touched you or made you think the most?"

"What I found most touching was the description of people experiencing great servitude and suffering emerging from that state and finding liberation, and how this symbolizes an inner journey, an inner freeing, gaining freedom from suffering, emerging from suffering.

"You all know that we experience bondage of some kind, and taking that external example reminds us of the need to emerge from that bondage.

"This is what I think."

"Thank you so much," I said. He had summarized in simple terms much of the teaching from Jonathan's reading of the Breslov Haggadah a year before.

"I want to thank you for everything that you prepared here."

"It was our pleasure," I said. "It was all pleasure. And now," I announced, "dessert!"

○

After my return from Dharamsala, I called Reb Zalman in Colorado to report back everything that had happened. I wanted him to know what had been said at the seder, and with His Holiness. I had done it, in many ways, for Reb Zalman—and because of him.

I had come full circle: the journey that began for me on a mountaintop in Dharamsala had taken me to Louisiana and Boulder, Los Angeles and Boston, and now back to Dharamsala. I had made that journey because of Reb Zalman.

Almost exactly a year had passed since our dinner at the Himalayan restaurant in Boulder, and now, talking to him and briefly to Eve Ilsen on the phone, I had the sense he was settling into a comfortable life in Colorado. He had wonderful *hevrah* [religious community], he said, davening in Rabbi Tirzah Firestone's shul in Boulder, content to relax and let others lead. Eve invited me to join them for Scrabble the next time I visited, but explained, "We use different rules." I wasn't entirely surprised: Reb Zalman has been tinkering with the rules all his life.

Reb Zalman came on the line from downstairs and explained that in their Scrabble game, you can bargain with other people for letters. "If they accept," Eve said, "they get twenty percent of the word." "We play a kind of collaborative game," Reb Zalman added. "We don't want adversarial stuff."

I asked Reb Zalman what he wanted to hear about first, and he said the seder, because he had an "applied" interest in it. Zalman shared an office at the Naropa Institute with a Tibetan lama, and he and Eve had conducted a Pesach seder for fourteen the first night, including several Tibetan guests. Now at the end of the eighth day of Passover, he considered my phone call a "*yuntif* [holiday] visit," which it certainly was.

I told him about the mysterious teacher we met on the streets of Dharamsala, who had called me rabbi. "Elijah" felt that Buddhism had a more direct approach to the path of the heart than the Judaism he'd been taught.

Reb Zalman said, "Right. It doesn't have so many tallisim and tefillin," all the particular ritual equipment and customs and practices Jews have accumulated over thousands of years.

All through the year I'd been struggling with this issue: we Jews, as Art Green said, have to drag our *fleishik* pots and *milchik* pots through the wilderness, and our multivolume commentaries on our backs. At this time, we sense that we need to let some of this go but don't have the criteria for letting go solidly in mind. Reb Zalman, as a bearer of the rich European Jewish tradition, had been living this problem and thinking and feeling it for us.

The seder itself is a dualistic vehicle. Actually it's not so much a Bentley, I've decided, as a station wagon. It doesn't go very fast, but it can carry the whole family. The seder is a good example. For many it is only for family and friends, and full of sentiment and nostalgia. Yet it can also provide an existential spiritual journey.

How do we travel from level to level? I don't believe we should abandon the form for the force, as Buber hoped to do. We need the old vehicle yet to travel back and forth, up and down. I told Reb Zalman about Geshe Sonam's question. Why were the hardships visited on the Egyptians? Reb Zalman replied, "It's so wonderful because it puts us always back at our dualism, which we are ashamed of. We'd like to be able to get beyond that."

"Right."

"But we do go beyond it on the eighth day of Pesach," he said. "Today, the *haftarah* was Isaiah 10, the peaceable kingdom, which is a way of saying, 'It takes a while.'"[1] He chuckled. In Isaiah's vision, "the wolf will dwell with the lamb; the leopard will lie down with the kid, the calf, the young lion, and the fatling together; and a little child will lead them."[2]

In the peaceable kingdom, all the dualism of our experience, symbolized by warring animals, is reconciled. Violence and conflict are banished. The prophet declares, "They will not hurt or destroy in all My holy mountain; for the earth will be full of knowledge of God, as the waters cover the sea."[3]

Reb Zalman explained that the Buddhists also speak of a pure land, and the Tibetans about Shambhala, an imaginary kingdom in which peace reigns.

The duality we are sometimes ashamed of is also Judaism's great strength. It keeps us solidly in the world, together, as a community while we work toward a time of perfection. But the key is to remember the practices that help us climb back to our unity, that make the *Shema* real. Behind the duality is the level of unity, which all people are trying to realize, and which we Jews realize in our own special language.

That language is very beautiful and has great depths in which I can see my life reflected. The seder speaks the language of food, of green and salt, of sweet and bitter, as the sweet and the bitter, the new and the old, mix in our lives. I told Reb Zalman about Geshe Sonam's comment on the Hillel sandwich—that it's very important to mix opposites.

He replied, "There's a beautiful story in which two worms meet. One worm is the worm in the horseradish, and he says, 'Oy, have I got a good home. You know, I have all the food there, I'm really very happy.' So the worm in the apple says, 'Have you ever tasted my home?'"

I laughed.

"'You don't know,'" Reb Zalman continued in the voice of the apple worm. "'You think horseradish life is the best you can get?'" He marveled at Geshe Sonam: "It's wonderful how he gets it." Reb Zalman explained that the urtext of kabbalah, the *Sefer Yetzirah*, or Book of Formation, unfolds creation as a series of oppositions.

"If it wouldn't be for sweet, how would you know what is bitter? If it wouldn't be for bitter, you wouldn't know sweet. It always takes the opposite to prove the quality. If it wouldn't be for darkness, how would you know how much greater is light?"

And if it wouldn't be for great pain, I thought, how would we know to open the heart?

I told Reb Zalman how quickly Geshe Sonam had grasped the seder as a theater of awareness.

"Isn't it wonderful what he does for us?" Zalman said. "To tell it back to people at that level, so when we come back to tell it to our people, they stand with their mouths open."

Certainly Jews can learn from the Tibetan Buddhist emphasis on the inner meaning, the inner vitality of our outward-seeming tradition, the inner life of the mezuzah, of the seder, of the *Shema*, of everything we Jews say and do, sometimes by rote or cultural habit, and sometimes with not enough awareness.

At the same time, Reb Zalman sees the Tibetans as people who can learn from the Jews. "They haven't done the sociology of ethnic survival. They are working in the dark. They don't even know what questions to ask. Geshe Sonam is wonderful, his *neshamah* [soul] is great, but when it comes to the applied questions, about what we need to do in Diaspora—it doesn't come so easy." For Zalman, the very duality that we are sometimes ashamed of as Jews is also a great strength. The machinery of our tradition, the old Bentley station wagon, has life not only for Jews, but as a model vehicle for others.

Reb Zalman had invited exiled Tibetan lamas to his seder that year. In his own contact with Tibetans in Boulder, "I kept working on this thing—that householders need to have some forms to tell the story and have the symbolic food which is memorable."

I was taken with Zalman's vision, though I knew in my heart we'd accomplished something much more modest, shown one Tibetan teacher what a seder is.

I thought about how my whole journey in the past six years had been a continuous education, how the exchanges I'd had with so many teachers, and not just teachers, had moved from exchanges of information to transformation. In Dharamsala I had called the Dalai Lama a rabbi—and a day later, a stranger on the street had called me a rabbi in turn. I didn't need to stalk Elijah; Elijah was stalking me.

He had come to remind me what I heard when I called out to the One on the San Bernardino Freeway: open the heart, open the heart. When I told Zalman about what the Elijah of Dharamsala had said about the *sha'ar ha-rahamim* [gate of mercy], my teacher replied with something amazing.

"There is a being in the universe—a bodhisattva, the sacred heart of Jesus, the heart of the *Yod Heh Vov Heh*. When you touch that part of compassion so that it comes alive for other beings, that's when you *are* the *sha'ar ha-rahamim*."

○

How do we teach and how do we learn? The Talmud asks, "Who is wise?" and answers, "One who learns from everyone."

The question is, How do I get to the state of mind where I can learn from every person? That is not so easy. But it seems to be the whole point of spiritual practice.

Every experience and every event has a voice, if only I keep my receiver in range. The blind man in an airport can be my teacher as well as Jonathan Omer-Man or Reb Zalman or Eve Ilsen—and how I play Scrabble can be as profound as how I daven, if I truly listen and learn from every person and every event. Then I will meet Elijah everywhere and in everyone.

The Jewish people have been blessed with many kinds of teachers and many teachings, but our richness can be sorted out only by heart. Some teachers are stern Shammais; others are sweet as Hillel. Certainly we hear such voices in today's interdenominational battles, and within denominations, as Jews argue about who is obedient, and who slack, and even who is and isn't a Jew.

As Geshe Sonam remarked, Shammai represents discipline (*gevurah*) and Hillel compassion (*hesed*). *Gevurah* and *hesed*, *keva* and *kavanna*—then as now in Jewish life, forms and forces do their dance. Today some Jews daydream of formless forces while others toil in the chains of empty, enervated forms. To Reb Zalman, who has struggled with both the meaning of forms and the power of what they contain, the lesson of Shammai and Hillel is that they are dialectical teachers.

When the Gentile first asked Shammai to explain Judaism while standing on one foot, Shammai struck him. "If it wouldn't have been for Shammai hitting the guy over the head," Zalman said, "what Hillel said in one sentence wouldn't have been enough. You know . . . because it was still rankling in him: 'Why did Shammai do that to me?' So when Hillel said, 'Don't do something to someone else that you wouldn't want done to you,' the Gentile had an experiential base."

"But could the same man have hit him on the head and then given him that lesson?"

"In Zen that's the way it would happen."

I laughed, admiring as always Zalman's range. We hung up, and I thought of many things on the eighth day of Passover. Of Isaiah's vision of the peaceable kingdom, of duality and monotheism, of Jonathan's soft voice and *Adonai* as doorsill, of Paul Wolff's intensity, and Art Green's affirming the voice I heard, a voice that said, "Open my heart." Of the seder Mark Borovitz had described in Chino prison and of how the home seder, as Lynn Gottlieb taught, is the spiritual gift of Jewish women from generation to generation.

Now we'd done a seder with Tibetans in India. One I hoped would be a model to get more people involved with the Tibetan cause of freedom. Paradoxically, by sharing the seder this way, donating part of it to other peoples, we begin to see the value of it more clearly for ourselves. In this time of pluralism, we Jews don't have to fear. Our tradition will only become more beautiful as we share it with others. No longer something to hold tightly and defensively to ourselves, our tradition is becoming what it was meant to be, foretold to Abraham so long ago: a blessing to humanity and a gift to bestow with open arms.

In that spirit we came to the end of the seder in Dharamsala, the messianic part of the evening. We opened the door for Elijah, *Eliahu ha-navi*, the prophet of hope and perfection. We'd set for him a brimming wine cup, and even though it wasn't really Passover, I checked its level all the same.

I had traveled from India to India. From the time Reb Zalman put his finger to my chest and said, "Your God is a true God," to another time, inside Kashmir Cottage, when, thinking of Reb Zalman, I raised the fourth cup and spoke a toast: "We're going to dedicate this last cup to the hope that the Jewish people and the Tibetan people will continue a friendship that will last for many years, and that we will continue to honor and comfort each other in years to come." Then I heard again our words, which express the hope of Elijah—redemption for Jews, redemption for Tibetans and, in some way, ultimately, for all the world.

"*Le-shanah ha-ba'ah Birushalayim!*" we called out, and I added, turning to Geshe Sonam, "*Le-shanah ha-ba'ah be-Lhasa!*"

Next Year in Jerusalem. Next Year in Lhasa.

*Afterword:* Teshuvah *and the Wisdom in Time*
APRIL–MAY 1997; NISAN–IYAR 5757

In Deuteronomy the Jewish people are commanded to teach the Torah diligently to our children. Every Jewish parent, then, is a full-time teacher, and the teaching goes on night and day, when you lie down and when you rise up. Clearly, the Jewish transmission is not genetic but educational. But what is education?

Today we live in an information-rich environment, but information is not meaning. When our Jewish education is reduced to information, it dies. As Rabbi Shefa Gold told me, it's "say these millions of things and do these millions of things," but the point of doing is lost. Often there's a confusion between having the right answer and being a righteous person. The ego comes into play, and unfortunately, much Jewish teaching is given in an atmosphere of intellectual one-upmanship, the power politics of knowing more than someone else. That's why I kept asking the teachers I met if God has any entrance requirements or knowledge requirements. And the answer from Art Green was, Yes, to treat every person as being in the image of God. That is especially important to remember when we teach and when we learn. To me, education means not dictation, but personal encounter.

In the traditional account that begins the Pirkei Avot, an Oral Torah was passed down from Sinai to Moses to Joshua to the men of the Great Assembly to the rabbinic sages to today. But Jewish women have also been passing down a Torah, and now we are beginning to learn it, as we have already lived it in our homes and families. However we read this statement of spiritual transmission, it's clear that in the holy chain of teachers, the holiness is not only in the content of the teaching, but also in the love passed down with it. The teaching of Judaism is brimming with love and light.

We are now entering a new stage in Judaism, a time of crisis but also of renewal. The old foundations, whether of Reform Judaism at one end or of Orthodoxy at the other, have been shaken. If I were to define myself denominationally, I'd say I'm an under-constructionist—and I wear a yellow hard-hat yarmulke.

We are building a new *mishkan*, and we have so many fine materials to draw on. We are looking for the light in the old kabbalah, but also in the new language of our experience. My teachers are women and men, my teachers are not all Jews—for I cannot assume any more triumphalism, whether the triumphalism of those segments of Orthodoxy that cannot acknowledge what is holy in the present or in other traditions, or the modernist triumphalism of a Reform Judaism that a hundred years ago discarded large parts of an ancient wisdom without due consideration. I have learned some of the richness of my Jewish language from teachers like Rabbi Jonathan Omer-Man and Rabbi Arthur Green and Reb Zalman, Rabbi Arthur Waskow and Rabbi Shefa Gold, but I have also learned it from many Buddhist teachers. When I called the Dalai Lama my rabbi, I meant that he too has shown me a pathway toward a deeper Jewish language. We don't have to be afraid of our dialogue with other traditions if we allow that dialogue to deepen our appreciation of our own. Just as Tibetans can hear Jewish questions about survival, so we Jews can begin to hear the deep Buddhist questions about our inner life.

I have also learned about the urgency of the search for new spiritual language from Rabbi Judith Halevy and from Mark Borovitz and from the *Maggid* of Hollywood and from Rabbi Lynn Gottlieb. In that richness, and with that personal urgency, I am part of a generation constructing a *mishkan* where the sacred and the everyday can be encountered. There's no part of my tradition I can afford to throw out without consideration, no richness I might not return to my life. It is a living tradition and a living process of interpretation, and I join it with joy.

I have explored here only a small part of a larger world of Jewish renewal, which in its broadest sense is a wave moving through the entire Jewish world. Although my work here has been primarily personal, holy work is not just prayers and meditation. I was impressed by the example of Mark Borovitz and Paul Wolff—that inner work did not preclude social action. The work we do on ourselves to increase our clarity, our humility, and our *hishtavut* should lead us to deeper and more constructive encounters with the world around us.

○

Even within the small part of the Jewish world I've explored, I've heard contradictions. Many have to do with language, and that is why one major resource for me has been that guide of the perplexed, Rabbi Moses Maimonides, the Rambam, whose philosophical examination of biblical language still speaks to the contemporary reader. I came to the Rambam from the Dalai Lama, for I first heard the challenge to Jewish language in Buddhism, with its emphasis on silence and emptiness.

Inspired in part by the example of Rabbi Zalman Schachter, two of my teachers, Rabbi Jonathan Omer-Man and Rabbi Arthur Green, have also responded to the challenge of Buddhist teaching, in part by searching the spiritual richness of kabbalah and *hasidut*, and transmitting these teachings and practices to contemporary heterodox Jews.

But in our time, another major challenge to Jewish language arises from listening to the voices of Jewish women, which for so long have been suppressed or ignored. When I first encountered Jewish renewal, I thought the feminine imagery of kabbalah might help us create a more inclusive prayer language, but I've come to think that the task is more complex. The kabbalah has a vital depth to offer any Judaism, but simple substitution of its rubrics or imagery will not resolve the deeper questions women are asking. For one thing, the kabbalah too readily equates masculine with active and feminine with passive. In our discussions, Art Green acknowledged this. "The question is," he said, "will there be a new kabbalah that will emerge in this age?" In regard to new forms of prayer that might emerge in response to meditative experience, he added that "other forms have to emerge. Some of them may have to be created by women. There may be some kind of Rosh Hodesh form that is going to emerge to renew our ritual life or renew Jewish women's ritual life. I think that's great."

In my view, this work not only is emerging, it's burgeoning. Creative work—like Lynn Gottlieb's *mishkan* or Torah-tarot, and Judith Halevy's theatrical interpretations of a Rebbe Nachman tale—joins a larger movement of women's midrash. But midrash has always been an area where the imagination has been fully engaged.

A more sensitive and conservative area, intimately connected with memory and nostalgia, is prayer. I could see the resistance to change in Rabbi Jonathan Omer-Man's preference for working with the traditional language and in Art Green's home davening, though he admitted that his attachment to the old prayer language is "vestigial." "The minyan I belong to," he said, "and the minyanim I support have always been egalitarian. I've spent my whole life that way." Yet he described with fondness a synagogue in Jerusalem he and Kathy go to, full of sixties people who made *aliyah*, but who are Orthodox and have a *meḥitzah*, or curtain separating men from women. "I like davening in a room immediately surrounded by men," he said, "with the women on the other side. Maybe it's the difference in what the prayer experience is for men and women, maybe it's a difference in our biological rhythms and style, the way we do it; it feels great for me to be praying among men."

Clearly the situation is quite complex. Art Green felt nostalgia for male-only worship. Men need a place, he said, to bond as Jews "not just on the golf course or the *shvitz*." Jewish women also feel this need, and many are working with separate prayer groups and Rosh Hodesh ceremonies. Anyone who thinks she or he has the answers to such questions, the right balance between competing claims of memory and justice, probably isn't paying full attention to all the voices out there. Some answers that satisfy the head, the heart can't go along with. For instance, when Moshe Waldoks told me he preferred the traditional *nusaḥ* [melodies] for prayer over Jewish renewal innovations, I understood that the old tunes have profound resonances for him. Yet they were also devised in exclusively male milieus where women's voices literally were not heard. So it's not surprising today's women might need to sing new songs.

Some women, among them Rabbi Shefa Gold and Hannah Tiferet Siegel, use the Shekhinah language of the kabbalists in their prayer. Others, like Marcia Falk in her *Book of Blessings*, have moved into new territory. Falk, a Hebrew scholar, translator, and poet, has spent the better part of two decades working on new paradigms for Jewish prayer, work that she presented last year, complete with scholarly apparatus, in her grand *Book of Blessings*. Her prayers work very much toward a sense of presence in the moment, in the act of blessing, that recalls Rabbi Omer-Man's kabbalah of the blessing path. The difference is that Falk does not practice an explicit triangulation between the blesser, the blessed, and the source of blessing. Indeed, she does not find it meaningful or powerful to address YHVH as an "other," and therefore she does not address YHVH as a "You."

The development of feminist reconstruction of prayer can be seen in a tale of three translations. When Jonathan taught me the blessing over bread, he worked with the traditional language: *Barukh Atah Adonai, Eloheinu melekh ha-olam, ha-motzi leḥem min ha-aretz*—Blessed art thou, *Adonai* our God, king of the universe who brings forth bread from the earth. Jewish renewal, in its prayers in the Or Chadash siddur, revises the *petiḥah*, or opening formula, to *Berukhah At Yah Eloheinu Ḥei Ha-olamim* . . . —Blessed art Thou (f.), Yah our God, life of all the worlds . . . This meets the problem of addressing God as a masculine You and as a king by substituting a feminine You and a traditional phrase in the feminine gender.

But Marcia Falk's blessing over bread eliminates the direct address and its grammar altogether: *N'vareykh et eyn ha-ḥayim hamotzi'ah leḥem min ha'aretz*—Let us bless the source of life that brings forth bread from the earth.[1] As a feminist, Falk clearly wishes to avoid the particular patriarchal associations of the rabbinic "*Adonai Eloheinu melekh ha-olam*": Lord—God—King. But the change in grammar also implies a theology that there is nothing else but God. The "source of life" in her prayer language hovers mysteriously in the words as it does in the experience, but we do not address it directly because that would imply a separation between the one reciting the blessing and the source of blessing— a separation Marcia Falk does not feel. Her prayer language speaks not only to issues raised by women, but to the theology articulated by Art Green as well.

Though we did not speak directly of Falk's work, Art Green told me that in general he welcomes such innovation in prayer and inner language: "I am waiting for the new kabbalah to emerge that will be created by women as well as by men. I'm very enthusiastic about that." On the other hand, Marcia Falk makes clear that she sees a discrepancy between Art Green's nondualistic theology and his prayer language.[2]

I wonder, though, if consistency is possible right now: in building the *mishkan* we work with all sorts of materials while transforming them. For myself, I find traditional Jewish prayer powerful in part because the old language is very new to me. The Hebrew still works as a koan and keeps me awake. But I respect what Marcia Falk and others are doing, because in the end, as

Shefa Gold said, God is not Jewish, and God is not the names we give to God. The mystery of unity expressed in the name YHVH goes beyond the complacency that the rote repetition of the rabbinic formulas can lead to. Like the *Shema*, all of our language needs shattering lest it become another idol.

In the end, the language of prayer should help us to an experience, not get in the way. Perhaps the most powerful language for Jews today is silence: we need more *shohin*—more emptying—in our prayer experience. One of Falk's points is that "no convention of prayer"—and she includes her own—"ought to become completely routine, lest it lose its ability to inspire authentic feeling." Rather, "we should set in motion *a process of ongoing naming*."[3] That to me seems exactly right. It is what Jonathan Omer-Man called the deepest form of prayer, calling things by their right names. That "ongoing naming" arises most profoundly from a depth of silence.

○

I first learned about that silence from my Tibetan friends. I had long wanted to repay that debt by helping the Tibetan political cause. After my return from Dharamsala in the spring of 1996, I joined the Interfaith Action Network of the International Campaign for Tibet, to mobilize people of all faiths in support of a free Tibet.

A new crisis with the Chinese arose after the Dalai Lama recognized a young boy, Gendun Choekyi Nyima, as the reincarnation of the eleventh Panchen Lama, the second highest religious position in Tibet. In November 1995, the Chinese government overruled his choice and selected their own candidate.

The young Panchen Lama and his family were placed under house arrest. The International Campaign for Tibet wished to organize a political campaign around his birthday, which fell on April 25, 1997. At age eight, he is the world's youngest prisoner of conscience.

Just back from our seder in Dharamsala, I was moved by the coincidence: April 25 fell during Passover week 1997. While young Jewish children could recite the four questions, a young Tibetan boy had been deprived of freedom on purely religious grounds. I proposed organizing a national campaign to help Jews become more involved with the campaign for Tibetan freedom. As we had done in Dharamsala, Jews everywhere would celebrate their Passover with Tibetan freedom in mind.

The idea spread nationally, through Hillels on college campuses, through an article in *Reform Judaism,* and through Aleph. From Dharamsala, the Dalai Lama sent the seders for Tibet a special message of greeting. Then, a month before Passover, I learned His Holiness wished to attend one himself, during a political visit to Washington, D.C.

Rabbi David Saperstein, of Reform Judaism's Religious Action Center, answered the call to host the event, and that is how I found myself on April 24, 1997, breaking matzah in such unfamiliar company as Supreme Court Justice Stephen Breyer and Adam Yauch of the Beastie Boys.

The Dalai Lama, with his glasses and black yarmulke (which I'd handed him just before we entered), looked very rabbinic and studious as he carefully followed the service in the Haggadah. Now once again, my younger daughter, Kezia, said the four questions, only this time before the Dalai Lama. He seemed touched by the recitation, and amused and delighted when David Saperstein's young son crawled under the head table to join him. The culinary delights of the seder were also not lost on His Holiness: as we ate our traditional boiled eggs with salt water, he pointed to a plate and said, "Bread? Bread?"

I said, "Matzah?"

He said, "Yes," taking some, and added cheerfully, "I like matzah!"

With politically important guests and rabbis from the major denominations, this wasn't like the intimate seder in Dharamsala. But it had its own beauty. At one point, the fifty of us crowded in a small room grew silent as we listened to a recording smuggled out of Tibet. We heard the quavering voice of Phuntsok Nyidron, a nineteen-year-old nun serving seventeen years in Drapchi prison. From far away, she sang to our seder about the meaning of freedom. Together we read the translation of her lyric, "We the captured friends in spirit. . . no matter how hard we are beaten/Our linked arms cannot be separated."

Reb Zalman's imaginative idea of doing a seder in Dharamsala had flowered and bloomed in an extraordinary way. The seder with the Dalai Lama was publicized around the world and, along with the Seders for Tibet, built a stronger connection between Jews and Tibetans. My hope is that Jews will continue to support the Tibetan cause until the Dalai Lama himself can say, "*This* year in Lhasa."

O

I began this account with a question I first heard from the Dalai Lama: What are our Jewish methods for genuine transformation?

For Paul Wolff, the blessing teaching is essential. Jonathan Omer-Man said that for him it is the blessing path and meditation. For Rabbi Judith Halevy, the holidays and cycles of time. For me, the most important practice I learned in this period among so many practices was the calling out, the *hitbodedut*, of Rebbe Nachman. Once I had this experience of personal prayer in my own language, I could read formal liturgical prayer in a whole new way. I heard my private thoughts and feelings echoed there.

But along with such private prayer, there is what Jonathan called *keva*, the discipline of daily and weekly practice. Our Jewish life is full of occasions for transformation, for *teshuvah*.

There are daily practices for inner transformation as well. I have described earlier the prayers on rising, and the morning prayer practice with which I began my explorations. There is also a prayer sequence for retiring at the end of the day.

The traditional bedtime *Shema* reminds us to review our actions. But before I can recite the *Shema*, which affirms the wholeness and unity of all being, I must repair the damages and cracks in my near relationships.

This can be done by recalling each person who this day has harmed me in some way. I call up each face in my imagination and forgive that person in my heart: I ask that no harm befalls that person because of what he or she has done to me. This is sometimes, I find, a difficult exercise. In fact there are many nights when I do not get to go to sleep for a long time. But it is powerful: I end my day in wholeness as I began it in gratitude.

In the weekly cycle, the Shabbat is our way of enacting perfection and wholeness; when the Dalai Lama first heard the customs of Shabbat described, he responded, "So it's a visualization." Shabbat then is, potentially, a daylong visualization of perfection, of peace, of *shelom-bayit*, peace in the family, peace in the home. It begins hours before sundown in the afternoon, when we clear the table at home, when we set a special tablecloth, when my daughter brings down the candlesticks—we use one for each daughter and two for my wife—and I run out to the bagel shop for our weekly challah. And then the actual candle lighting, the blessing of the children, the review of our week, the blessing over wine and over bread. Shabbat is a profound meditation on feeling at home.

There are larger cycles of time in our calendar, as Reb Zalman and Rabbi Judith Halevy taught me so well. In the fall, so many Jews, whether religious or not, feel a sense of return, a sense of *teshuvah*. They may feel it only as guilt, or perhaps express it mainly as a return to family and friends, or a visit to a synagogue. But for Rosh Hashanah and Yom Kippur, they do return, and try in their own way to make *teshuvah*.

Last year, I was asked by my synagogue in New Orleans to speak at Shabbat Shuvah, the Sabbath of Repentance (or turning), which falls between Rosh Hashanah and Yom Kippur. As I looked at the moon the night before, I saw by its shape how we were moving one day closer to Yom Kippur. I told my congregation what I'd learned from Arthur Green and Arthur Waskow: "The moon is our Jewish calendar. Our festivals begin on new or full moons, the new moon of Rosh Hashanah, the full moon of Pesach and Sukkot."

"Tonight," I said, "the moon tells us that we are in the eighth day of the ten days of *teshuvah*, of turning. Shabbat Shuvah is a special day in the ten days. It is said that the first seven days belong to Rosh Hashanah and the next three to Yom Kippur. Like the moon, we must turn toward the fullness of repentance because we stand before a darkness. We do not know what awaits in this coming year. And each year at this time we meditate on the past year, we do the bedtime *Shema* for an entire year. We seek to repair in person all our harms to others so we can stand on Erev Yom Kippur with an open heart and come before the Holy One, before the presence of that which rules in being."

So on the grand calendar of the Jewish year, the ten days of *teshuvah* provide an opportunity for internal audit and change. But *teshuvah* doesn't need to come only during the days of awe. For instance, the practice of counting the Omer between Pesach and Shavuot can be a powerful tool for self-reflection. *Teshuvah* can also be a daily practice of bedtime prayer, and a weekly practice at Shabbat. When Paul Wolff asked the men of Beit T'shuvah to go over their week, and discover what they felt gratitude for, they were taking the first step of *teshuvah*, an internal audit of change.

*Teshuvah*—turning—is our Jewish method of transformation, of "purification of our conflicting emotions" or, as the Tibetans put it so beautifully, "of our afflictive states of mind."

My own *teshuvah*, this year and next, will be to return to these practices more fully and faithfully, to live in the moment, and in the day and the week and the year, the wisdom embedded in Jewish time, the wisdom Reb Zalman first hinted at long ago in Dharamsala. "Teach us to number our days that we may get us a heart of wisdom."

NEW ORLEANS
MAY 28, 1997; 21 IYAR 5757, THE THIRTY-SIXTH DAY OF THE COUNTING OF THE OMER, *MALKHUT* OF *HOD*, THE NOBILITY IN HUMILITY

# Notes

## 2 GOD, ONE: NOTHING, NOTHING

1. In the *Shiur Komah.*
2. *Yevamot* 71a; *Bava Metzia* 31b.

## 3 MEDITATIONS ON THE BREATH

1. Joseph Goldstein and Jack Kornfield, *Seeking the Heart of Wisdom* (Boston: Shambhala, 1987).
2. Acharya Shantideva, *A Guide to the Bodhisattva's Way of Life*, trans. Stephen Batchelor (Dharamsala: Library of Tibetan Works and Archives, 1979).
3. The verb is in *vov* consecutive imperfect. See Ernest Klein, *A Comprehensive Etymological Dictionary of the Hebrew Language* (New York: Macmillan, 1987), p.422, s.v. See also Rashi's commentary on Exodus 31:17. Rashi affirms "restores one's soul and breath" and insists we must leave open what this might mean in the case of God.

## 4 RABBI ZALMAN SCHACHTER-SHALOMI: FOUR WORLDS, TEN *SEFIROT*

1. No hasidic sect has ever crossed into universalism, though in the prewar urban milieus of Vienna and Warsaw, as Zalman points out, Hillel Zeitlin, among others, approached it.
2. In Hebrew, *milei elohut*, "terms of divinity." See *Or Chadash*, 2d draft ed. (Philadelphia: Aleph, 1991), p. 35, for a discussion by David Cooper.

## 5 MOVING UNDER THE TREE OF LIFE

1. The Tanya, or *Likutei Amarim,* is the kabbalistic Torah treatise of Rabbi Schneur Zalman of Liadi, the founder of Chabad hasidism. A bilingual edition (Hebrew/English) is published by Kehot Publication Society, 770 Eastern Parkway, Brooklyn, New York 11213.

2. Zalman Schachter-Shalomi, *Spiritual Intimacy: A Study of Counseling in Hasidism* (New York: Jason Aronson, 1991), p. xii.

### 6 A Kabbalah Tourist

1. See R. Simon Jacobson, *A Spiritual Guide to Counting the Omer* (Brooklyn: Vaad Hanochos Hatmimim, 1996). A very helpful, usable guide.
2. Based on association. The letter *ayin* ע actually has the numerical equivalent of 70, and the word *ayin*, spelled ayin yod nun, means "eye"; however, the word *ein*, spelled aleph yod nun, means "nothingness."
3. 2 Kings 2:11.
4. Malachi 3:24.
5. Eduyyot, chap. 8, mishnah 7.
6. A *Tanna* (a teacher of the first and second centuries C.E.) of the fifth generation, 135–170 C.E.
7. Berakhot 3a.

### 7 Rabbi Shefa Gold: The Essential Vehicle

1. On the audiocassette *Tzuri (My Rock)*, available through Aleph.
2. *Dhikr* is an Arabic word meaning "remembrance." It also describes the Sufi practice of repeating a name of God or a phrase from the Qur'an to become aware of God.
3. Judith Plaskow, *Standing Again at Sinai* (San Francisco: HarperSanFrancisco, 1990).
4. Plaskow, *Standing Again at Sinai*, p. xvi.
5. Plaskow, *Standing Again at Sinai*, p. xiii.
6. Song of Songs 3:1: "By night on my bed I sought him whom my soul loves; I sought him, but I found him not."
7. For these kabbalistic terms and for a clear overview of kabbalah, I highly recommend Aryeh Kaplan, *Inner Space* (Jerusalem: Moznaim, 1990). Another stunning and penetrating introduction is Allen Afterman, *Kabbalah and Consciousness* (New York: Sheep Meadow Press, 1992).

### 8 Rabbi Zalman Schachter-Shalomi and Eve Ilsen: My Days Are Numbered

1. In his *Nine Gates to the Hasidic Mysteries*, an account of his life among the ḥasidim of Belz.

2. See Frantisek Langer, foreword to *Nine Gates to the Chassidic Mysteries*, by Jiri Langer (New York: Behrman House, 1976), p. xvii, where Kafka's "The Metamorphosis" is mentioned.

3. Cf., for instance, Rebbe Nachman's tale "The Prince Who Thought He Was a Turkey" as expounded in Avraham Greenbaum, *Under the Table and How to Get Up: Jewish Pathways of Spiritual Growth* (Tsohar Publishing, New York: 1991).

4. Zalman Schachter and Edward Hoffman, *Sparks of Light: Counseling in the Hasidic Tradition* (Boulder: Shambhala, 1983), pp. 174–75.

5. Deuteronomy 6:4–9.

## 9  RABBI JONATHAN OMER-MAN: THE SIDDUR IS A BOOK OF KOANS

1. Zohar I:4a–4b. See Isaiah Tishby, *The Wisdom of the Zohar: An Anthology of Texts* (Oxford: Oxford Univ. Press, 1989), vol. 1, p. 166; Harry Sperling et al., *The Zohar* (London: Soncino Press, 1984), vol. 1, pp. 15–18.

2. In Hebrew: *Modeh ani le-fanekha melekh hai ve-kayam. Shehehezarta bi nishmati be-hemlah. Rabbah emunatekha.*

3. In Hebrew, *Reishit hokhmah yirat Adonai.* See Psalm 20.

4. *Barukh Atah Adonai Eloheinu melekh ha-olam asher kideshanu be-mitzvotav vitzivanu al netilat yadayim.*

5. In Jewish renewal teaching, the word *mitzvah* is related to its Aramaic root, which means "connection." A mitzvah is to be seen not only as an order coming from the top down, but also as a connection between our scale of life and the divine scale.

## 10  PRAYER: THE WORLD IS WRONG NAMES

1. Moses Maimonides, *The Guide of the Perplexed*, trans. Shlomo Pines (Chicago: Univ. of Chicago Press, 1963), vol. 2, p. 526.

2. Maimonides, *Guide of the Perplexed*, vol. 1, p. 124.

3. Maimonides, *Guide of the Perplexed*, vol. 1, p. 126.

4. "In Memoriam: Richard Shapiro," *Metivta Newsletter* 1, no. 4 (August 1994).

## 11  TORAH AND THE STRANGE FIRE

1. A second *parashah*, Parah, on the red heifer, was also read because this was the third of four special Shabbats leading up to Passover. Cf. the chapter "Rabbi Judith Halevy: Cycles of Jewish Time" later in this book.

2. "Learn Torah with Rabbi Jonathan Omer-Man: Parashat Shemini," *Learn Torah with . . .* vol. 2, no. 26 (Shabbat, April 13, 1996); published by Torah Aura Productions, 4423 Fruitland Avenue, Los Angeles, CA 90058.
3. "Learn Torah with Rabbi Jonathan Omer-Man," vol. 2, no. 26.

### 13　RABBI LYNN GOTTLIEB: BUILDING THE NEW *MISHKAN*

1. Ellen Umansky, foreword to *She Who Dwells Within: A Feminist Vision of a Renewed Judaism*, by Lynn Gottlieb (San Francisco, HarperSanFrancisco, 1995), pp. xii–xiii.
2. For an anthology of such new rituals, see R. Debra Orenstein, ed., *Lifecycles: Jewish Women on Life Passages and Personal Milestones* (Woodstock, VT: Jewish Lights, 1994).
3. Gottlieb, *She Who Dwells Within*, p. 124.
4. Avivah Cantor, *Jewish Women/Jewish Men* (San Francisco: HarperSanFrancisco, 1995), pp. 101–2.

### 14　THE DOOR OF PAIN

1. Gershom Scholem, "Religious Authority and Mysticism," in *On the Kabbala and Its Symbolism* (New York: Shocken Books, 1965), pp. 29–30; he cites the source as R. Mendel Torum of Rymanov (d. 1814). See also Dov Levine, trans., *The Torah Discourses of the Holy Tzaddik Reb Menachem Mendel of Rimanov* (Hoboken, NJ: Ktav Publishing, 1996), p. 217.
2. See also Martin Buber in his exchange of letters with Franz Rosenzweig: "I do not believe that revelation is ever a formulation of law. It is only through man in his self-contradiction that revelation becomes legislation. This is the fact of man. I cannot admit the law transformed by man into the realm of my will, if I am to hold myself ready as well for the unmediated word of God directed to a specific hour of my life." (Heppenheim, June 24, 1924)
3. On her audiocassette *Chants Encounters* (Las Vegas, NM: B'emet Productions, 1994).
4. R. Yehoshua Starret, *The Breslov Haggadah* (Jerusalem and New York: Breslov Research Institute, 1989).

### 15　RABBI JUDITH HALEVY: CYCLES OF JEWISH TIME

1. Mekhilta, quoted by Rashi in his comment on Exodus 15:2.
2. Psalm 36:10: "For with you is the source of life [*mekor ḥayim*]; in your light shall we see light."

3. In addition to the Parshat Shemini, discussed earlier in this book in "Torah and the Strange Fire," Parshat Parah, the parashah of the red heifer, is added as the third of four special Shabbats leading up to Passover. By coincidence, it was Jonathan's bar mitzvah passage from forty-eight years before. He chanted it from memory.
4. E.g., Genesis Rabbah 8:12, Genesis Rabbah 18:2.
5. E.g., Genesis Rabbah 80:1.
6. Aryeh Kaplan, trans., *Rabbi Nachman's Stories* (Jerusalem and New York: Breslov Research Institute, 1983), p. 394.

## 16 MARK BOROVITZ: THE HOUSE OF RETURN

1. *Los Angeles Times*, April 19, 1993.
2. Quotation marks around a person's name upon its first introduction indicate that the name has been changed to protect that person's privacy.
3. See Phil Jacobs, "Addiction's Stepchildren," *Baltimore Jewish Times*, February 28, 1997, p. 69.

## 17 PAUL WOOLF: THE *MAGGID* OF HOLLYWOOD

1. *Metivta Newsletter* 1, no. 4 (August 1994).

## 19 LEARNING MEDITATION: DO THIS

1. Aryeh Kaplan, *Meditation and the Bible* (York Beach, ME: Samuel Weiser, 1978).
2. Kaplan, *Meditation and the Bible*, p. 1.
3. Aryeh Kaplan, *Meditation and Kabbalah* (York Beach, ME: Samuel Weiser, 1982). Kaplan writes, "The term 'Workings of the Merkava,' as used in the Talmud, refers to the mystery of Ezekiel's vision" (p. 19). The *merkavah* mystics attempted to replicate conditions under which they could have similar visions of God's throne. They date from at least the first century C.E.
4. Kaplan points out that the Talmud refers to them as the "first Hasidim." Cf. Nedarim 10a, Bava Kama 30a, Niddah 38a. They are not to be confused with the more familiar eighteenth-century movement of Hasidism.
5. Berakhot 32b.
6. Mark Verman, *The History and Varieties of Jewish Meditation* (Northvale, NJ: Jason Aronson, 1996), p. 8. I have altered his translation slightly.

7. Verman, *Varieties of Jewish Meditation*, pp. 8–9.
8. Reuven Hammer. *Entering Jewish Prayer* (New York: Schocken Books, 1994), pp. 104–5.
9. Verman, *Varieties of Jewish Meditation*, pp. 174–76.
10. His father, David Themanlys, was a disciple of Max Theon (1848–1927), a Polish kabbalist who led a circle of theosophists in Paris.
11. Verman, *Varieties of Jewish Meditation*, pp. 175–77.
12. Verman, *Varieties of Jewish Meditation*, pp. 175–76.

20  CORRECTIONS AND CONNECTIONS

1. Adin Steinsaltz, *The Thirteen Petalled Rose* (New York: Basic Books, 1980).
2. Dobh Baer of Lubavitch, *On Ecstasy*, trans. Louis Jacobs (New York: Rossell Books, 1963).
3. Steinsaltz, *Thirteen Petalled Rose*, p. 21.

22  DIVINE ALGEBRA: THE BLESSING PATH

1. According to Rabbi Meir, Menahot 43b.
2. See Arthur Green's discussion in *Seek My Face, Speak My Name*.
3. *The Complete ArtScroll Siddur*, ed. Rabbi Nosson Scherman (Brooklyn: Mesorah Publications, 1984), pp. 4–5.
4. The same movement from second to third person is even clearer in blessings involving commandments that begin with "You are Blessed, Lord our God" and continue, "who has sanctified us with his commandments." See Rabbi Dr. Elie Munk, *The World of Prayer* (New York: Philipp Feldheim, n.d.), vol. 1, p. 15. See also Reuven Hammer's helpful discussion in *Entering Jewish Prayer* (New York: Shocken Books, 1994), pp. 95 ff.
5. "Know that all the Holy Names in the Torah are intrinsically tied to the Tetragrammaton, which is YHVH." Rabbi Joseph Gikatilla, *Gates of Light (Sha'are Orah)*, trans. Avi Weinstein (San Francisco: Harper Collins, 1994), p. 6.
6. Gikatilla, *Gates of Light*, p. 247.
7. Gikatilla, *Gates of Light*, p. 245.
8. In contexts other than prayer, Orthodox Jews speak at even further remove, using *Adoshem* or *Hashem* (The Name). Likewise they would write YKVK or *Yod Kei Vov Kei*, not wishing in English or Hebrew to indicate this name.

9. The meaning is actually a base or pedestal, or the socket of a column. See Gikatilla, *Gates of Light*, p. 17: "AdoNaY contains the same root as AD'Nay He Chatzer (which are the foundations for the pillars of the courtyard)." Gikatilla relates the one hundred blessings a day to the one hundred sockets of the *mishkan*.

10. From "The Panther," *The Selected Poetry of Rainer Maria Rilke*, ed. and trans. Stephen Mitchell (New York: Vintage Books, 1984), p. 25.

11. For instance, when Moses meets YHVH at the burning bush, he's told "Ani Adonai—I am YHVH—and I appeared unto Abraham, unto Isaac and unto Jacob as El Shaddai—God Almighty, but by my name YHVH I made Me not known to them" (Exod. 6:2).

## 24 RABBI ARTHUR GREEN: DANCING ON THE SHORES OF THE SEA

1. English-only readers can taste a section of this enormous text, ably translated by the scholar Miles Krassen. See *Isaiah Horowitz: The Generations of Adam* (New York: Paulist Press, 1996).

2. From Mekilta, a midrash on Exodus, quoted by Rashi in his comment on Exodus 15:2.

3. William Novak, "A Conversation with Arthur Green," *Kerem*, spring 1995, p. 37.

4. Arthur Green, *Seek My Face, Speak My Name: A Contemporary Jewish Theology* (Northvale, NJ: Jason Aronson, 1994), p. 143.

5. Quoted by N. N. Glatzer, foreword to *Star of Redemption*, by Franz Rosenzweig (Notre Dame, IN: Univ. of Notre Dame Press, 1985), p. xii.

## 25 ALL ABOUT HALAKHAH: CORKSCREWS AND BY THE BOOK JEWS

1. Haim Soloveichik, "Rupture and Reconstruction: The Transformation of Contemporary Orthodoxy," *Tradition* 28:4, pp. 64–130.

2. Excerpted in *Modern Jewish Thought: A Source Reader*, ed. Nahum Glatzer (New York: Schocken Books, 1977).

3. Arthur Green, "Twin Centers: Sacred Time and Sacred Space," *Reconstructionist*, May–June 1990, pp. 16–22.

4. Avraham Greenbaum, ed., *Rabbi Nachman's Tikkun* (Jerusalem and New York: Breslov Research Institute, 1984).

5. Arthur Green, *Seek My Face, Speak My Name: A Contemporary Jewish Theology* (Northvale, TK: Jason Aronson, 1992), p. 7.

6. Green, *Seek My Face, Speak My Name*, p. 190.

7. Psalm 51:12.

8. Cf. the chapter "Learning Meditation: Do This" above.

### 26  A Seder in Dharamsala

1. On the last day of Passover, the *haftarah* is Isaiah 10:32–34, 11:1–16, and 12:1–6, the latter being Isaiah's vision of the Messianic age.
2. Isaiah 11:6.
3. Isaiah 11:9.

### Afterword

1. Marcia Falk, *The Book of Blessings* (San Francisco: HarperSanFrancisco, 1996), pp. 18–19. I have preserved Falk's transliteration, which differs slightly from the system I have used in this book.
2. Cf. Falk, *The Book of Blessing*, pp. 420–21. Falk explicitly comments on Green's nondualistic theology. She sees a discrepancy between Green's theology and his prayer language, and attributes it to "nostalgia" and "an entrenched conservatism on the part of the Jewish community at large in regard to liturgical change."
3. Falk, *The Book of Blessings*, p. xvii.

ABULAFIA, ABRAHAM: Thirteenth-century Spanish kabbalist who practiced an ecstatic kabbalah of letter combination and meditation on the divine name.

ADAM KADMON (Heb.): Primordial man. The fifth world (*olam*) of the *sefirot*, arrayed on the human body.

*AFIKOMAN:* The middle of three pieces of matzah, eaten at the conclusion of the seder. The custom is to break it, and hide half for the children to find.

AGGADAH: Jewish imaginative storytelling, commentary, theology; distinguished from legal discourse or halakhah.

*AKEIDAH:* The binding of Isaac (Gen. 22:9). Abraham prepares to sacrifice his son.

*ALEINU* (Heb., it is incumbent upon us): Prayer of divine sovereignty, originally part of the Rosh Hashanah service, but added since as the conclusion to all services.

ALEPH: The alliance of Jewish renewal havurot centered in Philadelphia; formerly P'nai Or and the Shalom Center.

*ALIYAH* (Heb., going up): 1. One who is called to read from the Torah. 2. One who ascends by going to live in Israel.

*AMIDAH* (Heb., standing): Also known as the *Shemoneh Esrei* (Eighteen Blessings) or *Tefillah* (Prayer). The blessings recited as the core of every Jewish prayer service.

*AM LEVANAH* (Heb.): People of the moon.

ASHKENAZIM: The Jews of Germany and eastern Europe, primarily Yiddish speakers, and their descendants who immigrated to the United States and Israel.

*ASSIYAH* (Heb., action, doing): One of four kabbalistic realms or *olamim*.

*ATZILUT* (Heb., nearness): One of four kabbalistic worlds.

AVALOKITESHVARA (Sanskrit): The bodhisattva of compassion. Tibetan Buddhists consider the Dalai Lama to be a manifestation of Avalokiteshvara.

*AVODAH* (Heb., work, service): Divine service, originally as sacrifice in the Temple.

BAAL SHEM TOV (Heb., "Master of the Good Name"): Rabbi Israel Ben Eliezer (ca.1700–1760), the founder of Hasidism.

*BA'AL TESHUVAH* (Heb., one who turns; fem. *BA'ALAT TESHUVAH*; pl. *BA'ALEI TESHUVAH*): One who repents or one who returns to Jewish observance.

*BALEBOOSTA* (Yiddish): A housewife.

*BALEBOOSTISM* (Yinglish): The *baleboosta* path.

BAR MITZVAH (Heb., son of the commandment): Male who has passed a Jewish literacy test by reading from the Torah and *haftarah* and is obliged to observe the commandments.

*BARUKH DAYAN HA-EMET* (Heb., "Blessed is the true Judge"): The prayer recited on the immediate occasion of a death.

*BARUKH HA-SHEM* (Heb., "Blessed is the Name"): A phrase in praise of God.

*BARUKH SHEM KEVOD* (Heb.): The opening of "*Barukh shem kevod malkhuto le-olam va'ed*," Blessed is His name whose glorious kingdom is forever." A phrase recited in response to the first verse of the *Shema*, said in an undertone.

BAT MITZVAH (Heb.): A daughter of the commandment. Cf. *bar mitzvah*.

*BEINONI* (Heb., average): In the *Tanya*, a person of intermediate spiritual attainment, neither a *tzaddik* nor a *rasha* (a wicked person). The *Tanya* is addressed to the *beinoni*. (See Tanya, chapter 1.)

*BEMIDBAR:* In the desert.

BEMIDBAR: The Hebrew name for the biblical book of Numbers.

*BERAKHAH* (Heb.; pl. *BERAKHOT*): Blessing.

BEREISHIT (Heb., in a beginning): The Hebrew name for the book of Genesis, and for the first *parashah* of the Book of Genesis; derived from the first significant word of the text.

*BERIYAH* (Heb.): Creation. One of four kabbalistic worlds.

*BIMAH* (Heb.): In Ashkenazi synagogues, the raised platform from which the service is conducted.

*BINAH* (Heb.): Understanding. One of the ten *sefirot*.

*BIRAH DOLEKET* (Heb.): A burning tower.

*BIRKAT HAMAZON:* Prayer after the meal.

BODHISATTVA (Sanskrit): One who forswears the achievement of nirvana to aid others. "The Bodhisattva ideal is the aspiration to practice infinite compassion with infinite wisdom" (XIV Dalai Lama).

BRATZLAV (also BRESLOV): Town in Ukraine where Rabbi Nachman served as rebbe.

BRATZLAVER: A follower of Rabbi Nachman of Bratzlav.

*BUBBE* (Yiddish): A Jewish grandmother.

*BUBBE MEISE* (Yiddish, grandmother story): Fairy tale.

CHABAD (cf. *ḥabad*): The movement of Lubavitcher *hasidim*. Derived from the initials for the *sefirot* of *ḥokhmah, binah, da'at*.

CHABADNIK: A member of Chabad; a follower of the Lubavitcher rebbe.

CHALLAH: The sweet Jewish bread of the Sabbath.

CHANUKAH (Heb. dedication): A historical Jewish holiday commemorating the defeat of the Greek Syrians by the Maccabees.

CHUBA: A Tibetan woman's peasant costume.

CHUTZPAH (Yiddish): Nerve.

*DA'AT* (Heb., knowing): The *sefirah* of knowledge.

*DARSHAN* (Heb., expounder): A public preacher in the synagogue.

*DARSHANA* (Sanskrit, seeing): A religious experience based on viewing an icon, or the gaze of the master.

DAVEN (Yiddish): To pray.

*DAVENNEN* (Yiddish): The act of prayer.

*DAVENNER* (Yinglish): One who davens.

*DAVENNOLOGY* (Yinglish): A coinage of Rabbi Zalman Schachter's to describe the study of Jewish prayer.

*DAVKA* (Heb.): Exactly.

*DERASH* (also *DRUSH*): A midrash or commentary on a Torah text.

*DESHEN* (Heb., sacrificial fat): Ashes of burnt sacrifice. (Cf. *Pesaḥim* 75b.)

*DEVAR TORAH* (Heb., word of Torah): An exposition of the Torah text, usually in the context of the reading of the Torah in a worship service.

*DEVEKUT* (Heb., clinging, cleaving to): Union with the divine.

DHARMA: The teachings of the Buddha; more generally, Buddhist wisdom.

DHARAMSALA: A small town in Himachal Pradesh in Northern India, seat of the Tibetan exile since 1959.

DIASPORA (Greek, dispersion): The Jewish people living outside of the Jewish homeland.

*DIVREI TORAH* (Heb., words of Torah): Active exposition of the Torah text; Oral Torah.

ECO-KOSHER: A Jewish renewal coinage. The concept of *kashrut* as applied to environmentalism.

*EIN SOF* (Heb., without bound): In kabbalah, the ultimate aspect of God about which nothing can be, properly, thought or said.

*ELIAHU HA-NAVI:* Elijah the prophet.

*EREV* (Heb.): Evening. Jewish days begin in the evening; hence Jewish holidays are celebrated commencing in the evening. Thus Erev Shabbat, Erev Yom Kippur, etc.

EVERFLOW: Cf. *shefa.*

*FLEISHIK* (Yiddish, meat [adj.]): Refers generally to dishes and utensils that come in contact with meat.

FOUR WORLDS: In Jewish renewal, the kabbalistic worlds (cf. *olam*) understood as spiritual and psychological categories.

*GABBAI* (Heb.): In talmudic times, a tax collector; later, treasurer of a synagogue; now, a synagogue official.

*GALUT:* Exile.

GAON OF VILNA: Rabbi Elijah ben Solomon Zalman of Vilna (1720–1797), an outstanding rabbinic authority known for his strong opposition to the hasidic movement. *Gaon* is an honorific, meaning "excellency."

GARTEL (Yiddish, girdle, belt): A belt of silk or wool worn by *hasidim* in prayer to make a division between the upper and lower halves of the body.

GEMARA (Aramaic, completion): Corpus of commentary on the Mishnah.

GEMILUT ḤASADIM: Deeds of loving-kindness. Cf. Simon the Righteous.

GESHE: Formal title for monk who has completed advanced study in Tibetan Buddhist teachings.

GEVURAH (Heb.): Strength, power. One of the ten *sefirot*.

GOYISHE (Yiddish): Gentile-like.

ḤAFTARAH (Heb., conclusion): Reading from the Prophets that follows the reading from the Torah in the morning Shabbat or holiday service.

HAGGADAH (Heb., narration; pl. HAGGADOT ): The prescribed format for telling the story of Exodus during the Passover seder.

HA-KADOSH BARUKH HU (Heb., "The Holy One, Blessed Is He"): A name associated with the *sefirah* of *gevurah* and with the first two letters of the tetragrammaton (*Yod Heh*).

HALAKHAH: The body of Jewish law.

ḤAMETZ: Leavened bread or leavening of any kind

ḤAREDI (Heb., one who trembles [i.e., in fear of God; cf. Quakers or Shakers]; pl. ḤAREDIM): The term many very traditional Jews—i.e., the so-called ultra-Orthodox—use to describe themselves.

HA-SHEM (Heb., the Name): A reverent expression for God, often used in observant Jewish communities.

ḤASID (pl. ḤASIDIM): Literally and in talmudic times, a saint or pious person (cf. *hasidim rishonim*, the pious ones of old; *Be-*

*rakhot* 32 b). In contemporary terms, an individual follower of a hasidic rebbe.

HASIDISM: A religious and mystical spiritual revival movement, beginning in the eighteenth century in the Ukraine and Poland.

ḤASIDUT: The body of hasidic teachings, lore, and texts.

HAVURAH (pl. HAVUROT): An intimate Jewish prayer and study group, especially any of the American groups arising in the late sixties.

ḤAYYUT: Vitality, the stream of life. Identified in hasidic writings with the concept of *shefa,* or the Everflow.

ḤESED (Heb.): Loving-kindness, mercy. One of the ten *sefirot.*

ḤEVRAH: Spiritual companions or those who share worship and fellowship.

ḤEVRUSA (Heb., companionship, society): Study partners or spiritual companions.

HIGH HOLY DAYS: The ten-day period from Rosh Hashanah to Yom Kippur.

*HILKHOT TESHUVAH* (Heb., Laws of Repentance): A tract by Maimonides on the concept of repentance or *teshuvah.*

HISHTAVUT (Heb., making equal): Term for equanimity, used by the Baal Shem Tov and others.

HITBODEDUT (Heb., self-isolation): A form of Jewish meditation taught by Rabbi Nachman of Bratzlav, involving a secluding of oneself to call out to God.

HITBONENUT (Heb., self-understanding): A form of Jewish meditation taught in the Lubavitch tradition, involving a contemplation of all things in relation to God.

HOD (Heb.): Glory or reverberation. One of the ten *sefirot.* Also identified with humility.

ḤOKHMAH: Wisdom. One of the ten *sefirot*.

ḤOSHEKH: Darkness. One of the Ten Plagues from the Exodus story.

THE IZBICER (pron. Izbitzer): Rabbi Mordecai Joseph Leiner (1800–1854), hasidic rebbe and founder of the Izbice dynasty, author of *Mei ha-Shiloaḥ* (Waters of Shiloah).

KABBALAH (Heb., tradition, that which is received): Jewish tradition in general, but in particular, the Jewish mystical tradition.

KABBALAT SHABBAT (Heb., receiving the Sabbath): A prayer service in the synagogue on Friday evenings (Erev Shabbat).

KADDISH (Aramaic, sanctification): An ancient Aramaic prayer in praise of God's powers, recited as prayers for the dead and at other points in a prayer service.

KADOSH BARUKH HU: Cf. *ha-Kadosh Barukh Hu*.

KALLAH (pl. KALLOT): A study convention. The term dates back to the time of the Babylonian academies.

KANGRA VALLEY: The valley below the slopes of Dharamsala's Dhaula Dhar range.

KASHER: To make kosher.

KASHRUT (Heb., fit): The dietary laws governing what is kosher.

KAVVANAH (Heb.; pl. KAVVANOT): Intention. Meditation prior to prayer or a holy act.

KEDUSHAH: A prayer incorporating "Holy, holy, holy [*kadosh, kadosh, kadosh*] is the Lord of Hosts."

KETER (Heb., crown): One of the ten *sefirot*. *Keter* represents the spiritual aspect of the divine.

KETER MALKHUT (Heb., crown of sovereignty): A phrase representing the enthronement of God by angels and man, through their offerings of praise. Hence, a Jewish spiritual path stressing humility and acceptance in the cultivation of personal sovereignty.

KEVA (Heb.): Regularity or discipline in spiritual practice.

KIDDUSH: Blessing over wine, recited at the Sabbath and on holidays.

KIPPAH (Heb.): A yarmulke.

KOHEIN (Heb.; pl. KOHANIM): Priest.

KORBAN ( Heb.): Sacrifice or offering.

LAMA (Tibetan): A Tibetan Buddhist sage.

LAM RIM (Tibetan): Graduated path. Teachings leading to enlightenment.

LEKH LEKHA (Heb., go forth): The *parashah* that describes the spiritual journey and transformation of Abram to Abraham (Gen. 12:1–17:27).

"LEKHAH DODI" (Heb., "Come, my beloved"): Sixteenth-century mystical Sabbath hymn, composed by Solomon Alkabetz, in Tzefat.

LOSAR: Tibetan New Year, celebrated in February.

LUBAVITCH: Town in Belorussia that became the center of Chabad in 1813.

LULAV (Heb.): Date-palm branch, one of four species carried for the festival of Sukkot.

LURIA, RABBI ISAAC: Sixteenth-century kabbalist of Tzefat. Also known as "the Ari."

LURIANIC KABBALAH: The development of the kabbalah of the Zohar by R. Isaac Luria and his followers in Tzefat.

MADHYAMIKA (Sanskrit, the middle): The middle-path school of Mahayana Buddhism.

*MAGGID* (Heb.): An itinerant preacher or storyteller, responsible for the spread of Hasidism in eastern Europe.

*MAGGID* OF MEZRITCH: Rabbi Dov Ber of Mezritch (d.1772), rabbi who took leadership of the hasidic movement after the death of the Baal Shem Tov. His disciples included R. Shneur Zalman of Liadi, founder of Chabad.

MAHABHARATA (Sanskrit): Ancient epic poem of India, that includes the *Bhagavad Gita*.

"MAH TOVU" ( Heb., how goodly): A text recited or sung upon entering a synagogue for morning services, derived from the blessing of Balaam (Num. 24:5).

*MALKHUT* (Heb.): Kingdom. One of the ten *sefirot*.

MANI WHEEL: A prayer wheel, a device for mechanically producing a mantra. May take the form of a large cylinder in a temple, or a small handheld cylinder with a handle that is whirled.

MANNA (Heb.): Miraculous food provided to the children of Israel in the desert (Exod. 16:2–36).

MANTRA (Sanskrit, instrument of thought): Verbal formula repeated as form of meditation—e.g., *om mani padme hum*.

*MAROR* (Heb.): Bitter herb. Eaten as part of Passover seder.

*MASHPI'A* (Heb., influencer): A teacher, usually of the younger students, in Chabad yeshivah, who serves as spiritual guide.

*MATIR ASURIM* (Heb, freer of captives): Epithet for God from the morning blessings and also from the *Amidah*.

MATZAH: Unleavened bread eaten during Passover.

ME'AH SHE'ARIM (Heb., hundred gates): An enclave neighborhood of ḥaredim in West Jerusalem.

*MEHAYEI HA-MEITIM* (Heb., who brings life to the dead): An epithet of God from the liturgy.

MEHITZAH (Heb., partition): A curtain or screen separating the men and women in the Orthodox prayer service.

MEKOR HAYIM (Heb.): Source of life. Cf. Psalm 36:10.

MELCHIZEDEK: The priest of Salem Abraham encounters in Genesis 14:18.

MELEKH HA-OLAM (Heb., king of the universe): Part of the blessing formula in Hebrew, as established by rabbinic teaching.

MERKAVAH (Heb., chariot): The merkavah meditators used visualizations of the divine chariot or throne derived from Ezekiel as a method of spiritual ascent.

MESHUGASS (Yiddish): Craziness.

METIVTA: (Aramaic): Yeshivah in the Zohar. Rabbi Jonathan Omer-Man's school of Jewish meditation in Los Angeles.

MEZUZAH: A small container or casing holding a scroll of parchment with paragraphs of the *Shema* (Deut. 6:4–9, 11:13–21) attached to the doorposts of a house. See *Shema*.

MIDDAH (Heb., quality; pl. MIDDOT): An attribute or emotional disposition.

MIDRASH (from Heb. *derash*, to delve): A commentary or extension of Torah. Generally refers to *midrash aggadah*, homiletical or theological exposition, as opposed to *midrash halakhah*, legal exposition.

MIKVEH: Pool of water for ritual immersion.

MILCHIK (Yiddish, milk [adj.]): Refers to those utensils or dishes that are reserved for dairy foods by those observing *kashrut*.

MINYAN (pl. MINYANIM): A quorum for prayer. Traditionally, ten Jewish males or today, in many Jewish circles, ten persons. Only in the presence of a minyan can certain prayers, such as the mourner's *Kaddish*, be recited.

MISHKAN (Heb., from root meaning "to dwell"): The Tabernacle, or portable sanctuary in which Jews carried the ark of the covenant in the desert. (Cf. Exod. 25:9 ff.)

MITNAGDIM (Heb., opponents): The opposition to the eighteenth-century hasidic movement, centering around the Gaon of Vilna.

MITZRAYIM (Heb., narrow place): Hebrew name for Egypt.

MITZVAH (pl. MITZVOT): Commandment; good deed.

MOMO: Tibetan dumpling. Cf. *kreplach*.

MOSHIAH (Heb.): The Messiah.

MOTZI: The blessing over bread.

MUSAR: A movement led by R. Israel Salanter (1810–1883), stressing ethics and moral development.

MYSTAGOGY: Religious mysteries or mystical doctrines. The term is often used pejoratively.

NESHAMAH: One of three biblical words used for the soul. See also *nefesh* and *ruah*.

NETZAH (Heb.): Reverberation or eternity. One of the ten *sefirot*.

NIGGUN: A hasidic wordless melody used in contemplation.

NITZOTZOT (Heb., sparks): The divine energy trapped in matter.

NOAHIDE: Referring to Noah, and specifically to those mitzvot, developed in rabbinic thought, governing the behavior of righteous Gentiles.

NOODGE (Yiddish): To provoke, or advocate in an annoying manner; also, one who does so.

NUSAH: Musical formulas for chanting the liturgy.

OLAM (Heb., world; pl. OLAMIM): A realm of divine activity or human perception.

OMER: The first offering of a new barley crop (Cf. Lev. 23:10). The mitzvah of counting the Omer involves noting each evening the forty-nine days between the second night of Passover and Shavuot.

OM MANI PADME HUM (Sanskrit, the jewel in the lotus): A mantra. According to the Dalai Lama, "This is almost our national mantra." The meaning is: jewel = thought of enlightenment; lotus = mind.

ORAL TORAH (Heb., *Torah she-be-al pe*): The divine revelation to Moses transmitted orally and passed down through oral tradition.

OTIYOT ḤAYYOT (Heb., living letters): Refers to the Jewish t'ai chi practice of Yehudit Goldfarb and her students in which Hebrew letters are spelled out with the body.

PANCHEN LAMA (Tibetan, great scholar): The second-highest position in the Tibetan Buddhist hierarchy. Traditionally the incarnate who serves as abbot of Tushilungbo Monastery in the Tsang region of Tibet.

PARAH ADUMAH (Heb., red cow): The red heifer. (Cf. Num. 19.)

PARASHAH (pl. PARASHIOT): The portion of Torah read on a particular Sabbath. There are fifty-four portions (sometimes two are combined). Each *parashah* is named for its opening word or first distinguishing word. (*See following.*)

PARSHAT LEKH LEKHA: Genesis 12:1–17:27.

PARSHAT PARAH: Numbers 19:1–22. A special portion read for Shabbat Parah, one of three Shabbats leading up to Passover.

PARSHAT SHEMINI: Leviticus 9:1–11:47. Describes the dedication of the *mishkan* and the disaster befalling Nadav and Abihu, the sons of Aaron.

PE'AH (Heb., corner): The mitzvah of reserving a corner of the harvested field for the poor to gather sustenance.

PERUGIN: Baked meat or cheese blintzes, especially delicious as prepared by my grandmother Dora Kamenetz.

PESADIK (adj. PESADIKA): Kosher for Passover.

PESHAT: Reading Torah in its plain exact sense. See also *remez*, *derash*, and *sod*.

PETIḤAH (Heb.): The opening formula of a blessing or prayer.

PIRKEI AVOT (Heb., chapters of the fathers): A mishnah that contains the lineages and wisdom of the rabbinic sages; known popularly in English as the "Ethics of the Fathers."

P'NAI OR (Heb., faces of light): The original Jewish renewal group centered around Rabbi Zalman Schachter in Philadelphia, renamed Aleph in 1993.

PSYCHO-HALAKHAH: Rabbi Zalman Schachter's term for analyzing halakhah based on its underlying intentions within its original setting, and revising it in accordance with more current understandings and technology.

PUSHKE (Yiddish): A small box or container, found in synagogue or the home, for use in collecting *tzedekah* or charity.

RAMBAM: Acronym for Rabbi Moses ben Maimon, or Moses Maimonides (1135–1204), a great philosopher and codifier.

RASHI: Acronym for Rabbi Shelomo Yitzhaki (1040–1105), preeminent Torah and Talmud commentator.

REBBE (Yiddish): Rabbi. Affectionate title for a hasidic rabbi.

RECONSTRUCTIONISM: A modernist movement in Judaism initiated by Rabbi Mordecai Kaplan (1881–1983).

REMEZ (Heb., hint): Reading of the Torah for its allusions or suggestions—i.e., at its contextual level.

RINPOCHE: Precious one. A Tibetan teacher or master. Often used for *tulkus*, or reincarnates.

ROSH HODESH (Heb.): New moon, the beginning of the Hebrew month. Marked by special prayers.

*RUAH HA-KODESH* (Heb., the holy spirit): The divine inspiration experienced by the prophets.

SADDHU: A Hindu ascetic holy man.

SECOND TEMPLE: The Temple in Jerusalem restored after the Babylonian exile.

SEDER (Heb., order): Ritual Passover meal.

SEFER YETZIRAH: Book of Formation. The earliest kabbalistic work, attributed in lore to Rabbi Akiva.

*SEFIRAH* (pl. *SEFIROT;* Heb., number): The supernal lights, divine grades, aspects, attributes of God. The names for the seven lower *sefirot* are derived from I Chronicles 29:11.

*SEIKHEL ELYON* (Heb.): Highest intelligence.

*SEMIKHAH* (Heb.): Rabbinic ordination.

*SHA'AR HA-RAHAMIM* (Heb.): Gate of mercy.

*SHA'AR YERUSHALAYIM* (Heb.): Gate of Jerusalem.

SHABBAS (Heb.; also SHABBAT, pl. SHABBATOT): Jewish Sabbath.

*SHABBASDIK* (Yiddish): Appropriate for Shabbas.

SHABBAT MEVAREKHIM (Heb.): A Sabbath preceding the new moon.

SHABBAT PARAH (see *Parshat Parah*): One of four special Shabbats preceding Pesach.

SHABBAT SHUVAH: The Sabbath of Repentance. A special Shabbat, falling between Rosh Hashanah and Yom Kippur.

*SHAHARIT* (Heb., dawn prayer): Morning prayer service. (In Ashkenazic pronunciation, *Shaharis.*)

SHAMBHALA: According to Robert Thurman, "a mythical country somewhere in the vicinity of Siberia or the North Pole where most of the population is enlightened and life is generally happy . . . the basis of the modern legends of Shangri-La."

SHAMMAI: A *tanna* and contemporary of Rabbi Hillel in the first decades C.E.

SHAVUOT (Heb., weeks): In ancient Israel, the second of the pilgrimage festivals, occurring seven weeks after Passover. Commemorates the Revelation at Sinai.

SHEFA (Heb., abundance): The Everflow or *hayyut*.

SHEKHINAH: God's indwelling presence, conceived as female.

SHEMA (Heb., hear): 1. Familiarly, Deuteronomy 6:4: "Hear O Israel, the Lord our God, the Lord is One." 2. The name given to three biblical passages (Deut 6:4–9, Deut. 11:13–21, Num. 15:37–41)that must be read in morning and evening prayer. The first passage (Deut. 6:4–9) is read before retiring as the bedtime *Shema*; the first two passages are inscribed on scrolls in the mezuzah and are also included, along with Exodus 13:1 and 13:11, in the tefillin.

SHEM HA-MEFORASH (Heb.): The proper or root name of God—i.e., YHVH.

SHEMONEH ESREI (Heb., eighteen benedictions): The eighteen—actually nineteen—benedictions of the *Amidah* in the weekday service.

SHEMOT (Heb.): Names.

SHEM YIHUD (Heb.): Unification of God's name.

SHI'UR (Heb.): Study session.

SHLAH: Acronym for the classic kabbalistic work *Two Tablets of the Covenant* and pseudonym for its author, Rabbi Isaiah Horowitz.

SHMOOZE (Yiddish): To chat socially.

SHMUTZ (Yiddish): Dirt.

SHOHIN (Heb.): To pause or wait.

SHOMER (Heb.): Observant.

SHOMER SHABBAS: A keeper of the Sabbath.

SHTIBL: A small Orthodox synagogue.

SHTREIML: A fur hat worn by men in the hasidic tradition.

SHUKEL: To pray by vigorously bending and moving.

SHUL (Yiddish): Synagogue.

SHVITZ (Yiddish): Steam bath.

SOD (Heb.): Secret. One of four levels of Torah interpretation.

SUAH (Heb.): A term in the Torah that seems to indicate meditation. Cf. Genesis 24:62: ". . . and Isaac went out to meditate (lasuah) in the field toward evening." Cf. also siah.

SUKKAH (Heb.; pl. SUKKOT): A harvest hut or temporary dwelling.

SUKKOT: The harvest festival, one of three great pilgrimage festivals in ancient Israel.

TALLIS (also TALLIT; pl. TALLISIM): Fringed prayer shawl.

TALMUD: Compendium of rabbinic law, stories, and wisdom, composed and compiled from 200 B.C.E. to 500 C.E. Consists of Mishnah and Gemara.

TANNA (Aramaic, one who studies and teaches): A rabbinic sage of the first and second centuries C.E., mentioned in the Mishnah or Baraita.

TANTRA (Sanskrit): 1. Collection of Hindu texts brought over to Tibet. 2. Practices associated with tantrayana.

TANTRAYANA: Esoteric Tibetan Buddhism; advanced meditation teachings, including deity yoga, said to promise speedy enlightenment. Same as *vajrayana*.

TANYA: Classic hasidic text of R. Shneur Zalman of Liadi, founder of Chabad.

TEFILLIN: Phylacteries. Prayer amulets containing biblical texts bound by leather straps to the forehead and the left arm.

*TESHUVAH* (Heb., turning, repentance): Repentance or return to observance.

TETRAGRAMMATON (Greek, four letters): The four-letter name of God, represented in this book as YHVH.

*THANKGA* (Tibetan): Tibetan devotional painting on a silk scroll.

*TIFERET* (Heb.): Beauty. One of the ten *sefirot*.

*TIKKUN* (Heb.): Repair. In Lurianic kabbalah, an act of devotion designed to raise sparks (*nitzotzot*) to a higher level.

*TIKKUN OLAM:* Repair of the world, whether manifested in the social realms as concrete acts of goodness, or as a mystical process of restoring the sparks (*nitzotzot*) to their proper place.

TORAH: Narrowly, the five books of Moses, and by extension, all of Jewish tradition and teaching.

TREIF (Heb., torn): Food that is not kosher.

TU BISHVAT: The New Year of the Trees, celebrated on the fifteenth of the Hebrew month of Shevat.

*TUMAT MEIT* (Heb.): Impurity of death.

*TZADDIK* (Heb., righteous one; pl. TZADDIKIM): In hasidic thought, the leader, generally the rebbe, who is considered to have great spiritual powers. Each generation, going back to Adam, is said to have its own *tzaddikim*.

*TZEDAKAH* (Heb., righteousness): Charity.

Tzefat (also Safed): A small town in northern Israel, the home of an extraordinary group of Jewish mystics in the sixteenth century, led by Rabbi Isaac Luria.

*TZIMTZUM* (Heb., contraction): In the Lurianic kabbalah, the theory that the act of creation was preceded by a concentration or occultation of the Divine.

*VE-AHAVATA* (Heb., "And you shall love"): Deuteronomy 6:5–9; part of the *Shema*.

*VIPASSANA:* Insight meditation.

*YAHRZEIT* (Yiddish): The yearly commemoration of a deceased person.

*YEHIDUT* (Heb.): One-on-one spiritual counseling in the hasidic tradition.

YESHIVAH (pl. YESHIVOT): School for rabbinic study.

*YESOD* (Heb.): Foundation. One of the ten *sefirot*.

*YETZIRAH* (Heb.): Formation. One of four kabbalistic worlds. See *olam*.

*YIDDISHE* (Yiddish): Jewish.

*YIHUD* (Heb.): Unification.

*YIRAH* (Heb.): Fear.

*YUNTIF* (Yiddish): Holiday, festival.

*ZADIE* (Yiddish): Grandfather.

Zohar (Heb., brilliance): The Book of Splendor; kabbalistic masterpiecc from thirteenth-century Spain.

*Books to Read and Places to Go*
*Bibliography*

## MAIMONIDES

Maimonides, Moses. *The Guide of the Perplexed.* Vols. 1 and 2. Translated by Shlomo Pines. Chicago: Univ. of Chicago Press, 1963.
————. *A Maimonides Reader.* Edited by Isadore Twersky. New York: Behrman House, 1972.
————. *Pirke Avot.* Translated by R. Eliyahu Touger. New York: Moznaim, 1994.

## THE JEWISH CALENDAR AND HOLIDAYS

Greenberg, R. Irving. *The Jewish Way: Living the Holidays.* New York: Summit Books, 1988.
Klagsbrun, Francine. *Jewish Days: A Book of Jewish Life and Culture Around the Year.* New York: Farrar, Straus and Giroux, 1996.
Waskow, Arthur. *Seasons of Our Joy.* Boston: Beacon Press, 1982.

## JEWISH MEDITATION

Adelman, Penina V. *Miriam's Well: Rituals for Jewish Women Around the Year.* 2d ed. New York: Biblio Press, 1990.
Buxbaum, Yitzhak. *Jewish Spiritual Practices.* Northvale, NJ: Jason Aronson, 1990.
Cooper, R. David. *Renewing Your Soul: A Guided Retreat for the Sabbath and Other Days of Rest.* San Francisco: HarperSanFrancisco, 1995.
Davis, Avram. *The Way of Flame: A Guide to the Forgotten Mystical Tradition of Jewish Meditation.* San Francisco: HarperSanFrancisco, 1996.
Dosick, Wayne. *Dancing with God: Everyday Steps to Jewish Spiritual Renewal.* San Francisco: HarperSanFrancisco, 1997.
Fisdel, Steven A. *The Practice of Kabbalah: Meditation in Judaism.* Northvale, NJ: Jason Aronson, 1996.

Frankiel, Tamar, and Judy Greenfeld. *Minding the Temple of the Soul.* Woodstock, VT: Jewish Lights, 1997.

Greenbaum, Avraham. *Under the Table and How to Get Up: Jewish Pathways of Spiritual Growth.* Jerusalem and New York: Tsohar, 1991.

Kaplan, Aryeh. *Jewish Meditation: A Practical Guide.* New York: Schocken Books, 1985.

———. *Meditation and the Bible.* York Beach, ME: Samuel Weiser, 1978.

———. *Meditation and Kabbalah.* York Beach, ME: Samuel Weiser, 1982.

Labowitz, Shoni. *Miraculous Living: A Guided Journey in Kabbalah Through the Ten Gates of the Tree of Life.* New York: Simon & Schuster, 1996.

*Opening the Inner Gates: New Paths in Kabbalah and Psychology.* Edited by Edward Hoffman. Boston and London: Shambhala, 1995.

Schachter-Shalomi, Zalman. "A First Step: A Devotional Guide." In *The First Jewish Catalog,* ed. Richard Siegel, Michael Strassfeld, and Sharon Strassfeld. Philadelphia: Jewish Publication Society, 1973.

———. *Gate to the Heart: An Evolving Process.* Philadelphia: Aleph, 1993.

———. *Paradigm Shift: From the Jewish Renewal Teachings of Reb Zalman Schachter-Shalomi.* Northvale, NJ: Jason Aronson, 1993.

Shapira, Kalonymus Kalman. *Conscious Community: A Guide to Inner Work.* Translated by Andrea Cohen-Kiener. Northvale, NJ: Jason Aronson, 1996..

Verman, Mark. *The History and Varieties of Jewish Meditation.* Northvale, NJ: Jason Aronson, 1996.

Wolfe-Blank, David. *Meta Siddur: A Jewish Soul-Development Workbook.* N.p., 1992.

## KABBALAH: INTRODUCTORY WORKS

Afterman, Alan. *Kabbalah and Consciousness.* New York: Sheep Meadow Press, 1992.

Ariel, David. *The Mystic Quest: An Introduction to Jewish Mysticism.* New York: Schocken Books, 1992.

Kaplan, Aryeh. *Inner Space.* Jerusalem: Moznaim, 1990.

Matt, Daniel. *Essential Kabbalah: The Heart of Jewish Mysticism.* San Francisco: HarperSanFrancisco, 1995.

Steinsaltz, Adin. *The Thirteen Petalled Rose*. New York: Basic Books, 1980.

## Scholarly Studies of Kabbalah and Translations of Original Source Materials

Fine, Lawrence, ed. *Essential Papers on Kabbalah*. New York: New York Univ. Press, 1995.

Ginsburg, Elliot. *Sod Ha-Shabbat (The Mysteries of the Sabbath)*. Albany, NY: SUNY Press, 1989.

Idel, Moshe. *Kabbalah: New Perspectives*. New Haven: Yale Univ. Press, 1988.

Jacobs, Louis. *Jewish Mystical Testimonies*. New York: Schocken Books, 1996.

Green Arthur, ed. *Jewish Spirituality*. Vol. 1, *From the Bible Through the Middle Ages*. Vol. 2, *From the Sixteenth-Century Revival to the Present*. New York: Crossroad, 1986, 1988.

*Safed Spirituality: Rules of Mystical Piety, the Beginning of Wisdom*. Classics of Western Spirituality. Mahwah, NJ: Paulist Press, 1985.

Scholem, Gershom. *Kabbalah*. Jerusalem: Keter, 1974.

————. *Major Trends in Jewish Mysticism*. 3d rev. ed. New York: Schocken Books, 1961.

————. *On the Kabbalah and Its Symbolism*. New York: Schocken Books, 1965.

Wolfson, Elliot. *Through a Speculum That Shines: Visions and Imagination in Medieval Jewish Mysticism*. Princeton, NJ: Princeton Univ. Press, 1994.

## Editions in English of Classic Kabbalistic Texts (in Historical Order)

*Sefer Yetzirah: The Book of Creation*. Translated and edited by Aryeh Kaplan. York Beach, ME: Samuel Weiser, 1997.

*The Bahir*. Translated by Aryeh Kaplan. York Beach, ME: Samuel Weiser, 1989.

Tishby, Isaiah. *The Wisdom of the Zohar: An Anthology of Texts*. 3 vols. Oxford: Oxford Univ. Press, 1989.

Wineman, R. Ariel. *Tales from the Zohar*. Philadelphia: Jewish Publication Society, 1996.

*Zohar*. Translated by Daniel Matt, with an introduction by Arthur Green. New York: Paulist Press, 1983.

Gikatilla, R. Joseph. *Gates of Light*. Translated by R. Ari Weinstein. San Francisco: HarperCollins, 1994.

Cordovero, R. Moshe. *The Palm Tree of Devorah*. Jerusalem: Feldheim, 1993.

Krassen, Miles, trans. *Isaiah Horowitz: The Generations of Adam*. New York: Paulist Press, 1996.

Luzzato, Moshe Chayim. *The Way of God*. Translated by Aryeh Kaplan. New York: Feldheim, 1988.

## CHABAD HASIDISM

Zalman, Rabbi Shneur, of Liadi. *Tanya*. Brooklyn: Kehot Publication Society, numerous editions. Generally available at Chabad centers. In addition to the *Tanya*, these editions include "Mystical Concepts in Chassidism," an excellent overview of the *sefirot* by R. Jacob Schochet.

## BRATZLAV HASIDISM

Green, Arthur. *Tormented Master: The Life and Spiritual Quest of Rabbi Nahman of Bratslav*. Woodstock, VT: Jewish Lights, 1992.

Greenbaum, Avraham, ed. *Rabbi Nachman's Tikkun*. Jerusalem and New York: Breslov Research Institute, 1984.

————, ed. and trans. *Garden of the Souls: Rebbe Nachman on Suffering*. Jerusalem: Breslov Research Institute, 1990.

Kaplan, Aryeh, trans. *Rabbi Nachman's Stories*. Jerusalem: Breslov Research Institute, 1983.

Starret, R. Yehoshua. *The Breslov Haggadah*. Jerusalem and New York: Breslov Research Institute, 1989.

## JEWISH RENEWAL

Petsonk, Judy. *Taking Judaism Personally: Creating a Meaningful Spiritual Life*. New York: Free Press, 1996.

Waskow, Arthur. *Down to Earth Judaism: Food, Money, Sex and the Rest of Life*. New York: Morrow, 1995.

## FEMINIST JUDAISM

Cantor, Aviva. *Jewish Women/Jewish Men: The Legacy of Patriarchy in Jewish Life*. San Francisco: HarperSanFrancisco, 1995.

Gottlieb, Lynn. *She Who Dwells Within: A Feminist Vision of a Renewed Judaism*. San Francisco: HarperSanFrancisco, 1995.

Heschel, Susannah, ed. *On Being a Jewish Feminist: A Reader*. New York: Schocken Books, 1983.

Orenstein, R. Debra, ed. *Lifecycles: Jewish Women on Life Passages and Personal Milestones*. Woodstock, VT: Jewish Lights, 1994.

Plaskow, Judith. *Standing Again at Sinai*. San Francisco: HarperSanFrancisco, 1990.

## Jewish Prayer

Falk, Marcia. *The Book of Blessings*. San Francisco: HarperSanFrancisco, 1996.

Green, Arthur, and Barry Holtz. *Your Word Is Fire: Hasidic Masters on Contemplative Prayer*. Woodstock, VT: Jewish Lights, 1993.

Hammer, Reuven. *Entering Jewish Prayer: A Guide to Personal Devotion and the Worship Service*. New York: Shocken Books, 1994.

Munk, R. Dr. Elie. *The World of Prayer*. 2 vols. New York: Philipp Feldheim, n.d.

*On Ecstasy: A Tract by Dobh Baer of Lubavitch*. Translated and annotated by Louis Jacobs. Chappaqua, NY: Rossell Books, 1963.

*Or Chadash: The Aleph Prayer Book*. 2d draft ed. Philadelphia: Aleph, 1991.

Zaslow, R. David, *Serve the Holy One with Joy: A Siddar*. Ashland: np., 1997. Available via Aleph.

## Judaism and Twelve Steps

Olitzky, R. Kerry, and Stuart Copans. *12 Jewish Steps to Recovery: A Personal Guide to Turning from Alcoholism and Other Addictions*. Woodstock VT: Jewish Lights, 1991.

## Works by Rabbi Zalman Schachter-Shalomi

Schachter, Zalman. *The First Step: A New Guide to the Jewish Spirit*. New York: Bantam, 1983.

Schachter, Zalman, and Edward Hoffman. *Sparks of Light: Counseling in the Hasidic Tradition*. Boulder: Shambhala, 1983.

Schachter-Shalomi, Zalman. *Gate to the Heart*. See above under "Meditation." This is Reb Zalman's guide to Jewish prayer and meditation.

————. *Spiritual Intimacy: A Study of Counseling in Hasidism*. Northvale, NJ: Jason Aronson, 1991.

## WORKS BY RABBI ARTHUR GREEN

Green, Arthur. *Keter: The Crown of God in Early Jewish Mysticism*. Princeton: Princeton Univ. Press, 1997.

————. *Seek My Face, Speak My Name: A Contemporary Jewish Theology*. Northvale, NJ: Jason Aronson, 1992.

————. *Tormented Master*. See above under "Bratzlav Hasidism."

## WORKS BY RABBI SHEFA GOLD

Gold, Shefa. *Chants Encounters*. Las Vegas, NM: B'emet Productions, 1994. Audiocassette.

————. *Tzuri*. Las Vegas, NM: B'emet Productions, 1991. Audiocassette. Includes morning prayers.

Both of these cassettes are available from Aleph.

## AUDIOTAPES

Cooper, David. *Kabbalah Meditation*. 2 tapes. Boulder, CO: Sounds True, 1994.

Gold, Shefa. *Chants Encounters* and *Tzuri*. See above under "Works by Rabbi Shefa Gold."

Klotz, Myriam. *Each and Every Day: Yoga and Meditation for Jewish Spirituality*. Atlanta: Synchronized Sound, 1995. Available from Aleph.

Zeller, David. *Good Night My Sweetest Children*. Efrat, Israel: Heartsong Productions, 1995.

————. *Let Go*. Efrat, Israel: Heartsong Productions, 1988.

————. *Ruach*. Efrat, Israel: Heartsong Productions, 1981.

————. *The Tree of Life: Meditations, Prayers, and Practices of Mystical Judaism*. 6 tapes with booklet. Boulder, CO: Sounds True, 1996.

## VIDEOTAPES

Goldfarb, Yehudit. *Otiyot Khayyot: Hebrew Letter Movements for Healing and Renewal*. Berkeley: L'haim Distributors, 1994.

*Places to Go*

### INTERNET RESOURCES

Virtual Yeshiva of Rabbi Rami Shapiro
http://www.rasheit.org/index.html

Yihud: The Jewish Meditation Web Site
http://rashi.tiac.net/yihud/index.html

### CORRESPONDENCE COURSE IN KABBALAH AND JEWISH SPIRITUALITY

A Still Small Voice
P.O.B. 14503
Jewish Quarter
Jerusalem, Israel 91141
Tel./fax: 011-972-2-6282988
E-mail: smlvoice@netvision.net.il
Web site: http://www.amyisrael.co.il/smallvoice/

### JEWISH RENEWAL AND HAVURAH ORGANIZATIONS

Aleph: Alliance for Jewish Renewal
7318 Germantown Road
Philadelphia, PA 19119-1793
(215) 242-4074
E-mail: Alephajr@aol.com

The Havurah Institute, National Havurah Committee
7318 Germantown Road
 Philadelphia, PA 19119-1793
(215) 248-9760

Jewish Reconstructionist Federation
1299 Church Road
Wyncote, PA, 19095
(215) 887–1988
E-mail: jrfnatl@aol.com

## MEDITATION AND RETREAT CENTERS

Chochmat HaLev
2525 Eighth Street, Suite 13
Berkeley, CA 94710
(510) 704-9687
E-mail: chochmat@best.com
Web site: http://www.chochmat.org

Elat Chayyim: A Center for Healing and Renewal
Rabbi Jeff Roth and Rabbi Joanna Katz
99 Mill Hook Road
Accord, NY 12404
(800) 398-2630
E-mail: elatchayyi@aol.com

Heart of Stillness Retreats
Rabbi David Cooper
P.O. Box 106
Jamestown, CO 80455
(303) 459-3431

Living Waters (a Jewish spiritual health spa)
Davie, FL
Director: Rabbi Shoni Labowitz
(954) 476-7466

Metivta: A Center for Jewish Wisdom
Rabbi Jonathan Omer-Man
2001 South Barrington Avenue, Suite 106
Los Angeles, CA 90025-5363
(310) 477-5370
Web site: http://www.metivta.org

Rose Mountain
Rabbi Shefa Gold and Andy Gold
P.O. Box 355
Las Vegas, NM 87701
(505) 425-5728

Sarah's Tent
Rabbi Judith Halevy
c/o Malibu Jewish Center and Synagogue
24855 Pacific Coast Highway
Malibu, CA 90265
(310) 456-2178

Yakar Center for Tradition and Creativity
Halamed He, 10
Jerusalem, Israel
Tel.: 011 972 2 612310
Director: Rabbi David Zeller

## MEDITATIONAL SYNAGOGUES

Bet Alef Meditational Synagogue
Seattle, WA
Rabbi: Ted Falcon
(206) 527-9399

Makom Ohr Shalom
Northridge, CA
Rabbis: David Cooper and Mordecai Finley
(818) 725-7600

## HALFWAY HOUSES AND TWELVE-STEP PROGRAMS

Gateway Rehabilitation Center
Aliquippa, Pennsylvania
(412) 378-4461

Gateways Beit T'shuvah
216 South Lake Street
Los Angeles, CA 90057
(213) 644-2026

JACS
(Jewish Alcoholics and Chemically Dependent and Significant Others)
426 West 58th Street
New York, NY 10019
(212) 397-4197
Fax: (212) 489-6224

## HELPING THE CAUSE OF TIBETAN FREEDOM

Seder for Tibet Project
1209 Pine Street
New Orleans, LA 70118
(504) 388-2984
Fax: (504) 866-6740
Web site: http://www.allcorp.com/TIBETSEDER

International Campaign for Tibet
1825 K Street, NW, Suite 520
Washington, DC 20006
(202) 785-1515
Fax: (202) 785-4343
E-mail: ict@peacenet.org

Students for a Free Tibet
241 East 32nd Street
New York, NY 10016
(212) 481-3569
Fax: (212) 779-9245
E-mail: ustcsft@igc.apc.org